T0337730

Peugeot Scooters
Service and Repair Manual

by Phil Mather

Models covered

(3920 - 4AH2 - 192)

50cc Speedfight, Prost and X-Team

50cc Speedfight 2, X-Team, X-Race, WRC 206, Furious, Silver Sport, Iron-X, Motorsport, R-Cup and Rally Victories

50cc Trekker Road, Off-Road, Urban Black, Streetboard and Metal-X

50cc TKR Street Zone, WRC 206, Metal-X Furious and Rally Victories

50cc Vivacity, Sportline, VS/X, X-Race and Compact

100cc Speedfight 100 and Prost

100cc Speedfight 2 100, X-Team, X-Race, WRC 206, Furious, Silver Sport, Rally Victories 100P and Advantage 100

100cc Trekker 100 and Metal-X

100cc Vivacity 100 and VS/X

© J H Haynes & Co. Ltd. 2008

ABCD

A book in the **Haynes Service and Repair Manual Series**

ISBN **978 1 84425 772 0**

British Library Cataloguing in Publication Data
A catalogue record for this book is available from the British Library.

Printed in Malaysia

J H Haynes & Co Ltd
Sparkford, Yeovil, Somerset BA22 7JJ, England

Haynes North America, Inc
859 Lawrence Drive, Newbury Park, California 91320, USA

Printed using NORBRITE BOOK 48.8gsm (CODE: 40N6533) from NORPAC; procurement system certified under Sustainable Forestry Initiative standard. Paper produced is certified to the SFI Certified Fiber Sourcing Standard (CERT - 0094271)

Contents

LIVING WITH YOUR SCOOTER

Introduction

Daily (pre-ride checks)

MAINTENANCE

Routine maintenance and servicing

Contents

The Peugeot Story

Peugeot celebrated its 100th automotive anniversary in 1998 but its history stretches back a further 88 years and encompasses an incredibly diverse range of products.

Now part of the massive PSA industrial conglomerate that includes Citroën and Peugeot, the Peugeot dynasty has classically humble beginnings.

Brothers, Jean-Pierre and Jean-Frederic Peugeot decided to manufacture cold rolled steel in the family mill on the Doubs river in eastern France. A far cry from the high-profile World Rally Championship, Le Mans and Formula One with which Peugeot has latterly become known. Fine steel strips and springs were sold to the nearby Swiss clock-making industry and by 1818 the brothers had moved into producing steel for tools, mainly saw blades. By 1824, 70 workers toiled in the factory at Herimoncourt and in 1850 the famous Peugeot trademark, the rampant Lion, was being used to mark their top grade of steel. The king of beasts was formerly registered as a trademark in 1858.

In a manner which reflected the innovative industrial production of Victorian Britain, Peugeot further diversified into coffee mills made of wood or metal, some for grocers' shops and cafes, others for the home. There followed pepper mills, washing machines, furniture, wireless sets, sewing machines, crinolines, umbrellas, irons and even shotguns. Much later, the first modern food processor, the Peugimix, was the talisman in a whole range of kitchen appliances.

The First Motor Vehicles

The first bicycles were made in 1882 at Beaulieu-Mandeure after Armand Peugeot was inspired by this new form of locomotion during his stay in England as a student.

In 1889, Peugeot took a leap of faith with its first 'car', actually a tricycle powered by a steam engine. From this inauspicious start they designed a four-wheeler the following year which used a Panhard-produced Daimler 565 cc V-twin engine. Cooled by water circulating in the frame tubes, it weighed 500 kg and produced 1hp at 1000 rpm. Top speed was little more than stationary.

The type 3 car of 1891 introduced mass production techniques for the day – 64 were made in four years. Six years on, the type 15 was the first car powered by an all-Peugeot engine.

The first Peugeot motor-bicycle appeared in 1902, a 1.5 bhp single cylinder engine in a cycle frame, and the company found itself in the heady position, repeated elsewhere across Europe, as newcomers to both car and motorcycle manufacturing.

The first Peugeot motor-bicycle appeared in 1902

A 5 hp machine was produced in tandem with the Bebe car designed by Ettore Bugatti. In 1905, a 12 hp racing motorcycle emerged to set two world records including the level kilometre at 76.612 mph. Peugeot's also featured in the first TT races on the Isle of Man in 1907.

After the First World War Peugeot won various Grands Prix races with a 500 cc machine and in 1925 rider Pean set a new world speed record at 103.15 mph on a 750 cc machine.

By 1929 Peugeot embarked on its first truly mass-produced car, the 201, and Peugeot motorcycles were selected for use by the French army, Gendarmerie and the national postal service. A new Peugeot bicycle was also coming off the assembly line every 45 seconds.

The motorcycle range expanded to include 175, 250, 350 and 500 cc machines but after the Second World War production focussed on smaller machines with the first scooters being made in 1955. Racing had taken a back seat but Peugeot won the 175 cc class at the 1952 Bol d'Or leading to the launch of the 175 cc Grand Sport road model.

The 100cc Speedfight 2

By 1970 their range had grown to include 23 models, mainly cycle-motors. It was not until 1982 that the first recognisably modern scooters were made with the SC/SX range and these were the first machines in Europe to use plastic bodywork. The formation of Peugeot Motocycles in 1987 acted as the catalyst for the new era of modern scooter production.

Scooter Production

Scooter and cycle-motor production at Peugeot is centred on two contrasting manufacturing plants close to the small town of Sochaux famous as the heartland of the Peugeot dynasty and the faded glory of a once famous football team.

Less than an hour's drive from Basle airport on the Franco-Swiss border, Beaulieu-Mandeure is home to the Peugeot Motocycles assembly plant. Here, tubes are bent into frames, electrical wire is made into looms, silencers are fabricated, bodywork and chassis are painted and largely home-produced components are assembled by the workforce of over 1000 people. Approximately 60% of the machines produced are for export, with the remainder consumed by the home market.

Back along the autoroute towards Basle, Peugeot's modern engine plant at Dannemarie produce the company's four-stroke engines fitted to the Elystar and Elyseo 125 and 150 luxury scooters, using technology from Peugeot's car engine division. At Dannemarie, where the legend 'Honda Engineering' adorns many a high tech machine tool, they produce seven different types of engine, but in a

The 50cc Speedfight 2 X-Race

The 50cc Speedfight 2 X-Team

The 50cc Trekker Road

The 50cc Trekker Off Road

bewildering 190 different specifications. This compact facility has the capacity to produce 2000 engines per day and has its own pressure and gravity die-casting plants.

Many engine components are sourced from Mahle, Mikuni and Dell'Orto and parts such as pistons, clutches, cylinders and crankshafts are machined on site. The factory has its own nickel and zinc coating facility and heat-treating plant.

While Peugeot's success in Britain has been meteoric it's not without parallel as Peugeot seeks an ever larger share of the massive European scooter market. The Italian 50 cc scooter sector alone accounts for 570,000 machines a year; together with Spain, Germany, France and Holland the total tops a million.

Peugeot leads markets in France, Finland, Belgium, Holland and Denmark and is aggressively pursuing the German and Italian markets where it established subsidiaries in 1997. Despite stiff competition from Piaggio, Aprilia and Malaguti, Peugeot see the Italian market as the key to its greatest expansion.

Speedfight, Trekker and Vivacity

The mainstay of Peugeot's twist-and-go scooter range are the Speedfight 50 and 100 cc models. Unveiled in the UK in late 1996 as a 50 cc, and then joined by a 100 cc model the following summer, the Speedfight's success was responsible for Peugeot becoming the most popular scooter marque in the UK market.

The 50cc Trekker Streetboard

The 50cc Vivacity

The original Speedfight was superseded by the Speedfight 2 in 2000, most noticeable by its sharper body styling with V-shaped air intake grille in the front panel with asymmetric headlights above. Technical improvements were also made to the steering, suspension and instrumentation.

All models use a two-stroke engine and are either air- or liquid-cooled. Special editions included the Prost model, the multi-coloured X-Team, the X-Race, and the WRC 206 to commemorate Peugeot's success in the World Rally Championship. Reflecting the customising trend amongst scooter owners, the Furious model features exposed motorcycle-style handlebars with a mini all-electronic instrument cluster, carbon fibre-look mirrors and a piggy-back competition style exhaust system. Since 2005 the Speedfight range has seen the introduction of the Iron-X, Motorsport, R-Cup, Rally Victories the Silversport and the Advantage 100 all of which come with their own graphics and paint schemes and two-tone seats.

The Trekker superseded the Squab model in 1997 and was aimed at the adventure scooter market, being a machine suitable for road and gentle off-road use. It had the rugged looks of an off-road machine, with knobbly tyres on certain models. All Trekker models use an air-cooled two-stroke engine.

Special versions of the Trekker are the Streetboard, Urban Black, Metal-X, Street Zone and WRC 206, broadening the models appeal with a variety of styling options and colour schemes. In 2003 the Trekker was re-named TKR and versions were produced in Street Zone, WRC 206 and Metal-X Furious livery; a Rally Victories version followed in 2004.

The Vivacity was introduced to the range in 1999 in 50 and 100 cc sizes, and provided a

The 50cc Vivacity Sportline

softer less radical styling to the Speedfight. The Vivacity range was supplemented by the Sportline model in 2000 which featured electronic instrumentation and restyled graphics. Special editions of the Vivacity include the VS/X and X-Race. The Vivacity Compact was introduced in 2003 – with shortened front suspension and smaller diameter wheels it boasts a seat height of only

76 cm – and while the standard Vivacity 50 remained in the line-up, the Silver Sport continued the sports trend of the earlier X-Race.

Peugeot have addressed the problem of security on their machines, with the fitting of an integral Boa lock and ignition immobiliser system fitted either as standard or available as optional equipment.

Acknowledgements

Our thanks are due to Three Cross Motorcycles Ltd of Wimborne, Dorset, and to Andy Legg, who supplied the scooters featured in the photographs throughout this manual. We are also indepted to the technical staff of Three Cross Motorcycles Ltd for the provision of technical literature and advice and to Graham Sanderson who wrote the introduction 'The Peugeot Story'. We would also like to thank NGK Spark Plugs (UK) Ltd for supplying the colour spark plug condition photos and Draper Tools Ltd for some of the workshop tools shown.

About this Manual

The aim of this manual is to help you get the best value from your scooter. It can do so in several ways. It can help you decide what work must be done, even if you choose to have it done by a dealer; it provides information and procedures for routine maintenance and servicing; and it offers diagnostic and repair procedures to follow when trouble occurs.

We hope you use the manual to tackle the work yourself. For many simpler jobs, doing it yourself may be quicker than arranging an appointment to get the scooter into a dealer and making the trips to leave it and pick it up. More importantly, a lot of money can be saved by avoiding the expense the shop must pass on to you to cover its labour and overhead costs. An added benefit is the sense of satisfaction and accomplishment that you feel after doing the job yourself.

References to the left or right side of the scooter assume you are sitting on the seat, facing forward.

We take great pride in the accuracy of information given in this manual, but motorcycle manufacturers make alterations and design changes during the production run of a particular motorcycle of which they do not inform us. No liability can be accepted by the authors or publishers for loss, damage or injury caused by any errors in, or omissions from, the information given.

Illegal Copying

The frame number is stamped into the frame . . .

. . . and also appears on the identification plate

The engine number is stamped into the rear of the transmission casing

Identification numbers

Frame and engine numbers

The frame serial number, or VIN (Vehicle Identification Number) as it is often known, is stamped into the frame, and also appears on the identification plate. The engine number is stamped into the rear of the transmission casing. Both of these numbers should be recorded and kept in a safe place so they can be furnished to law enforcement officials in the event of a theft.

The frame and engine numbers should also be kept in a handy place (such as with your driving licence) so they are always available when purchasing or ordering parts for your scooter.

Each model type can be identified by its engine and frame number prefix – refer to *Model identification* in the service schedule pages of Chapter 1. A full list of the models covered in this manual is given in the table below.

Models covered	Capacity	Introduced
Speedfight 50	50 cc	Dec 1996
Speedfight 100	100 cc	Aug 1997
Speedfight 50 LCD and LCDP	50 cc	Nov 1997
Speedfight 50 M and MP	50 cc	Nov 1998
Speedfight Prost 50 LCD and LCDP	50 cc	Nov 1998
Speedfight Prost 100	100 cc	May 1999
Speedfight X-Team	50 cc	May 1999
Speedfight 50 LBD and LBDP	50 cc	Nov 1999
Speedfight 50 B and BP	50 cc	Nov 1999
Speedfight Prost 50	50 cc	Nov 1999
Speedfight X-Team BP and LBDP	50 cc	Nov 1999
Speedfight 100 P	100 cc	Nov 1999
Speedfight 2 50 M and MP	50 cc	Mar 2000
Speedfight 2 50 B and BP	50 cc	Mar 2000
Speedfight 2 50 LCDP and LBDP	50 cc	Mar 2000
Speedfight 2 100 P	100 cc	Mar 2000
Speedfight 2 50 N, NP and X-Team NP	50 cc	Nov 2000
Speedfight 2 50 LNDP and X-Team LNDP	50 cc	Nov 2000
Speedfight 2 X-Race 50 NP and LNDP	50 cc	Nov 2000
Speedfight 2 100 NP	100 cc	Nov 2000
Speedfight 2 X-Team 100	100 cc	Nov 2000
Speedfight 2 X-Race 100	100 cc	Nov 2000
Speedfight 2 WRC 206 50	50 cc	Nov 2001
Speedfight 2 WRC 206 100	100 cc	Nov 2001
Speedfight 2 50 E, EP and LEDP	50 cc	2002
Speedfight 2 100 EP	100 cc	2002
Speedfight 2 Furious	50 cc	2003
Speedfight 2 Furious	100 cc	2003
Speedfight Rally Victories	50 cc	2004

Models covered	Capacity	Introduced
Speedfight Rally Victories 100P	100 cc	2004
Speedfight 2 Silver Sport	50 cc	2005
Speedfight 2 Silver Sport	100 cc	2005
Speedfight 50 Iron-X	50 cc	2005
Speedfight Motorsport 50	50 cc	2005
Speedfight R-Cup 50	50 cc	2005
Speedfight Advantage	100 cc	2007
Trekker Road	50 cc	Nov 1997
Trekker Off Road	50 cc	Nov 1997
Trekker 100	100 cc	Nov 1997
Trekker Urban Black	50 cc	Nov 1999
Trekker Streetboard	50 cc	Nov 1999
Trekker Metal-X	50 cc	Nov 2001
Trekker Metal-X 100	100 cc	2002
TKR Street Zone	50 cc	2003
TKR WRC 206	50 cc	2003
Metal-X Furious	50 cc	2003
TKR Rally Victories	50 cc	2004
Vivacity 50	50 cc	Feb 1999
Vivacity 100	100 cc	Feb 1999
Vivacity Sportline	50 cc	Feb 2000
Vivacity X-Race	50 cc	Nov 2001
Vivacity VS/X	50 cc	2002
Vivacity VS/X 100	100 cc	2002
Vivacity Compact	50 cc	2003
Vivacity Silver Sport	50 cc	2004
Vivacity 100 T	100 cc	2005

Buying spare parts

When ordering replacement parts, it is essential to identify exactly the machine for which the parts are required. While in some cases it is sufficient to identify the machine by its title e.g. 'Speedfight 50', any modifications made to components mean that it is usually essential to identify the scooter by its year of production, or better still by its frame or engine number prefix.

To identify your own scooter, refer to the engine and frame number prefix information in refer to 'Model identification' in the service schedule pages of Chapter 1.

To be absolutely certain of receiving the correct part, not only is it essential to have the scooter's engine or frame number prefix to hand, but it is also useful to take the old part for comparison (where possible). Note that where a modified component has superseded the original, a careful check must be made that there are no related parts which have also been modified and must be used to enable the replacement to be correctly refitted; where such a situation is found, purchase all the necessary parts and fit them, even if this means renewing apparently unworn items.

Purchase replacement parts from an authorised Peugeot dealer or someone who specialises in scooter parts; they are more likely to have the parts in stock or can order them quickly from the importer. Pattern parts are available for certain components; if used, ensure these are of recognised quality brands which will perform as well as the original.

Expendable items such as lubricants, spark plugs, some electrical components, bearings, bulbs and tyres can usually be obtained at lower prices from accessory shops, motor factors or from specialists advertising in the national motorcycle press.

Trekker model development

Trekker Road, Trekker Off Road and TKR

The 50 cc Trekker models were introduced in November 1997, replacing the Squab model. All were fitted with an air- cooled two-stroke engine.

The Trekker Road featured 12 inch wheels, 32 mm Paioli front forks and a rear spoiler. It was available in metallic black, Grenade Red and Magic Blue, although the metallic black colour option was dropped in November 1999.

The Trekker Off Road featured 10 inch wheels and upside-down front forks. It was available in amber, metallic black, Excaliber Silver and Torero Red. The Excaliber Silver colour option was dropped in November 1998 and the colour options were further revised in November 1999 to amber and Manganese.

The Urban Black (matt black) and Streetboard (Technium Satin) variants of the Off Road were introduced in November 1999. At the same time, all 50 cc Trekker models were fitted with an ignition immobiliser and Boa lock as standard equipment and redesignated with a 'P' suffix.

In November 2000, the colour range for the Trekker Off Road was revised to black, Torero Red and Acid Green and the Boa lock became an optional extra.

The Metal-X variant was introduced in November 2001, featuring revised body styling, a separate front mudguard mounted directly above the wheel, motorcycle-style handlebars and a digital instrument display. An ignition immobiliser and Boa lock were fitted as standard equipment. Available in either graphite/blue or graphite/red colour options.

The TKR model replaced the Trekker in 2003, with Street Zone and WRC 206 variants, and the Metal-X Furious was introduced at the same time. The TKR Rally Victories was introduced in 2004 and finished in technium silver/red. All models had air-cooled two-stroke engines, 10 inch wheels and upside-down front forks.

Trekker 100

The Trekker 100 was introduced at the same time as the Trekker 50. It was fitted with an air-cooled two-stroke engine and was available as an 'On-road' variant only.

Available in Excaliber Silver, Grenade Red and Magic Blue. The Magic Blue colour option was dropped in November 1999.

Redesignated Trekker 100 P in November 1999.

The Metal-X was introduced for 2002. It has the same features as the 50 cc Metal-X, plus a sidestand.

Vivacity model development

Vivacity 50 and Vivacity 100

The Vivacity 50 and Vivacity 100 were introduced in February 1999. Both models were fitted with an air-cooled two-stroke engine, a single headlight and upside-down front forks. A steering lock, ignition immobiliser and Boa lock were standard equipment.

Available in Night Blue, Grenade Red, Oxo Yellow, amber and metallic black. Additional colour options (Mint Green and Plumb) were introduced in November 1999.

The ignition immobiliser was dropped from the Vivacity 50 in November 1999, but remained standard equipment on the Vivacity 100. The Boa lock became an optional extra on both models. Machines fitted with an ignition immobiliser and Boa lock as standard were identified with the model suffix 'P'.

In November 2000, the colour range for both models was revised to black, Night Blue, Grenade Red and Technium Grey and the 50 cc model was also available in Atoll Blue. The X-Race model was introduced in November 2001.

The Vivacity VS/X 50P and VS/X 100P were introduced in 2002. They differ from the standard models in the fitting of a rear spoiler and alloy footboards and have distinctive white stripes running through their Pulsar blue bodypanels.

The Vivacity Compact was introduced in 2003. It had a 50 cc air-cooled two-stroke engine, disc front brake, shortened front suspension and 10 inch wheels. The Compact was available in Maori Green and Technium Silver.

Vivacity Sportline

Introduced in February 2000. It had the same size engine and specification as the Vivacity 50, with the addition of a rear spoiler and restyled mirrors. A revised Sportline was introduced in November 2000, differing from the original model in having an electrically operated speedometer, digital odometer, clock and fuel gauge. The Sportline models were available in Torero red, Magic Blue/Technium Grey and Torero Red/Technium Grey. The Silver Sport colour option was introduced in 2004 for the 50 cc variant.

Speedfight model development

Speedfight 50

The first Speedfight model was the Speedfight 50 introduced in December 1996. It was available with a liquid-cooled, 50 cc two-stroke engine, monolever front suspension, disc front brake and drum rear brake.

Available in four colours: Excaliber Silver, Torero Red, metallic black and blue/yellow.

Speedfight 50 LCD and LCDP

Introduced in November 1997. It was fitted with a liquid-cooled two-stroke engine, but differed from the original Speedfight 50 model in its use of a rear disc brake. New style mirrors were fitted.

The LCDP had a steering lock, transponder ignition immobiliser and Boa lock as standard equipment. The Boa lock was available as an optional extra on the LCD model.

Available in six colours: Excaliber Silver, Torero Red, metallic black, blue/yellow, Grenade Red/silver and amber/silver.

The model was redesignated Speedfight 50 LBD and LBDP in November 1999.

Speedfight 50 MP

Introduced in November 1998. It was fitted with an air-cooled two-stroke engine and drum rear brake, but was otherwise a similar specification to the LCDP model.

Initially available in Torero Red, Excaliber Silver, Night Blue and metallic black, then the colours were revised in November 1999 in line with LCD and LCDP models.

The model was redesignated Speedfight 50 BP in November 1999.

Speedfight 50 M

Introduced in November 1998. Same specification and colours as the MP model but without the immobiliser – Boa lock available as an optional extra. Redesignated Speedfight 50 B in November 1999.

In November 1999, the colour range for all the 50 cc Speedfight models, with the exception of the Prost and X-Team, was revised to amber/silver, metallic black/silver, Night Blue/silver and Grenade Red/silver.

Speedfight Prost 50 LCD and LCDP

Introduced in November 1998. Prost model was based on the existing LCD and LCDP models, with the addition of a competition style exhaust, rear spoiler and aluminium footboard trims. It was available in Pulsor Blue with Prost decals.

An air-cooled variant, the Prost 50 AC, was introduced in November 1999 and the liquid-cooled variant was redesignated the Prost 50 LC.

Speedfight X-Team

Introduced in May 1999. Same specification as the MP model with blue, white and red colour scheme. Competition style exhaust, rear spoiler and aluminium footboard trims.

A liquid-cooled variant with disc rear brake, the X-Team LBDP, was introduced in November 1999 and the air-cooled variant was redesignated the X-Team BP.

Speedfight 100

The Speedfight 100 was introduced in August 1997. It has an air-cooled 100 cc two-stroke engine, disc brakes front and rear, an immobiliser and Boa lock, and was available in metallic black, Excaliber Silver, Torero Red and Night Blue.

New mirrors and an additional colour option (Grenade Red) were introduced November 1997.

In November 1999, the colour range was revised to Night Blue and Grenade Red and the model was redesignated the Speedfight 100 P.

Speedfight Prost 100

Introduced in May 1999. Same specification as the Speedfight 100 plus rear spoiler and aluminium footboard trims. Same colour scheme as the Prost 50.

Speedfight 2

The entire Speedfight range was revised in March 2000 with new body styling, headlights and instrument panel, re-engineered monolever front suspension and uprated shock absorbers front and rear. The 50 cc models continued to be available in air- and liquid-cooled two-stroke engine variants, and the 100 cc models were available with air-cooled two-stroke engines only.

Machines fitted with a transponder ignition immobiliser and Boa lock as standard continued to be identified with the model suffix 'P'.

Colour options for the 50 cc models were Torero Red, Magic Blue, Technium Grey and Formula Yellow. Colour options for the 100 cc model were Night Blue, Grenade Red and Technium Grey.

In November 2000, an additional colour option (Acid Green) was introduced for the 50 cc models, and the colour range for the 100 cc models was revised to Pulsar Blue, Black and Technium Grey. At the same time, air-cooled models previously designated M(P) and B(P) were redesignated N(P), and liquid-cooled models previously designated LCDP and LBDP were redesignated LNDP. 2002 models were designated E(P) and LEDP. The Silver Sport colour option was introduced in 2003 for both 50 cc and 100 cc variants.

Speedfight 2 X-Race 50 NP and 50 LNDP

Introduced in November 2000 in air-cooled (NP) and liquid-cooled (LNDP) variants. Apart from the different engines, both models had the same specification as the X-Team LNDP (formerly LBDP), with a new Pulsar Blue/orange colour scheme.

Speedfight 2 X-Team 100 and X-Race 100

Introduced in November 2000. Both models had the same engine and specification as the Speedfight 2 100, with the addition of a rear spoiler and aluminium footboard trims. The X-Team 100 had the same colour scheme as the 50 cc X-Team and the X-Race 100 had the new Pulsar Blue/orange colour scheme.

Speedfight 2 WRC 206

Introduced in November 2001 in both 50 cc and 100 cc variants to commemorate Peugeot's success in the World Rally Championship.

The 50 cc model had the same specification and liquid-cooled engine as the X-Race 50, and the 100 cc model had the same engine and specification as the X-Race 100. Both models had a new Technium Silver colour scheme and 206 graphics.

Speedfight 2 Furious

Introduced in November 2001 in both 50 cc and 100 cc variants, the Furious featured motorcycle-style handlebars and digital instrument display. The 50 cc model was available with either an air- or liquid-cooled engine, the 100 cc model had an air-cooled engine.

Speedfight Rally Victories 50 and 100P

Introduced in 2004 in both 50 cc and 100 cc air-cooled and liquid-cooled variants. The Rally Victories versions have race graphics, aluminium footplates and rear spoiler. Finished in Torero Red or Technium Silver.

Speedfight Iron-X 50

Introduced in 2005 the Iron-X features new decals, carbon-look mirrors, aluminium footplates and a rear spoiler and two-tone seat. Finished in red or Pulsar blue/white.

Speedfight Motorsport 50

Introduced in 2005 in air-cooled and liquid-cooled variants. The Motorsport special edition comes with motorsport graphics, two-tone seat, aluminium footplates and a rear spoiler. Colour blue.

Speedfight R-Cup 50

Introduced in 2005 in air-cooled and liquid-cooled variants. The R-Cup versions come with race graphics and aluminium footplates and a rear spoiler. Finished in red.

Speedfight Silversport 50P

Introduced in 2005 with snakebite exhaust, asymmetric trim headlights, race graphics, aluminium footrests and a rear spoiler.

Speedfight Advantage 100

Introduced in 2007 with colour options yellow/silver and Torero red/silver.

Professional mechanics are trained in safe working procedures. However enthusiastic you may be about getting on with the job at hand, take the time to ensure that your safety is not put at risk. A moment's lack of attention can result in an accident, as can failure to observe simple precautions.

There will always be new ways of having accidents, and the following is not a comprehensive list of all dangers; it is intended rather to make you aware of the risks and to encourage a safe approach to all work you carry out on your bike.

Asbestos

● Certain friction, insulating, sealing and other products - such as brake pads, clutch linings, gaskets, etc. - contain asbestos. Extreme care must be taken to avoid inhalation of dust from such products since it is hazardous to health. If in doubt, assume that they do contain asbestos.

Fire

● Remember at all times that petrol is highly flammable. Never smoke or have any kind of naked flame around, when working on the vehicle. But the risk does not end there - a spark caused by an electrical short-circuit, by two metal surfaces contacting each other, by careless use of tools, or even by static electricity built up in your body under certain conditions, can ignite petrol vapour, which in a confined space is highly explosive. Never use petrol as a cleaning solvent. Use an approved safety solvent.

● Always disconnect the battery earth terminal before working on any part of the fuel or electrical system, and never risk spilling fuel on to a hot engine or exhaust.

● It is recommended that a fire extinguisher of a type suitable for fuel and electrical fires is kept handy in the garage or workplace at all times. Never try to extinguish a fuel or electrical fire with water.

Fumes

● Certain fumes are highly toxic and can quickly cause unconsciousness and even death if inhaled to any extent. Petrol vapour comes into this category, as do the vapours from certain solvents such as trichloro-ethylene. Any draining or pouring of such volatile fluids should be done in a well ventilated area.

● When using cleaning fluids and solvents, read the instructions carefully. Never use materials from unmarked containers - they may give off poisonous vapours.

● Never run the engine of a motor vehicle in an enclosed space such as a garage. Exhaust fumes contain carbon monoxide which is extremely poisonous; if you need to run the engine, always do so in the open air or at least have the rear of the vehicle outside the workplace.

The battery

● Never cause a spark, or allow a naked light near the vehicle's battery. It will normally be giving off a certain amount of hydrogen gas, which is highly explosive.

● Always disconnect the battery ground (earth) terminal before working on the fuel or electrical systems (except where noted).

● If possible, loosen the filler plugs or cover when charging the battery from an external source. Do not charge at an excessive rate or the battery may burst.

● Take care when topping up, cleaning or carrying the battery. The acid electrolyte, evenwhen diluted, is very corrosive and should not be allowed to contact the eyes or skin. Always wear rubber gloves and goggles or a face shield. If you ever need to prepare electrolyte yourself, always add the acid slowly to the water; never add the water to the acid.

Electricity

● When using an electric power tool, inspection light etc., always ensure that the appliance is correctly connected to its plug and that, where necessary, it is properly grounded (earthed). Do not use such appliances in damp conditions and, again, beware of creating a spark or applying excessive heat in the vicinity of fuel or fuel vapour. Also ensure that the appliances meet national safety standards.

● A severe electric shock can result from touching certain parts of the electrical system, such as the spark plug wires (HT leads), when the engine is running or being cranked, particularly if components are damp or the insulation is defective. Where an electronic ignition system is used, the secondary (HT) voltage is much higher and could prove fatal.

Remember...

✗ **Don't** start the engine without first ascertaining that the transmission is in neutral.

✗ **Don't** suddenly remove the pressure cap from a hot cooling system - cover it with a cloth and release the pressure gradually first, or you may get scalded by escaping coolant.

✗ **Don't** attempt to drain oil until you are sure it has cooled sufficiently to avoid scalding you.

✗ **Don't** grasp any part of the engine or exhaust system without first ascertaining that it is cool enough not to burn you.

✗ **Don't** allow brake fluid or antifreeze to contact the machine's paintwork or plastic components.

✗ **Don't** siphon toxic liquids such as fuel, hydraulic fluid or antifreeze by mouth, or allow them to remain on your skin.

✗ **Don't** inhale dust - it may be injurious to health (see Asbestos heading).

✗ **Don't** allow any spilled oil or grease to remain on the floor - wipe it up right away, before someone slips on it.

✗ **Don't** use ill-fitting spanners or other tools which may slip and cause injury.

✗ **Don't** lift a heavy component which may be beyond your capability - get assistance.

✗ **Don't** rush to finish a job or take unverified short cuts.

✗ **Don't** allow children or animals in or around an unattended vehicle.

✗ **Don't** inflate a tyre above the recommended pressure. Apart from overstressing the carcass, in extreme cases the tyre may blow off forcibly.

✔ **Do** ensure that the machine is supported securely at all times. This is especially important when the machine is blocked up to aid wheel or fork removal.

✔ **Do** take care when attempting to loosen a stubborn nut or bolt. It is generally better to pull on a spanner, rather than push, so that if you slip, you fall away from the machine rather than onto it.

✔ **Do** wear eye protection when using power tools such as drill, sander, bench grinder etc.

✔ **Do** use a barrier cream on your hands prior to undertaking dirty jobs - it will protect your skin from infection as well as making the dirt easier to remove afterwards; but make sure your hands aren't left slippery. Note that long-term contact with used engine oil can be a health hazard.

✔ **Do** keep loose clothing (cuffs, ties etc. and long hair) well out of the way of moving mechanical parts.

✔ **Do** remove rings, wristwatch etc., before working on the vehicle - especially the electrical system.

✔ **Do** keep your work area tidy - it is only too easy to fall over articles left lying around.

✔ **Do** exercise caution when compressing springs for removal or installation. Ensure that the tension is applied and released in a controlled manner, using suitable tools which preclude the possibility of the spring escaping violently.

✔ **Do** ensure that any lifting tackle used has a safe working load rating adequate for the job.

✔ **Do** get someone to check periodically that all is well, when working alone on the vehicle.

✔ **Do** carry out work in a logical sequence and check that everything is correctly assembled and tightened afterwards.

✔ **Do** remember that your vehicle's safety affects that of yourself and others. If in doubt on any point, get professional advice.

● **If** in spite of following these precautions, you are unfortunate enough to injure yourself, seek medical attention as soon as possible.

Note: *The daily (pre-ride) checks outlined in your owner's manual covers those items which should be inspected on a daily basis.*

Engine oil level check

Before you start:
✔ Make sure you have a supply of the correct oil available.
✔ Support the machine in an upright position whilst checking the level. Make sure it is on level ground.

The correct oil:
● Modern engines place great demands on their oil. It is very important that the correct oil for your bike is used.
● Always top up with a good quality oil of the specified type. Peugeot specify a semi-synthetic, JASO FC SAE20 oil for two-stroke engines with separate lubrication.
● If the oil level warning light comes on the oil tank requires topping up immediately or at the earliest opportunity. However, do not rely on the oil warning light to tell you that the oil tank needs topping up. Get into the habit of checking the oil level in the oil tank regularly, such as at the same time as you fill up with fuel.
● If the engine is run without oil, even for a short time, engine damage and very soon engine seizure will occur. It is advised that a bottle of two-stroke oil is carried in the storage compartment for such emergencies.

1 Remove the filler cap to check the oil level; it should be up to the bottom of the filler neck when full.

2 If the level is low, top the tank up with the recommended oil, then fit the filler cap securely.

Coolant level check (liquid-cooled models)

 Warning: DO NOT leave open containers of coolant about, as it is poisonous.

 Warning: Do not remove the reservoir cap when the engine is hot. It is good practice to cover the cap with a heavy cloth and turn the cap slowly anti-clockwise. If you hear a hissing sound (indicating that there is still pressure in the system), wait until it stops, then continue turning the cap until it can be removed.

Before you start:
✔ Make sure you have a supply of coolant available (a mixture of 50% distilled water and 50% Procor 3000 anti-freeze is needed). Peugeot state that other anti-freeze products will not mix with Procor 3000. If you are in any doubt about the type of coolant already in the system, it is advised that you drain and flush the cooling system (see Chapter 3) and refill with the specified coolant mixture.
✔ Always check the coolant level when the engine is cold.
✔ Support the machine in an upright position whilst checking the level. Make sure it is on level ground.

Bike care:
● Use only the specified coolant mixture. It is important that anti-freeze is used in the system all year round, and not just in the winter. Do not top-up the system with water only, as the coolant will become too diluted.
● Do not overfill the reservoir tank, which is located behind the front panel on all models. The coolant level should be just below the bottom of the filler neck. Any surplus should be siphoned or drained off to prevent the possibility of it being expelled.
● If the coolant level falls steadily, check the system for leaks (see Chapter 1). If no leaks are found and the level continues to fall, it is recommended that the machine is taken to a Peugeot dealer for a pressure test.

1 Undo the screws securing the front panel and remove the panel.

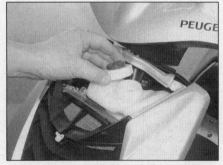

2 Unscrew the reservoir cap – see *Warning* above. The reservoir should be at least half full.

3 Top-up if necessary with the specified coolant mixture.

Brake fluid level check (disc braked models)

⚠️ **Warning: Brake hydraulic fluid can harm your eyes and damage painted surfaces, so use extreme caution when handling and pouring it and cover surrounding surfaces with rag. Do not use fluid that has been standing open for some time, as it absorbs moisture from the air which can cause a dangerous loss of braking effectiveness.**

Before you start:

✔ Support the machine in an upright position on level ground and turn the handlebars until the hydraulic reservoir is as level as possible – remember to check both reservoirs if your scooter is equipped with front and rear disc brakes.

✔ Make sure you have a supply of DOT 4 hydraulic fluid.

✔ Access to the reservoir is restricted on most models by the upper handlebar cover. Remove the cover if the reservoir requires topping-up.

✔ Wrap a rag around the reservoir to ensure that any spillage does not come into contact with painted or plastic surfaces. If any fluid is spilt wash it off immediately with cold water.

Bike care:

● The fluid in the hydraulic reservoir will drop slightly as the brake pads wear down.

● If the reservoir requires repeated topping-up this is an indication of a fluid leak somewhere in the system, which should be investigated immediately.

● Check for signs of fluid leakage from the brake hoses and components – if found, rectify immediately.

● Check the operation of the brake before riding the machine; if there is evidence of air in the system (a spongy feel to the lever), it must be bled as described in Chapter 8.

1 The brake fluid level is visible through the sightglass in the reservoir body – it must be half way up the glass when the reservoir is level.

2 Remove the reservoir cap screws and remove the cover, the diaphragm plate and the diaphragm.

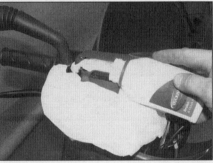

3 Top-up with new DOT 4 hydraulic fluid until the level is half way up the sightglass. Do not overfill and take care to avoid spills (see **Warning** above).

4 Ensure that the diaphragm is correctly seated before installing the plate and cover. Tighten the cover screws securely.

Fuel check

● This may seem obvious, but check that you have enough fuel to complete your journey. Do not wait until the fuel gauge or warning light to tell you that the level in the tank is low before filling up.

● If you notice signs of leakage you must rectify the cause immediately.

● Ensure you use the correct grade unleaded petrol, minimum 95 octane. Note that the use of unleaded petrol will increase spark plug life and have obvious benefits to the environment.

Suspension and steering checks

● Check that the front and rear suspension operates smoothly without binding.

● Check that the steering moves smoothly from lock-to-lock.

Tyre checks

The correct pressures:
● The tyres must be checked when **cold**, not immediately after riding. Note that low tyre pressures may cause the tyre to slip on the rim or come off. High tyre pressures will cause abnormal tread wear and unsafe handling.

● Use an accurate pressure gauge.

● Proper air pressure will increase tyre life and provide maximum stability and ride comfort.

● Refer to *Service specifications* in Chapter 1 for the correct tyre pressures for your model.

Tyre care:
● Check the tyres carefully for cuts, tears, embedded nails or other sharp objects and excessive wear. Operation of the scooter with excessively worn tyres is extremely hazardous as handling will be directly affected.
● Check the condition of the tyre valve and ensure the dust cap is in place.
● Pick out any stones or nails which may have become embedded in the tyre tread. If left, they will eventually penetrate through the casing and cause a puncture.
● If tyre damage is apparent, or unexplained loss of pressure is experienced, seek the advice of a tyre fitting specialist without delay. Peugeot do not recommend the use of tyres repaired after a puncture.

Tyre tread depth:
● At the time of writing UK law for machines over 50 cc requires that tread depth must be at least 1 mm over 3/4 of the tread breadth all the way around the tyre, with no bald patches. Many riders, however, consider 2 mm tread depth minimum to be a safer limit. Note that UK law for machines of 50 cc and under only requires that the original tyre tread is visible, although in the interest of safety owners may wish to apply the above limit.
● Many tyres now incorporate wear indicators in the tread. Identify the triangular pointer on the tyre sidewall to locate the indicator bar and renew the tyre if the tread has worn down to the bar.

1 Check the tyre pressures when the tyres are **cold** and keep them properly inflated.

2 Measure tread depth at the centre of the tyre using a tread depth gauge.

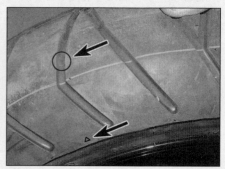

3 Tyre tread wear indicator bar and its location marking (usually either an arrow, a triangle or the letters TWI) on the sidewall (arrowed).

Legal and safety checks

Lighting and signalling:
● Take a minute to check that the headlight, tail light, brake light, instrument lights and turn signals all work correctly.
● Check that the horn sounds when the switch is operated.
● A working speedometer graduated in mph is a statutory requirement in the UK.

Safety:
● Check that the throttle grip rotates smoothly and snaps shut when released, in all steering positions.
● Check that stand return spring holds the stand securely up when retracted.
● Check that both brakes work correctly when applied and free off when released.

Chapter 1
Routine maintenance and servicing

Contents

Degrees of difficulty

Easy, suitable for novice with little experience	Fairly easy, suitable for beginner with some experience	Fairly difficult, suitable for competent DIY mechanic 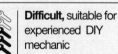	Difficult, suitable for experienced DIY mechanic	Very difficult, suitable for expert DIY or professional

Introduction

1 This Chapter is designed to help the home mechanic maintain his/her scooter for safety, economy, long life and peak performance.

2 Deciding where to start or plug into the service schedule depends on several factors. If the warranty period on your machine has just expired, and if it has been maintained according to the warranty standards, you may want to pick up routine maintenance as it coincides with the next mileage or calendar interval. If you have owned the machine for some time but have never performed any maintenance on it, then you may want to start at the nearest interval and include some additional procedures to ensure that nothing important is overlooked. If you have just had a major engine overhaul, then you may want to start the maintenance routine from the beginning. If you have a used machine and have no knowledge of its history or maintenance record, you may desire to combine all the checks into one large service initially and then settle into the maintenance schedule prescribed.

3 Before beginning any maintenance or repair, the machine should be cleaned thoroughly, especially around the engine and transmission covers. Cleaning will help ensure that dirt does not contaminate the engine and will allow you to detect wear and damage that could otherwise easily go unnoticed.

4 Certain maintenance information is sometimes printed on decals attached to the machine. If the information on the decals differs from that included here, use the information on the decal.

Note 1: *The daily (pre-ride) checks detailed at the beginning of this Manual cover those items which should be inspected on a daily basis. Always perform the pre-ride inspection at every maintenance interval (in addition to the procedures listed).*

The intervals listed below are the intervals recommended by the manufacturer for each particular operation during the model years covered in this manual. Your owner's manual may have different intervals for your model.

Note 2: *An initial service should be performed by a Peugeot dealer after the first 300 miles (500 km) from new. Thereafter, the machine should be serviced according to the intervals specified in the service schedules which follow.*

Note 3: *Refer to the Maintenance Plan in the maintenance booklet supplied with the machine for the correct intervals.*

Speedfight 50

Model identification

Engine	49 cc single cylinder liquid-cooled two-stroke
Transmission	Variable speed automatic, belt driven
Ignition	Capacitor discharge ignition (CDI)
Front suspension	Leading link monolever
Rear suspension	Swingarm and single shock
Front brake	180 mm disc
Rear brake	110 mm drum
Front tyre size	120/70 x 12
Rear type size	140/70 x 12
Engine no. suffix	FL1
Frame no. prefix	VGAS1B
Wheelbase	1225 mm
Overall length	1730 mm
Overall width (excl. mirrors)	700 mm
Overall height (excl. mirrors)	1155 mm
Weight (dry)	90 kg
Fuel tank capacity	7.2 litres

Servicing specifications and lubricants

Spark plug type	NGK BR7HS
Spark plug electrode gap	0.6 mm
Idle speed	1500 rpm
Front tyre pressure	19 psi (1.3 Bar)
Rear tyre pressure	23 psi (1.6 Bar)
Disc brake pad minimum thickness	1.5 mm
Rear drum brake lever freeplay	10 to 20 mm
Throttle twistgrip freeplay	2 to 5 mm
Fuel	Unleaded petrol (gasoline) min 95 octane
Engine oil	JASO FC, SAE 20 semi-synthetic
Engine oil tank capacity	1.3 litres
Relay box oil	80W-90 scooter gear oil
Relay box oil capacity	120 ml
Brake fluid	DOT 4
Coolant	50% distilled water and 50% Procor 3000 anti-freeze is needed). Peugeot state that other anti-freeze products will not mix with Procor 3000.

Service intervals – Speedfight 50

Note: *Always perform the Daily (pre-ride) checks before every service interval – see the beginning of this Manual. Severe conditions are regarded as intensive urban use, short journeys with cold engine or use in dusty conditions.*

	Text section in this Chapter	Every 3000 miles (5000 km) or 1500 miles (2500 km) for severe conditions	Every 6000 miles (10,000 km) or 3000 miles (5000 km) for severe conditions
Air filter – clean/renew	1	✔	
Battery – check	2	✔	
Brake cable – check and lubricate	5	✔	
Brake fluid – check*	6	✔	
Brake hose – check*	7	✔	
Brake levers – lubricate	4	✔	
Brake pads – check	8	✔	
Brake shoes – check	9	✔	
Brake system – check	3	✔	
Carburettor – clean	16		✔
Clutch pulley and bearing – check and lubricate	26		✔
Cooling system – check**	19	✔	
Cylinder head – decarbonise	23		✔
Drive belt – check	24	✔	
Drive belt – renew	25		✔
Engine oil system – check	11	✔	
Engine oil filter – change	12		✔
Fuel system – check	14	✔	
Headlight, brake light and horn – check	21	✔	
Idle speed – check and adjust	15	✔	
Kickstart gear and spindle bush – check	27		✔
Nuts and bolts – tightness check	20	✔	
Oil pump cable – check and adjust	13	✔	
Rear drum brake cam – check and lubricate	29		✔
Stand – check and lubricate	22	✔	
Spark plug – gap check and adjust	17	✔	
Spark plug – renew	18		✔
Throttle cable – check and adjust	10	✔	
Relay box oil level – check	28		✔
Variator pulley and rollers – check and lubricate	24	✔	
Wheels and tyres – check	30	✔	

* The brake fluid must be changed every 2 years and the brake hose renewed every 3 years, irrespective of mileage
**Drain and refill with fresh coolant every 2 years, irrespective of mileage

Speedfight 50 LCD/LBD/Prost, LCDP/LBDP/Prost, Prost 50 LC, X-Team LBDP

Model identification

Engine	49 cc single cylinder liquid-cooled two-stroke
Transmission	Variable speed automatic, belt driven
Ignition	Capacitor discharge ignition (CDI)
Front suspension	Leading link monolever
Rear suspension	Swingarm and single shock
Front brake	180 mm disc
Rear brake	180 mm disc
Front tyre size	120/70 x 12
Rear tyre size	140/70 x 12
Engine no. suffix	FL1
Frame no. prefix	VGAS1B
Wheelbase	1225 mm
Overall length	1730 mm
Overall width (excl. mirrors)	700 mm
Overall height (excl. mirrors)	1155 mm
Weight (dry)	90 kg
Fuel tank capacity	7.2 litres

Servicing specifications and lubricants

Spark plug type	NGK BR7HS
Spark plug electrode gap	0.6 mm
Idle speed	1500 rpm
Front tyre pressure	17 psi (1.3 Bar)
Rear tyre pressure	19 psi (1.6 Bar)
Disc brake pad minimum thickness	1.5 mm
Throttle twistgrip freeplay	2 to 5 mm
Fuel	Unleaded petrol (gasoline) min 95 octane
Engine oil	JASO FC, SAE 20 semi-synthetic
Engine oil tank capacity	1.3 litres
Relay box oil	80W-90 scooter gear oil
Relay box oil capacity	120 ml
Brake fluid	DOT 4
Coolant	50% distilled water and 50% Procor 3000 anti-freeze is needed). Peugeot state that other anti-freeze products will not mix with Procor 3000.

Service intervals – Speedfight 50 LCD/LBD/Prost, LCDP/LBDP/Prost, Prost 50 LC , X-Team LBDP

Note: *Always perform the Daily (pre-ride) checks before every service interval – see the beginning of this Manual. Severe conditions are regarded as intensive urban use, short journeys with cold engine or use in dusty conditions.*

	Text section in this Chapter	Every 3000 miles (5000 km) or 1500 miles (2500 km) for severe conditions	Every 6000 miles (10,000 km) or 3000 miles (5000 km) for severe conditions
Air filter – clean/renew	1	✔	
Battery – check	2	✔	
Brake fluid – check*	6	✔	
Brake hoses – check*	7	✔	
Brake levers – lubricate	4	✔	
Brake pads – check	8	✔	
Brake system – check	3	✔	
Carburettor – clean	16		✔
Clutch pulley and bearing – check and lubricate	26		✔
Cooling system – check**	19	✔	
Cylinder head – decarbonise	23		✔
Drive belt – check	24	✔	
Drive belt – renew	25		✔
Engine oil system – check	11	✔	
Engine oil filter – change	12		✔
Fuel system – check	14	✔	
Headlight, brake light and horn – check	21	✔	
Idle speed – check and adjust	15	✔	
Kickstart gear and spindle bush – check	27		✔
Nuts and bolts – tightness check	20	✔	
Oil pump cable – check and adjust	13	✔	
Stand – check and lubricate	22	✔	
Spark plug – gap check and adjust	17	✔	
Spark plug – renew	18		✔
Throttle cable – check and adjust	10	✔	
Relay box oil level – check	28		✔
Variator pulley and rollers – check and lubricate	24	✔	
Wheels and tyres – check	30	✔	

* The brake fluid must be changed every 2 years and the brake hose renewed every 3 years, irrespective of mileage
**Drain and refill with fresh coolant every 2 years, irrespective of mileage

Speedfight 50 M/B, 50 MP/BP, Prost 50 AC, X-Team, X-Team BP

Model identification

Engine	50 cc single cylinder air-cooled two-stroke
Transmission	Variable speed automatic, belt driven
Ignition	Capacitor discharge ignition (CDI)
Front suspension	Leading link monolever
Rear suspension	Swingarm and single shock
Front brake	180 mm disc
Rear brake	110 mm drum
Front tyre size	120/70 x 12
Rear tyre size	130/70 x 12
Engine no. suffix	FB4
Frame no. prefix	VGAS1A
Wheelbase	1225 mm
Overall length	1730 mm
Overall width (excl. mirrors)	700 mm
Overall height (excl. mirrors)	1155 mm
Weight (dry)	94 kg
Fuel tank capacity	7.2 litres

Servicing specifications and lubricants

Spark plug type	NGK BR7HS
Spark plug electrode gap	0.6 mm
Idle speed	1500 rpm
Front tyre pressure	19 psi (1.3 Bar)
Rear tyre pressure	23 psi (1.6 Bar)
Disc brake pad minimum thickness	1.5 mm
Rear drum brake lever freeplay	10 to 20 mm
Throttle twistgrip freeplay	2 to 5 mm
Fuel	Unleaded petrol (gasoline) min 95 octane
Engine oil	JASO FC, SAE 20 semi-synthetic
Engine oil tank capacity	1.3 litres
Relay box oil	80W-90 scooter gear oil
Relay box oil capacity	120 ml
Brake fluid	DOT 4

Service intervals – Speedfight 50 M/B, 50 MP/BP, Prost 50 AC, X-Team, X-Team BP

Note: *Always perform the Daily (pre-ride) checks before every service interval – see the beginning of this Manual. Severe conditions are regarded as intensive urban use, short journeys with cold engine or use in dusty conditions.*

	Text section in this Chapter	Every 3000 miles (5000 km) or 1500 miles (2500 km) for severe conditions	Every 6000 miles (10,000 km) or 3000 miles (5000 km) for severe conditions
Air filter – clean/renew	1	✔	
Battery – check	2	✔	
Brake cable – check and lubricate	5	✔	
Brake fluid – check*	6	✔	
Brake hose – check*	7	✔	
Brake levers – lubricate	4	✔	
Brake pads – check	8	✔	
Brake shoes – check	9	✔	
Brake system – check	3	✔	
Carburettor – clean	16		✔
Clutch pulley and bearing – check and lubricate	26		✔
Cylinder head – decarbonise	23		✔
Drive belt – check	24	✔	
Drive belt – renew	25		✔
Engine oil system – check	11	✔	
Engine oil filter – change	12		✔
Fuel system – check	14	✔	
Headlight, brake light and horn – check	21	✔	
Idle speed – check and adjust	15	✔	
Kickstart gear and spindle bush – check	27		✔
Nuts and bolts – tightness check	20	✔	
Oil pump cable – check and adjust	13	✔	
Rear drum brake cam – check and lubricate	29		✔
Stand – check and lubricate	22	✔	
Spark plug – gap check and adjust	17	✔	
Spark plug – renew	18		✔
Throttle cable – check and adjust	10	✔	
Relay box oil level – check	28		✔
Variator pulley and rollers – check and lubricate	24	✔	
Wheels and tyres – check	30	✔	

* The brake fluid must be changed every 2 years and the brake hose renewed every 3 years, irrespective of mileage

Speedfight 2 50 LCDP/LBDP/LNDP/LEDP, X-Team 50 LNDP, X-Race 50 LNDP, WRC 206 50, Furious, Iron-X 50, Motorsport 50, R-Cup 50

Model identification

Engine	49 cc single cylinder liquid-cooled two-stroke
Transmission	Variable speed automatic, belt driven
Ignition	Capacitor discharge ignition (CDI)
Front suspension	Leading link monolever
Rear suspension	Swingarm and single shock
Front brake	180 mm disc
Rear brake	180 mm disc
Front tyre size	120/70 x 12
Rear tyre size	
2000 to 2002 models	140/70 x 12
2003-on models	130/70 x 12
Engine no. suffix	FL1
Frame no. prefix	VGAS1B
Wheelbase	1225 mm
Overall length	1730 mm
Overall width (excl. mirrors)	700 mm
Overall height (excl. mirrors)	1155 mm
Weight (dry)	90 kg
Fuel tank capacity	7.2 litres

Servicing specifications and lubricants

Spark plug type	NGK BR7HS
Spark plug electrode gap	0.6 mm
Idle speed	1500 rpm
Front tyre pressure	19 psi (1.3 Bar)
Rear tyre pressure	23 psi (1.6 Bar)
Disc brake pad minimum thickness	1.5 mm
Throttle twistgrip freeplay	2 to 5 mm
Fuel	Unleaded petrol (gasoline) min 95 octane
Engine oil	JASO FC, SAE 20 semi-synthetic
Engine oil tank capacity	1.3 litres
Relay box oil	80W-90 scooter gear oil
Relay box oil capacity	120 ml
Brake fluid	DOT 4
Coolant	50% distilled water and 50% Procor 3000 anti-freeze is needed). Peugeot state that other anti-freeze products will not mix with Procor 3000.

Service intervals – Speedfight 2 50 LCDP/LBDP/LNDP/LEDP, X-Team 50 LNDP, X-Race 50 LNDP, WRC 206 50, Furious, Iron-X 50, Motorsport 50, R-Cup 50

Note: *Always perform the Daily (pre-ride) checks before every service interval – see the beginning of this Manual. Severe conditions are regarded as intensive urban use, short journeys with cold engine or use in dusty conditions.*

	Text section in this Chapter	Every 3000 miles (5000 km) or 1500 miles (2500 km) for severe conditions	Every 6000 miles (10,000 km) or 3000 miles (5000 km) for severe conditions
Air filter – clean/renew	1	✔	
Battery – check	2	✔	
Brake fluid – check*	6	✔	
Brake hoses – check*	7	✔	
Brake levers – lubricate	4	✔	
Brake pads – check	8	✔	
Brake system – check	3	✔	
Carburettor – clean	16		✔
Clutch pulley and bearing – check and lubricate	26		✔
Cooling system – check**	19	✔	
Cylinder head – decarbonise	23		✔
Drive belt – check	24	✔	
Drive belt – renew	25		✔
Engine oil system – check	11	✔	
Engine oil filter – renew	12		✔
Fuel system – check	14	✔	
Headlight, brake light and horn – check	21	✔	
Idle speed – check and adjust	15	✔	
Kickstart gear and spindle bush – check	27		✔
Nuts and bolts – tightness check	20	✔	
Oil pump cable – check and adjust	13	✔	
Stand – check and lubricate	22	✔	
Spark plug – gap check and adjust	17	✔	
Spark plug – renew	18		✔
Throttle cable – check and adjust	10	✔	
Relay box oil level – check	28		✔
Variator pulley and rollers – check and lubricate	24	✔	
Wheels and tyres – check	30	✔	

* The brake fluid must be changed every 2 years and the brake hose renewed every 3 years, irrespective of mileage
**Drain and refill with fresh coolant every 2 years, irrespective of mileage

Speedfight 2 50 B/N/E, 50 BP/NP/EP, X-Team 50 NP, WRC 206 50, Furious, Silver Sport, Iron-X, Motorsport 50 AC, R-Cup 50 AC, Rally Victories

Model identification

Engine	50 cc single cylinder air-cooled two-stroke
Transmission	Variable speed automatic, belt driven
Ignition	Capacitor discharge ignition (CDI)
Front suspension	Leading link monolever
Rear suspension	Swingarm and single shock
Front brake	180 mm disc
Rear brake	110 mm drum
Front tyre size	120/70 x 12
Rear tyre size	130/70 x 12
Engine no. suffix	FB4
Frame no. prefix	VGAS1A
Wheelbase	1225 mm
Overall length	1730 mm
Overall width (excl. mirrors)	700 mm
Overall height (excl. mirrors)	1155 mm
Weight (dry)	94 kg
Fuel tank capacity	7.2 litres

Servicing specifications and lubricants

Spark plug type	NGK BR7HS
Spark plug electrode gap	0.6 mm
Idle speed	1500 rpm
Front tyre pressure	19 psi (1.3 Bar)
Rear tyre pressure	23 psi (1.6 Bar)
Disc brake pad minimum thickness	1.5 mm
Rear drum brake lever freeplay	10 to 20 mm
Throttle twistgrip freeplay	2 to 5 mm
Fuel	Unleaded petrol (gasoline) min 95 octane
Engine oil	JASO FC, SAE 20 semi-synthetic
Engine oil tank capacity	1.3 litres
Relay box oil	80W-90 scooter gear oil
Relay box oil capacity	120 ml
Brake fluid	DOT 4

Service intervals – Speedfight 2 50 B/N/E, 50 BP/NP/EP, X-Team 50 NP, WRC 206 50, Furious, Silver Sport, Iron-X, Motorsport 50 AC, R-Cup 50 AC, Rally Victories

Note: *Always perform the Daily (pre-ride) checks before every service interval – see the beginning of this Manual. Severe conditions are regarded as intensive urban use, short journeys with cold engine or use in dusty conditions.*

	Text section in this Chapter	Every 3000 miles (5000 km) or 1500 miles (2500 km) for severe conditions	Every 6000 miles (10,000 km) or 3000 miles (5000 km) for severe conditions
Air filter – clean/renew	1	✔	
Battery – check	2	✔	
Brake cable – check and lubricate	5	✔	
Brake fluid – check*	6	✔	
Brake hose – check*	7	✔	
Brake levers – lubricate	4	✔	
Brake pads – check	8	✔	
Brake shoes – check	9	✔	
Brake system – check	3	✔	
Carburettor – clean	16		✔
Clutch pulley and bearing – check and lubricate	26		✔
Cylinder head – decarbonise	19		✔
Drive belt – check	24	✔	
Drive belt – renew	25		✔
Engine oil system – check	11	✔	
Engine oil filter – renew	12		✔
Fuel system – check	14	✔	
Headlight, brake light and horn – check	21	✔	
Idle speed – check and adjust	15	✔	
Kickstart gear and spindle bush – check	27		✔
Nuts and bolts – tightness check	20	✔	
Oil pump cable – check and adjust	13	✔	
Rear drum brake cam – check and lubricate	29		✔
Stand – check and lubricate	22	✔	
Spark plug – gap check and adjust	17	✔	
Spark plug – renew	18		✔
Throttle cable – check and adjust	10	✔	
Relay box oil level – check	28		✔
Variator pulley and rollers – check and lubricate	24	✔	
Wheels and tyres – check	30	✔	

* The brake fluid must be changed every 2 years and the brake hose renewed every 3 years, irrespective of mileage

Speedfight 2 X-Race 50 NP

Model identification

Engine	49 cc single cylinder air-cooled two-stroke
Transmission	Variable speed automatic, belt driven
Ignition	Capacitor discharge ignition (CDI)
Front suspension	Leading link monolever
Rear suspension	Swingarm and single shock
Front brake	180 mm disc
Rear brake	180 mm disc
Front tyre size	120/70 x 12
Rear tyre size	140/70 x 12
Engine no. suffix	FB4
Frame no. prefix	VGAS1A
Wheelbase	1225 mm
Overall length	1730 mm
Overall width (excl. mirrors)	700 mm
Overall height (excl. mirrors)	1155 mm
Weight (dry)	90 kg
Fuel tank capacity	7.2 litres

Servicing specifications and lubricants

Spark plug type	NGK BR7HS
Spark plug electrode gap	0.6 mm
Idle speed	1500 rpm
Front tyre pressure	19 psi (1.3 Bar)
Rear tyre pressure	23 psi (1.6 Bar)
Disc brake pad minimum thickness	1.5 mm
Throttle twistgrip freeplay	2 to 5 mm
Fuel	Unleaded petrol (gasoline) min 95 octane
Engine oil	JASO FC, SAE 20 semi-synthetic
Engine oil tank capacity	1.3 litres
Relay box oil	80W-90 scooter gear oil
Relay box oil capacity	120 ml
Brake fluid	DOT 4

Service intervals – Speedfight 2 X-Race 50 NP

Note: *Always perform the Daily (pre-ride) checks before every service interval – see the beginning of this Manual. Severe conditions are regarded as intensive urban use, short journeys with cold engine or use in dusty conditions.*

	Text section in this Chapter	Every 3000 miles (5000 km) or 1500 miles (2500 km) for severe conditions	Every 6000 miles (10,000 km) or 3000 miles (5000 km) for severe conditions
Air filter – clean/renew	1	✔	
Battery – check	2	✔	
Brake fluid – check*	6	✔	
Brake hoses – check*	7	✔	
Brake levers – lubricate	4	✔	
Brake pads – check	8	✔	
Brake system – check	3	✔	
Carburettor – clean	16		✔
Clutch pulley and bearing – check and lubricate	26		✔
Cylinder head – decarbonise	23		✔
Drive belt – check	24	✔	
Drive belt – renew	25		✔
Engine oil system – check	11	✔	
Engine oil filter – renew	12		✔
Fuel system – check	14	✔	
Headlight, brake light and horn – check	21	✔	
Idle speed – check and adjust	15	✔	
Kickstart gear and spindle bush – check	27		✔
Nuts and bolts – tightness check	20	✔	
Oil pump cable – check and adjust	13	✔	
Stand – check and lubricate	22	✔	
Spark plug – gap check and adjust	17	✔	
Spark plug – renew	18		✔
Throttle cable – check and adjust	10	✔	
Relay box oil level – check	28		✔
Variator pulley and rollers – check and lubricate	24	✔	
Wheels and tyres – check	30	✔	

* The brake fluid must be changed every 2 years and the brake hose renewed every 3 years, irrespective of mileage

Speedfight 100, 100P and Prost 100
Speedfight 2 100 NP, X-Team 100, X-Race 100, WRC 206 100, Furious, Silver Sport, Rally Victories 100P, Advantage 100

Model identification

Engine	100 cc single cylinder air-cooled two-stroke
Transmission	Variable speed automatic, belt driven
Ignition	Capacitor discharge ignition (CDI)
Front suspension	Leading link monolever
Rear suspension	Swingarm and single shock
Front brake	180 mm disc
Rear brake	180 mm disc
Front tyre size	120/70 x 12
Rear tyre size	
1997 to 2002 models	130/70 x 12
2003-on models	140/70 x 12
Engine no. suffix	FB6
Frame no. prefix	VGAS2A
Wheelbase	1225 mm
Overall length	1730 mm
Overall width (excl. mirrors)	700 mm
Overall height (excl. mirrors)	1155 mm
Weight (dry)	94 kg
Fuel tank capacity	7.2 litres

Servicing specifications and lubricants

Spark plug type	
Normal use	NGK BR8ES
Frequent stop/start riding	NGK BPR7ES
Spark plug electrode gap	0.6 mm
Idle speed	1600 rpm
Front tyre pressure	19 psi (1.3 Bar)
Rear tyre pressure	23 psi (1.6 Bar)
Disc brake pad minimum thickness	1.5 mm
Throttle twistgrip freeplay	2 to 5 mm
Fuel	Unleaded petrol (gasoline) min 95 octane
Engine oil	JASO FC, SAE 20 semi-synthetic
Engine oil tank capacity	1.3 litres
Relay box oil	80W-90 scooter gear oil
Relay box oil capacity	120 ml
Brake fluid	DOT 4

Service intervals – Speedfight 100, 100P and Prost 100, Speedfight 2 100 NP, X-Team 100, X-Race 100, WRC 206 100, Furious, Silver Sport, Rally Victories 100P, Advantage 100

Note: *Always perform the Daily (pre-ride) checks before every service interval – see the beginning of this Manual. Severe conditions are regarded as intensive urban use, short journeys with cold engine or use in dusty conditions.*

	Text section in this Chapter	Every 3000 miles (5000 km) or 1500 miles (2500 km) for severe conditions	Every 6000 miles (10,000 km) or 3000 miles (5000 km) for severe conditions
Air filter – clean/renew	1	✔	
Battery – check	2	✔	
Brake fluid – check*	6	✔	
Brake hoses – check*	7	✔	
Brake levers – lubricate	4	✔	
Brake pads – check	8	✔	
Brake system – check	3	✔	
Carburettor – clean	16		✔
Clutch pulley and bearing – check and lubricate	26		✔
Cylinder head – decarbonise	23		✔
Drive belt – check	24	✔	
Drive belt – renew	25		✔
Engine oil system – check	11	✔	
Engine oil filter – renew	12		✔
Fuel system – check	14	✔	
Headlight, brake light and horn – check	21	✔	
Idle speed – check and adjust	15	✔	
Kickstart gear and spindle bush – check	27		✔
Nuts and bolts – tightness check	20	✔	
Oil pump cable – check and adjust	13	✔	
Stand – check and lubricate	22	✔	
Spark plug – gap check and adjust	17	✔	
Spark plug – renew	18		✔
Throttle cable – check and adjust	10	✔	
Relay box oil level – check	28		✔
Variator pulley and rollers – check and lubricate	24	✔	
Wheels and tyres – check	30	✔	

* The brake fluid must be changed every 2 years and the brake hose renewed every 3 years, irrespective of mileage

Trekker Road, Road P

Model identification

Engine	49 cc single cylinder air-cooled two-stroke
Transmission	Variable speed automatic, belt driven
Ignition	Capacitor discharge ignition (CDI)
Front suspension	Telescopic fork
Rear suspension	Swingarm and single shock
Front brake	190 mm disc
Rear brake	110 mm drum
Front tyre size	120/70 x 12
Rear tyre size	130/70 x 12
Engine no. suffix	FB2
Frame no. prefix	VGAS1A
Wheelbase	1250 mm
Overall length	1760 mm
Overall width (excl. mirrors)	670 mm
Overall height (excl. mirrors)	1100 mm
Weight (dry)	83 kg
Fuel tank capacity	6 litres

Servicing specifications and lubricants

Spark plug type	NGK BR7HS
Spark plug electrode gap	0.6 mm
Idle speed	1600 rpm
Front tyre pressure	19 psi (1.3 Bar)
Rear tyre pressure	23 psi (1.6 Bar)
Disc brake pad minimum thickness	1.5 mm
Rear drum brake lever freeplay	10 to 20 mm
Throttle twistgrip freeplay	2 to 5 mm
Fuel	Unleaded petrol (gasoline) min 95 octane
Engine oil	JASO FC, SAE 20 semi-synthetic
Engine oil tank capacity	1.3 litres
Relay box oil	80W-90 scooter gear oil
Relay box oil capacity	120 ml
Brake fluid	DOT 4

Service intervals – Trekker Road, Road P

Note: *Always perform the Daily (pre-ride) checks before every service interval – see the beginning of this Manual. Severe conditions are regarded as intensive urban use, short journeys with cold engine or use in dusty conditions.*

	Text section in this Chapter	Every 3000 miles (5000 km) or 1500 miles (2500 km) for severe conditions	Every 6000 miles (10,000 km) or 3000 miles (5000 km) for severe conditions
Air filter – clean/renew	1	✔	
Battery – check	2	✔	
Brake cable – check and lubricate	5	✔	
Brake fluid – check*	6	✔	
Brake hose – check*	7	✔	
Brake levers – lubricate	4	✔	
Brake pads – check	8	✔	
Brake shoes – check	9	✔	
Brake system – check	3	✔	
Carburettor – clean	16		✔
Clutch pulley and bearing – check and lubricate	26		✔
Cylinder head – decarbonise	23		✔
Drive belt – check	24	✔	
Drive belt – renew	25		✔
Engine oil system – check	11	✔	
Engine oil filter – renew	12		✔
Fuel system – check	14	✔	
Headlight, brake light and horn – check	21	✔	
Idle speed – check and adjust	15	✔	
Kickstart gear and spindle bush – check	27		✔
Nuts and bolts – tightness check	20	✔	
Oil pump cable – check and adjust	13	✔	
Rear drum brake cam – check and lubricate	29		✔
Stand – check and lubricate	22	✔	
Spark plug – gap check and adjust	17	✔	
Spark plug – renew	18		✔
Throttle cable – check and adjust	10	✔	
Relay box oil level – check	28		✔
Variator pulley and rollers – check and lubricate	24	✔	
Wheels and tyres – check	30	✔	

* *The brake fluid must be changed every 2 years and the brake hose renewed every 3 years, irrespective of mileage*

Trekker 100, 100P, Metal-X

Model identification

Engine	100 cc single cylinder air-cooled two-stroke
Transmission	Variable speed automatic, belt driven
Ignition	Capacitor discharge ignition (CDI)
Front suspension	Telescopic fork
Rear suspension	Swingarm and single shock
Front brake	190 mm disc
Rear brake	110 mm drum
Front tyre size	120/70 x 12
Rear tyre size	130/90 x 12
Engine no. suffix	FB6
Frame no. prefix	VGAS2A
Wheelbase	1250 mm
Overall length	1760 mm
Overall width (excl. mirrors)	670 mm
Overall height (excl. mirrors)	1110 mm
Weight (dry)	91 kg
Fuel tank capacity	7.2 litres

Servicing specifications and lubricants

Spark plug type	
Normal use	NGK BR8ES
Frequent stop/start riding	NGK BPR7ES
Spark plug electrode gap	0.6 mm
Idle speed	1600 rpm
Front tyre pressure	19 psi (1.3 Bar)
Rear tyre pressure	23 psi (1.6 Bar)
Disc brake pad minimum thickness	1.5 mm
Rear drum brake lever freeplay	10 to 20 mm
Throttle twistgrip freeplay	2 to 5 mm
Fuel	Unleaded petrol (gasoline) min 95 octane
Engine oil	JASO FC, SAE 20 semi-synthetic
Engine oil tank capacity	1.3 litres
Relay box oil	80W-90 scooter gear oil
Relay box oil capacity	120 ml
Brake fluid	DOT 4

Service intervals – Trekker 100, 100P, Metal-X

Note: *Always perform the Daily (pre-ride) checks before every service interval – see the beginning of this Manual. Severe conditions are regarded as intensive urban use, short journeys with cold engine or use in dusty conditions.*

	Text section in this Chapter	Every 3000 miles (5000 km) or 1500 miles (2500 km) for severe conditions	Every 6000 miles (10,000 km) or 3000 miles (5000 km) for severe conditions
Air filter – clean/renew	1	✔	
Battery – check	2	✔	
Brake cable – check and lubricate	5	✔	
Brake fluid – check*	6	✔	
Brake hose – check*	7	✔	
Brake levers – lubricate	4	✔	
Brake pads – check	8	✔	
Brake shoes – check	9	✔	
Brake system – check	3	✔	
Carburettor – clean	16		✔
Clutch pulley and bearing – check and lubricate	26		✔
Cylinder head – decarbonise	23		✔
Drive belt – check	24	✔	
Drive belt – renew	25		✔
Engine oil system – check	11	✔	
Engine oil filter – renew	12		✔
Fuel system – check	14	✔	
Headlight, brake light and horn – check	21	✔	
Idle speed – check and adjust	15	✔	
Kickstart gear and spindle bush – check	27		✔
Nuts and bolts – tightness check	20	✔	
Oil pump cable – check and adjust	13	✔	
Rear drum brake cam – check and lubricate	29		✔
Stand – check and lubricate	22	✔	
Spark plug – gap check and adjust	17	✔	
Spark plug – renew	18		✔
Throttle cable – check and adjust	10	✔	
Relay box oil level – check	28		✔
Variator pulley and rollers – check and lubricate	24	✔	
Wheels and tyres – check	30	✔	

* The brake fluid must be changed every 2 years and the brake hose renewed every 3 years, irrespective of mileage

Trekker Off Road, Urban Black, Streetboard, Metal-X, TKR Street Zone, TKR WRC 206, Metal-X Furious, TKR Rally Victories

Model identification

Engine	49 cc single cylinder air-cooled two-stroke
Transmission	Variable speed automatic, belt driven
Ignition	Capacitor discharge ignition (CDI)
Front suspension	Upside down telescopic fork
Rear suspension	Swingarm and single shock
Front brake	190 mm disc
Rear brake	110 mm drum
Front tyre size	120/90 x 10
Rear tyre size	130/90 x 10
Engine no. suffix	FB2
Frame no. prefix	VGAS1A
Wheelbase	1250 mm
Overall length	1760 mm
Overall width (excl. mirrors)	670 mm
Overall height (excl. mirrors)	1110 mm
Weight (dry)	88 kg
Fuel tank capacity	6 litres

Servicing specifications and lubricants

Spark plug type	NGK BR7HS
Spark plug electrode gap	0.6 mm
Idle speed	1600 rpm
Front tyre pressure	19 psi (1.3 Bar)
Rear tyre pressure	23 psi (1.6 Bar)
Disc brake pad minimum thickness	1.5 mm
Rear drum brake lever freeplay	10 to 20 mm
Throttle twistgrip freeplay	2 to 5 mm
Fuel	Unleaded petrol (gasoline) min 95 octane
Engine oil	JASO FC, SAE 20 semi-synthetic
Engine oil tank capacity	1.3 litres
Relay box oil	80W-90 scooter gear oil
Relay box oil capacity	120 ml
Brake fluid	DOT 4

Service intervals – Trekker Off Road, Urban Black, Streetboard, Metal-X, TKR Street Zone, TKR WRC 206, Metal-X Furious, TKR Rally Victories

Note: Always perform the Daily (pre-ride) checks before every service interval – see the beginning of this Manual. Severe conditions are regarded as intensive urban use, short journeys with cold engine or use in dusty conditions.

	Text section in this Chapter	Every 3000 miles (5000 km) or 1500 miles (2500 km) for severe conditions	Every 6000 miles (10,000 km) or 3000 miles (5000 km) for severe conditions
Air filter – clean/renew	1	✔	
Battery – check	2	✔	
Brake cable – check and lubricate	5	✔	
Brake fluid – check*	6	✔	
Brake hose – check*	7	✔	
Brake levers – lubricate	4	✔	
Brake pads – check	8	✔	
Brake shoes – check	9	✔	
Brake system – check	3	✔	
Carburettor – clean	16		✔
Clutch pulley and bearing – check and lubricate	26		✔
Cylinder head – decarbonise	23		✔
Drive belt – check	24	✔	
Drive belt – renew	25		✔
Engine oil system – check	11	✔	
Engine oil filter – renew	12		✔
Fuel system – check	14	✔	
Headlight, brake light and horn – check	21	✔	
Idle speed – check and adjust	15	✔	
Kickstart gear and spindle bush – check	27		✔
Nuts and bolts – tightness check	20	✔	
Oil pump cable – check and adjust	13	✔	
Rear drum brake cam – check and lubricate	29		✔
Stand – check and lubricate	22	✔	
Spark plug – gap check and adjust	17	✔	
Spark plug – renew	18		✔
Throttle cable – check and adjust	10	✔	
Relay box oil level – check	28		✔
Variator pulley and rollers – check and lubricate	24	✔	
Wheels and tyres – check	30	✔	

* The brake fluid must be changed every 2 years and the brake hose renewed every 3 years, irrespective of mileage

Vivacity 50, Sportline, VS/X, X-Race, Compact, Silver Sport

Model identification

Engine	49 cc single cylinder air-cooled two-stroke
Transmission	Variable speed automatic, belt driven
Ignition	Capacitor discharge ignition (CDI)
Front suspension	Upside down telescopic fork
Rear suspension	Swingarm and single shock
Front brake	190 mm disc
Rear brake	110 mm drum
Front tyre size	
Compact	110/80 x 10
All other models	120/70 x 12
Rear tyre size	
Compact	120/70 x 10
All other models	130/70 x 12
Engine no. suffix	FB2
Frame no. prefix	VGAS1A
Wheelbase	1249 mm
Overall length	1740 mm
Overall width (excl. mirrors)	700 mm
Overall height (excl. mirrors)	
Compact	1090 mm
All other models	1140 mm
Weight (dry)	
Compact	79.3 kg
All other models	81 kg
Fuel tank capacity	6 litres

Servicing specifications and lubricants

Spark plug type	NGK BR7HS
Spark plug electrode gap	0.6 mm
Idle speed	1600 rpm
Front tyre pressure	19 psi (1.3 Bar)
Rear tyre pressure	23 psi (1.6 Bar)
Disc brake pad minimum thickness	1.5 mm
Rear drum brake lever freeplay	10 to 20 mm
Throttle twistgrip freeplay	2 to 5 mm
Fuel	Unleaded petrol (gasoline) min 95 octane
Engine oil	JASO FC, SAE 20 semi-synthetic
Engine oil tank capacity	1.3 litres
Relay box oil	80W-90 scooter gear oil
Relay box oil capacity	120 ml
Brake fluid	DOT 4

Service intervals – Vivacity 50, Sportline, VS/X, X-Race, Compact, Silver Sport

Note: *Always perform the Daily (pre-ride) checks before every service interval – see the beginning of this Manual. Severe conditions are regarded as intensive urban use, short journeys with cold engine or use in dusty conditions.*

	Text section in this Chapter	Every 3000 miles (5000 km) or 1500 miles (2500 km) for severe conditions	Every 6000 miles (10,000 km) or 3000 miles (5000 km) for severe conditions
Air filter – clean/renew	1	✔	
Battery – check	2	✔	
Brake cable – check and lubricate	5	✔	
Brake fluid – check*	6	✔	
Brake hose – check*	7	✔	
Brake levers – lubricate	4	✔	
Brake pads – check	8	✔	
Brake shoes – check	9	✔	
Brake system – check	3	✔	
Carburettor – clean	16		✔
Clutch pulley and bearing – check and lubricate	26		✔
Cylinder head – decarbonise	23		✔
Drive belt – check	24	✔	
Drive belt – renew	25		✔
Engine oil system – check	11	✔	
Engine oil filter – renew	12		✔
Fuel system – check	14	✔	
Headlight, brake light and horn – check	21	✔	
Idle speed – check and adjust	15	✔	
Kickstart gear and spindle bush – check	27		✔
Nuts and bolts – tightness check	20	✔	
Oil pump cable – check and adjust	13	✔	
Rear drum brake cam – check and lubricate	29		✔
Stand – check and lubricate	22	✔	
Spark plug – gap check and adjust	17	✔	
Spark plug – renew	18		✔
Throttle cable – check and adjust	10	✔	
Relay box oil level – check	28		✔
Variator pulley and rollers – check and lubricate	24	✔	
Wheels and tyres – check	30	✔	

* The brake fluid must be changed every 2 years and the brake hose renewed every 3 years, irrespective of mileage

Vivacity 100, VS/X, 100T

Model identification

Engine	100 cc single cylinder air-cooled two-stroke
Transmission	Variable speed automatic, belt driven
Ignition	Capacitor discharge ignition (CDI)
Front suspension	Upside down telescopic fork
Rear suspension	Swingarm and single shock
Front brake	190 mm disc
Rear brake	110 mm drum
Front tyre size	120/70 x 12
Rear tyre size	130/70 x 12
Engine no. suffix	FB6
Frame no. prefix	VGAS2A
Wheelbase	1250 mm
Overall length	1740 mm
Overall width (excl. mirrors)	700 mm
Overall height (excl. mirrors)	1140 mm
Weight (dry)	90 kg
Fuel tank capacity	6 litres

Servicing specifications and lubricants

Spark plug type	
Normal use	NGK BR8ES
Frequent stop/start riding	NGK BPR7ES
Spark plug electrode gap	0.6 mm
Idle speed	1600 rpm
Front tyre pressure	19 psi (1.3 Bar)
Rear tyre pressure	23 psi (1.6 Bar)
Disc brake pad minimum thickness	1.5 mm
Rear drum brake lever freeplay	10 to 20 mm
Throttle twistgrip freeplay	2 to 5 mm
Fuel	Unleaded petrol (gasoline) min 95 octane
Engine oil	JASO FC, SAE 20 semi-synthetic
Engine oil tank capacity	1.3 litres
Relay box oil	80W-90 scooter gear oil
Relay box oil capacity	120 ml
Brake fluid	DOT 4

Service intervals – Vivacity 100, VS/X, 100T

Note: *Always perform the Daily (pre-ride) checks before every service interval – see the beginning of this Manual. Severe conditions are regarded as intensive urban use, short journeys with cold engine or use in dusty conditions.*

	Text section in this Chapter	Every 3000 miles (5000 km) or 1500 miles (2500 km) for severe conditions	Every 6000 miles (10,000 km) or 3000 miles (5000 km) for severe conditions
Air filter – clean/renew	1	✔	
Battery – check	2	✔	
Brake cable – check and lubricate	5	✔	
Brake fluid – check*	6	✔	
Brake hose – check*	7	✔	
Brake levers – lubricate	4	✔	
Brake pads – check	8	✔	
Brake shoes – check	9	✔	
Brake system – check	3	✔	
Carburettor – clean	16		✔
Clutch pulley and bearing – check and lubricate	26		✔
Cylinder head – decarbonise	23		✔
Drive belt – check	24	✔	
Drive belt – renew	25		✔
Engine oil system – check	11	✔	
Engine oil filter – renew	12		✔
Fuel system – check	14	✔	
Headlight, brake light and horn – check	21	✔	
Idle speed – check and adjust	15	✔	
Kickstart gear and spindle bush – check	27		✔
Nuts and bolts – tightness check	20	✔	
Oil pump cable – check and adjust	13	✔	
Rear drum brake cam – check and lubricate	29		✔
Stand – check and lubricate	22	✔	
Spark plug – gap check and adjust	17	✔	
Spark plug – renew	18		✔
Throttle cable – check and adjust	10	✔	
Relay box oil level – check	28		✔
Variator pulley and rollers – check and lubricate	24	✔	
Wheels and tyres – check	30	✔	

* The brake fluid must be changed every 2 years and the brake hose renewed every 3 years, irrespective of mileage

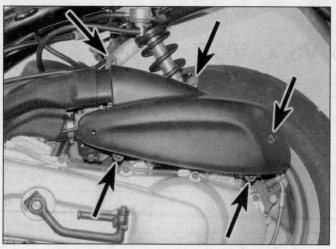

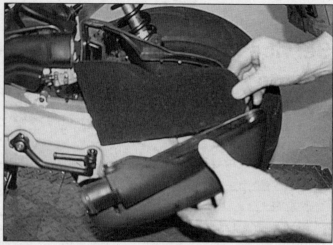

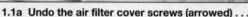

1.1a Undo the air filter cover screws (arrowed) . . .

1.1b . . . and remove the cover and filter element

Routine maintenance and servicing procedures

Note: *Refer to the model specifications at the beginning of this Chapter for service intervals.*

1 Air filter – cleaning and renewal

Caution: If the machine is continually ridden in continuously wet or dusty conditions, the filter should be cleaned more frequently.

1 Remove the screws securing the air filter cover and detach the cover **(see illustration)**. Remove the filter element **(see illustration)**.

2 Wash the filter in hot soapy water, then blow dry using compressed air.

3 Soak the air filter in a mixture of petrol and 10% two-stroke oil, then squeeze out the excess liquid, making sure you do not damage the filter by twisting it.

4 Allow the filter to dry for a while, then fit it back into the housing and install the cover and tighten the screws securely.

5 If the filter is excessively dirty and cannot be cleaned properly, or is torn or damaged in any way, renew it. *The element can be cleaned as described, although note that Peugeot actually recommend fitting a new element at 3000 mile (5000 km) intervals.*

2.2 Remove the cell caps to top-up the battery

2 Battery – check

Caution: Be extremely careful when handling or working around the battery. The electrolyte is very caustic and an explosive gas (hydrogen) is given off when the battery is charging.

Conventional battery

1 Remove the battery access panel and the battery retaining strap, and partially lift the battery out of its holder (see Chapter 9). Check the electrolyte level which is visible through the translucent battery case – it should be between the UPPER and LOWER level marks.

2 If the electrolyte is low, disconnect the battery terminals (see Chapter 9) and move the battery to the work bench. Remove the cell caps and fill each cell to the upper level mark with distilled water **(see illustration)**. Do not use tap water, and do not overfill. The cell holes are quite small, so it may help to use a clean plastic squeeze bottle with a small spout to add the water. Install the battery cell caps, tightening them securely, then install the battery (see Chapter 9).

Maintenance-free battery

3 On machines fitted with a sealed battery, no maintenance is required. **Note:** *Do not attempt to remove the battery caps to check the electrolyte level or battery specific gravity. Removal will damage the caps, resulting in electrolyte leakage and battery damage. All that should be done is to check that its terminals are clean and tight and that the casing is not damaged or leaking. See Chapter 9 for further details.*

3 Brake system – check

1 A routine check of the brake system will ensure that any problems are discovered and remedied before the rider's safety is jeopardised.

2 Check the brake levers for looseness, rough action, excessive play and other damage. Replace any worn or damaged parts with new ones (see Chapter 8).

3 Make sure all brake fasteners are tight. Check the brake pads (disc brake) and brake shoes (drum brake) for wear (see Sections 8 and 9).

4 Where disc brakes are fitted, make sure the fluid level in the hydraulic reservoir is correct (see *Daily (pre-ride) checks*). Look for leaks at the hose connections and check for cracks and abrasions in the hoses and renew them if necessary (see Chapter 8). If the lever action is spongy, bleed the brakes (see Chapter 8).

5 Where drum brakes are fitted, check the cable for damage or stiff action (see Section 5).

6 Make sure the brake light operates when each brake lever is pulled in. The brake light switches are not adjustable. If they fail to operate properly, check them (see Chapter 9).

4 Brake levers – lubrication

1 The lever pivots should be lubricated periodically to reduce wear and ensure safe and trouble-free operation.

2 In order for the lubricant to be applied where it will do the most good, the lever should be removed (see Chapter 8). However, if chain and cable lubricant is being used, it can be applied to the pivot joint gaps and will

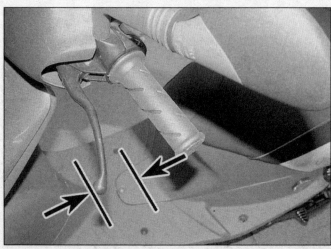

5.1 Measuring rear brake lever freeplay

5.2 Rear drum brake adjuster nut

usually work its way into the areas where friction occurs. If motor oil or light grease is being used, apply it sparingly as it may attract dirt (which could cause the controls to bind or wear at an accelerated rate). **Note:** *One of the best lubricants for the control lever pivots is a dry-film lubricant.*

5 Brake cable – check, adjustment and lubrication

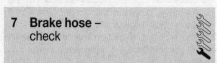

Check and adjustment

1 On machines with a drum rear brake, check that there is no excessive freeplay in the handlebar lever before the brake takes effect. Peugeot specify 10 to 20 mm freeplay at the ball end of the lever **(see illustration)**.
2 To reduce freeplay in the lever, turn the adjuster nut on the brake drum end of the cable clockwise; to increase freeplay, turn the adjuster nut anti-clockwise **(see illustration)**.
3 The wheel should spin freely when the brake is not activated. If the brake is binding without the lever being pulled, first check that the lever is moving freely (see Section 4). Next, disconnect the cable from the handlebar lever (see Chapter 8) and check that the inner cable slides smoothly in the outer cable. If the action is stiff, inspect along the length of the outer cable for splits and kinks, and the ends of the inner cable for frays, and replace it with a new one if necessary (see Chapter 8).
4 If there are no signs of damage, lubricate the cable (see Step 7). If the cable is still stiff after lubrication, replace it with a new one (see Chapter 8).
5 If the handlebar lever and brake cable are in good condition, check the operation of the brake cam (see Section 29).

Lubrication

6 The cable should be lubricated periodically to ensure safe and trouble-free operation.

7 To lubricate the cable, disconnect it at its upper end and lubricate it with a pressure adapter, or using the set-up shown **(see illustration)**.
8 Reconnect the cable and adjust the handlebar lever freeplay (see Step 2).

6 Brake fluid – check

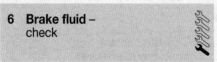

1 The fluid level in the hydraulic reservoir should be checked before riding the machine (see *Daily (pre-ride) checks*).
2 Brake fluid will degrade over a period of time. It should be changed every two years or whenever a new master cylinder or caliper is

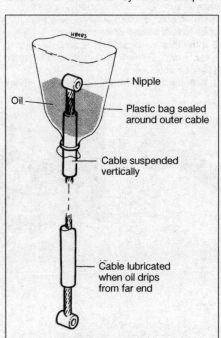

5.7 Lubricating a cable with a makeshift funnel and motor oil

Oil

Nipple

Plastic bag sealed around outer cable

Cable suspended vertically

Cable lubricated when oil drips from far end

fitted. Refer to the brake bleeding and fluid change section in Chapter 8.

7 Brake hose – check

1 Twist and flex the hose while looking for cracks, bulges and seeping fluid. Check extra carefully where the hose connects to the banjo fittings as this is a common area for hose failure **(see illustration)**.
2 Inspect the banjo fittings; if they are rusted, cracked or damaged, fit new hoses.
3 Inspect the banjo union connections for leaking fluid. If they leak when tightened securely, unscrew the banjo bolt and fit new washers (see Chapter 8).
4 The flexible hydraulic hose will deteriorate with age and should be renewed every three years regardless of its apparent condition (see Chapter 8).

8 Brake pads – check

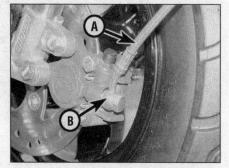

1 The disc brake pads are not marked with wear indicators. The amount of friction

7.1 Inspect the brake hose (A) and banjo fitting (B)

8.1 Check brake pad wear at the underside of the caliper

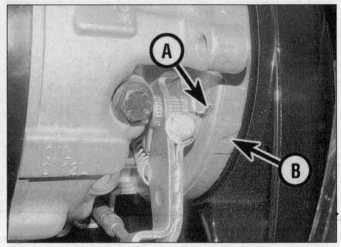

9.1 Rear drum brake wear indicator (A) and index mark (B)

material wear can be checked by looking at the underside of the caliper (see illustration). Alternatively, displace the caliper (see Chapter 8) to check the amount of wear.

2 If the amount of friction material remaining on the pads is below 1.5 mm, new pads must be fitted.

⚠️ *Warning: Brake pads often wear at different rates. If there is any doubt about the condition of either of the pads in a caliper, remove the caliper and check. Brake failure will result if the friction material wears away completely.*

3 Refer to Chapter 8 for details of pad removal, inspection and replacement.

9 Brake shoes – check 🔧

1 The rear drum brake is equipped with a wear indicator (see illustration).
2 As the brake shoes wear and the cable is

adjusted to compensate, the indicator moves closer to the index mark on the casing. To check the extent of brake wear, have an assistant apply the brake firmly; if the indicator aligns with the index mark, the brake shoes must be replaced with new ones (see Chapter 8).

10 Throttle cable – check and adjustment 🔧

All models

1 Ensure the throttle twistgrip rotates easily from fully closed to fully open with the handlebars turned at various angles. The twistgrip should return automatically from fully open to fully closed when released.
2 If the throttle sticks, this is probably due to a cable fault. Remove the cable and lubricate it (see Chapter 4).
3 With the throttle operating smoothly, check

for a small amount of freeplay in the cable, measured in terms of the amount of twistgrip rotation before the throttle opens, and compare the amount to the Specifications at the beginning of this Chapter (see illustration).
4 If there is insufficient or excessive freeplay, loosen the locknut on the cable adjuster, then turn the adjuster until the specified amount of freeplay is evident, then retighten the locknut (see illustration). If the adjuster has reached its limit of adjustment, replace the cable with a new one (see Chapter 4).
5 Start the engine and check the idle speed. If the idle speed is too high, this could be due to incorrect adjustment of the cable. Loosen the locknut and turn the adjuster in – if the idle speed falls as you do, there is insufficient freeplay in the cable. Reset the adjuster (see Step 4). **Note:** *The idle speed should not change as the handlebars are turned. If it does, the throttle cable is routed incorrectly. Rectify the problem before riding the scooter (see Chapter 4).*

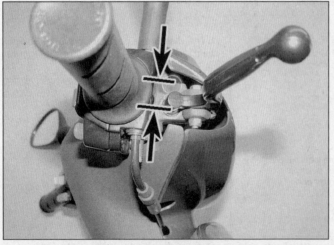

10.3 Throttle cable freeplay is measured in terms of twistgrip rotation

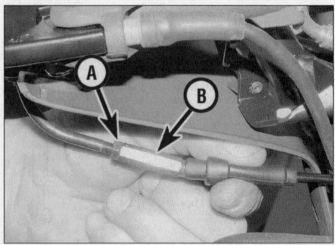

10.4 Throttle cable locknut (A) and adjuster (B)

Models fitted with a cable operated oil pump

Note: *Generally speaking, all 100 cc models and 50 cc models manufactured before 2000 are fitted with a cable operated pump; all other models are fitted with a centrifugal pump. A quick visual check will confirm which pump is fitted to your machine.*

6 There should be no discernable freeplay in the cable from the splitter to the carburettor **(see illustration)**.

7 Remove the air filter housing (see Chapter 4) and pull back the boot on the cable adjuster on the top of the carburettor.

8 Screw the adjuster into the top of the carburettor to create a small amount of freeplay in the cable, then screw the adjuster out until the carburettor slide just begins to lift. Now turn the adjuster in a quarter turn **(see illustration)**. Refit the boot and the filter housing.

9 Check the adjustment of the oil pump cable (see Section 13).

11 Engine oil system – check

1 A routine check of the engine oil system will ensure that any problems are discovered and remedied before the engine is damaged.

2 Check the engine oil level (see *Daily (pre-ride) checks*).

3 Check the operation of the oil level warning light in the instrument cluster. The light should come on temporarily when the ignition is first turned on as a check of the warning circuit and then extinguish. If the light stays on the oil level is low and should be topped up. If the light doesn't come on at all, check the bulb and circuit as described in Chapter 9.

4 Remove the storage compartment (see Chapter 7) and inspect the oil filter **(see**

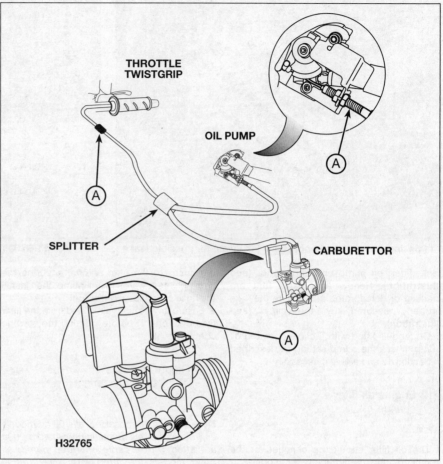

10.6 Cable arrangement for models fitted with a cable operated oil pump

Location of cable adjusters (A)

illustration). Air bubbles should be bled from the filter by tilting it to allow trapped air to rise through the hose into the oil tank. Check for sediment in the filter and replace the filter with

a new one if necessary (see Section 12).

5 Check the condition of the oil inlet and outlet hoses. In particular check that there are no leaks from the hose connections to the oil

10.8 Adjusting the cable at the carburettor end

11.4 Inspect the oil filter (arrowed)

11.5a Inspect oil hose connections (arrowed) for possible leaks

11.5b Oil hose to carburettor secured by clip

tank, filter, oil pump and carburettor **(see illustration)**. Renew any hoses that are cracked or deteriorated and ensure they are properly secured by the clips **(see illustration)**.
6 On models fitted with a cable operated oil pump, check the pump setting as described in Section 13 and adjust if necessary.

12 Engine oil filter – change

1 The oil filter should be changed at the specified service interval, or sooner if necessary (see Section 11).
2 Remove the storage compartment to access the oil filter (see Chapter 7). Release the clips securing the inlet hoses to the filter and slide them along the hoses away from the filter. Detach the hoses and clamp them to prevent oil loss.
3 The oil filter body is marked with an arrow indicating the direction of oil flow. Connect

the hoses to the filter unions, ensuring the arrow points towards the oil pump, then install the hose clips **(see illustration)**.
4 Ensure any trapped air is bled from the filter (see Section 11) before refitting the storage compartment.

13 Oil pump cable – check and adjustment

Note 1: *Generally speaking, all 100 cc models and 50 cc models manufactured before 2000 are fitted with a cable operated pump; all other models are fitted with a centrifugal pump. A quick visual check will confirm which pump is fitted to your machine.*
1 Ensure the throttle twistgrip rotates easily from fully closed to fully open with the handlebars turned at various angles, and check the cable freeplay with the Specifications at the beginning of this Chapter (see Section 10).
2 Remove the storage compartment (see Chapter 7). With the throttle fully open, the

index mark on the pump cam should align with the mark on the pump body **(see illustration)**.
3 If the marks are not aligned, slacken the cable adjuster locknuts and screw them up or down the threaded adjuster as required until the marks align, then retighten the locknuts **(see illustration 13.2)**. If the adjuster has reached its limit of adjustment, replace the cable with a new one (see Chapter 4). Once adjustment is complete install the storage compartment (see Chapter 7).

14 Fuel system – check

⚠️ *Warning: Petrol is extremely flammable, so take extra precautions when you work on any part of the fuel system. Don't smoke or allow open flames or bare light bulbs near the work area, and don't work in a garage where a natural gas-type appliance is*

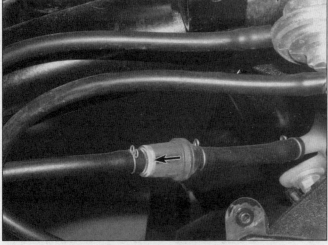

12.3 Arrow on filter indicates direction of oil flow

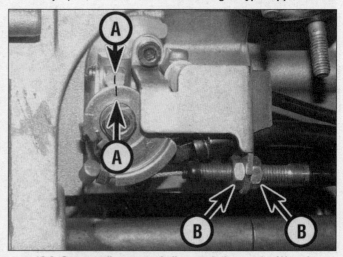

13.2 Correct alignment of oil pump index marks (A) and adjuster locknuts (B)

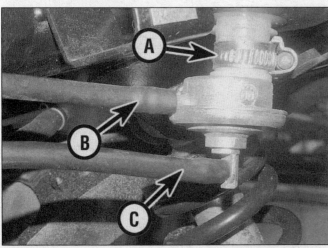

14.2 Fuel tap union clip (A), fuel hose (B) and vacuum hose (C)

15.4a Adjusting the idle speed screw on the Speedfight . . .

15.4b . . . and on the Trekker and Vivacity

present. If you spill any fuel on your skin, rinse it off immediately with soap and water. When you perform any kind of work on the fuel system, wear safety glasses and have a fire extinguisher suitable for a Class B type fire (flammable liquids) on hand.

1 Remove the body panels as necessary to access the fuel tank, tap and carburettor (see Chapter 7). Check the fuel tank, the tap and the fuel hose for signs of leakage, deterioration or damage; in particular check that there is no leakage from the fuel hose. Replace the fuel hose if it is cracked or deteriorated.

2 Inspect the fuel tap to tank union and ensure that the hose clip around the union is tight **(see illustration)**. If the union is leaking, remove the tank and check the condition of the fuel tap O-ring (see Chapter 4).

3 The fuel tap is vacuum operated and should be closed when the engine is not running. Disconnect the hose from the tap to check that the valve inside is not leaking **(see illustration 14.2)**. If the valve is leaking, fit a new tap (see Chapter 4).

4 Cleaning or replacement of the fuel filter is advised after a particularly high mileage has been covered or if fuel starvation is suspected (see Chapter 4).

5 Check that the fuel tank cap breather hole is clear. If the hole becomes blocked, fuel starvation will occur.

6 If the carburettor gaskets are leaking, the carburettor should be disassembled and rebuilt using new gaskets and seals (see Chapter 4).

7 If the fuel gauge is believed to be faulty, check the operation of the sender (see Chapter 9).

15 Idle speed – check and adjustment

1 The idle speed (engine running with the throttle twistgrip closed) should be checked and adjusted when it is obviously too high or too low. Before adjusting the idle speed, make sure the throttle cable is correctly adjusted (see Section 10) and check the spark plug gap (see Section 17).

2 The engine should be at normal operating temperature, which is usually reached after 10 to 15 minutes of stop-and-go riding. Place the machine on its stand and make sure the rear wheel is clear of the ground.

⚠ *Warning: Do not allow exhaust gases to build up in the work area; either perform the check outside or use an exhaust gas extraction system*

3 No tachometer is fitted as standard equipment to enable the idle speed to be compared with that specified. However, it is sufficient to ensure that at idle the engine speed is steady and does not falter, and that it is not so high that the automatic transmission engages.

4 The idle speed adjuster screw is located on the carburettor **(see illustrations)**. With the engine running, turn the screw clockwise to increase idle speed, and anti-clockwise to decrease it.

5 Snap the throttle open and shut a few times, then recheck the idle speed. If necessary, repeat the adjustment procedure.

6 If a smooth, steady idle can't be achieved, the fuel/air mixture may be incorrect (see Chapter 4) or the carburettor may need cleaning (see Section 16)

7 With the idle speed correctly adjusted, recheck the throttle cable freeplay (see Section 10).

16 Carburettor – cleaning

1 Provided the air filter element is kept clean (see Section 1) the carburettor will give many thousands of miles of satisfactory service. However, dirt particles and varnish which gradually accumulate inside the carburettor will eventually lead to running problems and necessitate that the carburettor be removed as described in Chapter 4, Section 9, then dismantled and cleaned as described in Section 10 of the same Chapter. Note that a new carburettor gasket set will be required if it is to be dismantled.

2 Note that the exterior of the carburettor should be kept clean and free of road dirt. Remove the air filter housing cover and the air intake duct (see Chapter 4) for access.

17 Spark plug – gap check and adjustment

1 Make sure your spark plug socket is the correct size (14 mm) before attempting to remove the plug. Open the engine access panel in the bottom of the storage compartment and pull off the spark plug cap **(see illustrations)**.

2 Ensure the spark plug socket is located correctly over the plug and unscrew the plug from the cylinder head.

3 Inspect the electrodes for wear. Both the centre and side electrode should have square edges and the side electrode should be of uniform thickness. Look for excessive deposits and evidence of a cracked or chipped insulator around the centre electrode. Compare your spark plug to the colour spark plug reading chart at the end of this manual.

17.1a Open the engine access panel . . .

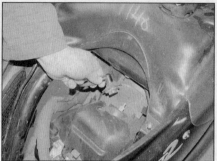

17.1b . . . and remove the spark plug cap

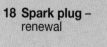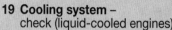

18 Spark plug – renewal

1 Remove the old spark plug as described in Section 17 and install a new one.

19 Cooling system – check (liquid-cooled engines)

Warning: The engine must be cool before beginning this procedure.

Warning: Do not remove the reservoir cap when the engine is hot. It is good practice to cover the cap with a heavy cloth and turn the cap slowly anti-clockwise. If you hear a hissing sound (indicating that there is still pressure in the system), wait until it stops, then continue turning the cap until it can be removed.

1 Check the coolant level (see *Daily (pre-ride) checks*).
2 The entire cooling system should be checked for evidence of leaks. Examine each coolant hose along its entire length, noting that you will need to remove the body panels on the right-hand side to access the hoses **(see illustration)**. Look for cracks, abrasions and other damage. Squeeze the hoses at various points. They should feel firm, yet pliable, and return to their original shape when released. If they are hard or perished, replace them with new ones (see Chapter 3).
3 Check for evidence of leaks at each cooling system joint. Ensure that the hoses are pushed fully onto their unions and that the hose clips are tight. **Note:** *Check the tension of the hose spring clips and replace them with new ones if they are loose.*

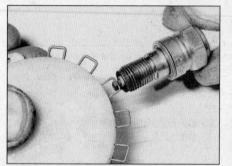

17.5a Using a wire type gauge to measure the spark plug electrode gap

17.5b Using a feeler gauge to measure the spark plug electrode gap

Check the condition of the threads and washer, and the ceramic insulator body for cracks and other damage.
4 If the electrodes are not excessively worn, and if the deposits can be easily removed with a wire brush, the plug can be re-gapped and re-used (if no cracks or chips are visible in the insulator). If in doubt concerning the condition of the plug, replace it with a new one, as the expense is minimal.
5 Before installing the plug, make sure it is the correct type and heat range and check the gap between the electrodes **(see illustrations)**. Compare the gap to that specified and adjust as necessary. If the gap must be adjusted,

bend the side electrode only and be very careful not to chip or crack the insulator nose **(see illustration)**. Make sure the washer is in place before installing the plug.
6 Since the cylinder head is made of aluminium, which is soft and easily damaged, first thread the plug into the head by hand. Once the plug is finger-tight, tighten it securely with the spark plug socket, then reconnect the plug cap.

HAYNES HINT *A stripped plug thread in the cylinder head can be repaired with a thread insert.*

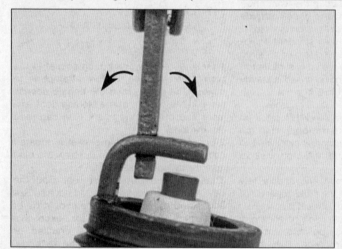

17.5c Adjust the electrode gap by bending the side electrode only

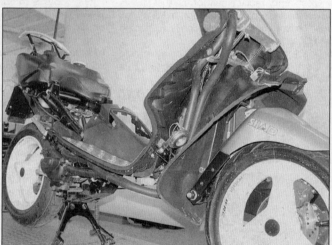

19.2 The coolant hoses run along the right-hand side of the scooter

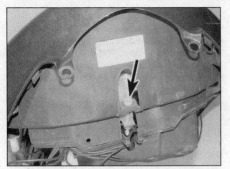

21.2a Headlight adjuster screw on Speedfight models

4 Check the underside of the water pump for evidence of leaks (see Chapter 3).

5 Check the radiator for leaks and other damage. Leaks in the radiator leave tell-tale scale deposits or coolant stains on the outside of the core below the leak. If leaks are noted, remove the radiator (see Chapter 3) and have it repaired or replace it with a new one.

Caution: Do not use a liquid leak stopping compound to try to repair leaks.

6 Inspect the radiator fins for mud, dirt and insects which will impede the flow of air through the radiator. If the fins are dirty, remove the radiator (see Chapter 3) and clean it using water or low pressure compressed air directed through the fins from the back. If the fins are bent or distorted, straighten them carefully with a screwdriver. If the air flow is restricted by bent or damaged fins over more than 30% of the radiator's surface area, fit a new radiator.

7 Remove the reservoir pressure cap (see **Warning**). Check the condition of the coolant in the reservoir. If it is rust-coloured or if accumulations of scale are visible, drain, flush and refill the system with new coolant (see Chapter 3).

8 Check the antifreeze content of the coolant with an antifreeze hydrometer. Sometimes coolant looks like it's in good condition, but is too weak to offer adequate protection. If the hydrometer indicates a weak mixture, drain, flush and refill the system (see Chapter 3). **Note:** *Peugeot recommend draining and refilling the cooling system with fresh coolant every 2 years.*

9 Start the engine and let it reach normal operating temperature, then check for leaks again.

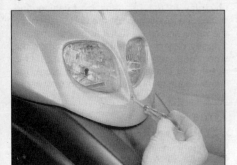

21.2b Adjusting the headlight beam on Trekker models

10 If the coolant level is consistently low, and no evidence of leaks can be found, have the entire system pressure checked by a Peugeot dealer.

20 Nuts and bolts – tightness check

1 Since vibration tends to loosen fasteners, all nuts, bolts, screws, etc. should be periodically checked for proper tightness.

2 Pay particular attention to the following:
    Spark plug
    Carburettor clamps
    Relay box oil plug (where fitted)
    Stand bolts
    Engine mounting bolts
    Suspension bolts
    Wheel bolts
    Brake caliper mounting bolts (disc brakes)
    Brake hose banjo bolts (disc brakes)
    Exhaust system bolts/nuts

3 If a torque wrench is available, use it along with the torque specifications given in this manual.

21 Headlight, brake light and horn – check

Note: *An improperly adjusted headlight may cause problems for oncoming traffic or provide poor, unsafe illumination of the road ahead. Before adjusting the headlight aim, be sure to consult with local traffic laws and regulations.*

1 The headlight beam can adjusted vertically. Before making any adjustment, check that the tyre pressures are correct and the suspension is adjusted as required. Make any adjustments to the headlight aim with the machine on level ground, with the fuel tank half full and with an assistant sitting on the seat. If the bike is usually ridden with a passenger on the back, have a second assistant to do this.

2 Adjustment is made by turning the adjuster screw clockwise to move the beam up, and anti-clockwise to move it down. The adjuster screw is located on the underside of the headlight panel on Speedfight and Vivacity models, and between the headlights on Trekker models **(see illustrations)**.

3 Check the operation of the brake light with the engine running. The brake light should come on when either the front or rear brake levers are pulled in. If it does not, check the operation of the brake light switch and rear/brake light bulb (see Chapter 9).

4 Check the operation of the horn with the engine running. If it fails to work, check the operation of the handlebar switch and the horn itself (see Chapter 9).

22 Stand – check and lubrication

1 Since the stand is exposed to the elements, it should be lubricated periodically to ensure safe and trouble-free operation.

2 In order for the lubricant to be applied where it will do the most good, the component should be disassembled. However, if chain and cable lubricant is being used, it can be applied to the pivot joint gaps and will usually work its way into the areas where friction occurs. If motor oil or light grease is being used, apply it sparingly as it may attract dirt (which could cause the controls to bind or wear at an accelerated rate).

3 The return spring must be capable of retracting the stand fully and holding it retracted when the machine is in use. If the spring has sagged or broken it must be replaced (see Chapter 6).

23 Cylinder head – decarbonisation

Caution: If the machine is continually ridden on short journeys which do not allow the engine to reach and maintain its normal operating temperature, the cylinder head should be decarbonised more frequently.

1 Remove the cylinder head (see Chapter 2A for air-cooled engines, or 2B for liquid-cooled engines).

2 Remove all accumulated carbon from the cylinder head using a blunt scraper. Small traces of carbon can be removed with very fine abrasive paper or a kitchen scourer.

Caution: The cylinder head and piston are made of aluminium which is relatively soft. Take great care not to gouge or score the surface when scraping.

3 Press the cylinder down against the crankcase to avoid breaking the cylinder base gasket seal, then turn the engine over until the piston is at the very top of its stroke. Smear grease all around the edge of the piston to trap any particles of carbon, then clean the piston crown, again taking care not to score or gouge it or the cylinder bore.

4 Clean off the carbon, then lower the piston and wipe away the grease and any remaining particles. Also scrape or wipe clean the intake and exhaust ports in the cylinder. If the exhaust port is heavily coked, remove the exhaust system and clean the port and the exhaust pipe thoroughly (see Chapter 4).

5 Install the cylinder head (see Chapter 2A or 2B).

 HAYNES HiNT *Finish the piston head and combustion chamber off using a metal polish. A shiny surface is more resistant to the build-up of carbon deposits.*

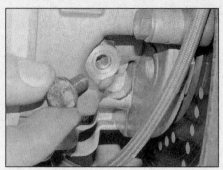

28.2 Unscrew the plug to check the oil level

24 Variator pulley and rollers and drive belt – check

Variator pulley and rollers

1 Referring to Chapter 2C, remove the drive belt cover.
2 A Peugeot service tool or home made alternative is required to remove the variator (see Chapter 2C). Dismantle the variator and renew any parts that are worn; if applicable, lubricate the rollers, ramp plate and housing with high temperature grease (Peugeot recommend Esso SKF LGHT 3/0.4) before reassembly. **Note:** *The variator housing O-ring and variator centre nut must be replaced with a new one on reassembly.*

Drive belt

3 Inspect the drive belt when checking the variator pulley and rollers. No specifications are available regarding belt wear limits but signs of premature belt wear should be investigated. Refer to Chapter 2C, Section 5 for more details.

25 Drive belt – renewal

1 The drive belt must be renewed at the specified service interval (see Chapter 2C).

28.4 Top-up with the specified oil only

26 Clutch pulley and bearing – check and lubrication

1 Referring to Chapter 2C, remove the drive belt cover. The outer half of the clutch pulley should slide outwards on the clutch hub, against the pressure of the clutch centre spring.
2 Grasp the pulley assembly and check for play in the pulley hub bearings. A Peugeot service tool or home made alternative is required to dismantle the clutch and pulley assembly (see Chapter 2C). Renew any parts that are worn and lubricate the pulley needle bearing and the pulley guide pins with high temperature grease (Peugeot recommend Esso SKF LGHT 3/0.4) before reassembly. **Note:** *The clutch centre nut must be replaced with a new one on reassembly.*

27 Kickstart gear and spindle bush – check

1 Referring to Chapter 2C, remove the driver belt cover. The kickstart lever should move smoothly and return to the rest position under the tension of the return spring.
2 Inspect the component parts for damage and wear and renew any parts as necessary (see Chapter 2C). Lubricate the kickstart spindle with high temperature grease (Peugeot recommend Esso SKF LGHT 3/0.4) before reassembly.

28 Relay box oil level – check

Note 1: *Early models were fitted with a relay box drain plug. For those models Peugeot recommend changing the oil every 10,000 km. For all models without a drain plug, it is sufficient to check the oil level at 10,000 km as described below.*
Note 2: *From mid-2002 the oil level plug was deleted from the casing – it is not necessary to change the oil during the life of the scooter, except in the event of relay box overhaul. The level can however be checked if desired when the drive belt cover is removed for inspection of the belt and rollers (see Section 24); with the cover removed the relay box oil level plug is accessible.*
1 Support the machine in an upright position on its stand on level ground. Raise the front wheel, if necessary, so that the rear wheel is touching the ground.
2 Clean the area around the oil level plug on the back of the casing, then unscrew the plug **(see illustration)**.

3 The oil level should come up to the plug threads so that it is just visible on the threads.
4 If the oil is below the level of the plug threads, add the specified grade and type of oil to bring it up to the correct level **(see illustration)**. Do not overfill. Note that Peugeot specify 120 ml of 80W-90 scooter gear oil and specifically advise against the use of a hypoid oil.
5 If the oil level is very low, or oil is leaking from the relay box case, refer to Chapter 2C and inspect the condition of the case seals and gaskets and replace them with new ones if necessary.

29 Rear drum brake cam – check and lubrication

1 Remove the rear wheel and brake shoes, then remove the brake arm and pull the brake cam out of the casing (see Chapter 8).
2 Clean the shaft and cam and inspect the bearing surfaces for wear; replace the cam with a new one if necessary.
3 Apply some copper grease to the bearing surfaces of the cam and the shaft before reassembly.
Caution: Do not apply too much grease otherwise there is a risk of it contaminating the brake drum and shoe linings.

30 Wheels and tyres – general check

Wheels

1 Cast wheels are virtually maintenance free, but they should be kept clean and checked periodically for cracks and other damage. Also check the wheel runout and alignment (see Chapter 8). Never attempt to repair damaged cast wheels; they must be replaced with new ones.
2 Wheel bearings will wear over a period of time and result in handling problems. Support the machine on its centre stand and check for any play in the bearings by pushing and pulling the wheel against the hub. Also rotate the wheel and check that it turns smoothly.
3 If any play is detected in the hub, or if the wheel does not rotate smoothly (and this is not due to brake or transmission drag), the wheel bearings must be inspected for wear or damage (see Chapter 8).

Tyres

4 Check the tyre condition and tread depth thoroughly – see *Daily (pre-ride) checks*. Check the valve rubber for signs of damage or deterioration and have it replaced if necessary. Also, make sure the valve stem cap is in place and tight.

Chapter 2 Part A:
Air-cooled two-stroke engine

Refer to Chapter 1 for model identification details

Contents

Degrees of difficulty

Easy, suitable for novice with little experience		Fairly easy, suitable for beginner with some experience		Fairly difficult, suitable for competent DIY mechanic		Difficult, suitable for experienced DIY mechanic		Very difficult, suitable for expert DIY or professional	

Specifications

50 cc FB2 and FB4 engines

General

Type	Single cylinder two-stroke
Capacity	49.13 cc
Bore	40.0 mm
Stroke	39.1 mm
Compression ratio	6.6 to 1

Piston

Piston diameter (measured 25 mm down from lower ring groove, at 90° to piston pin axis)	
Standard	39.85 mm
Piston pin diameter	12 mm

50 cc FB2 and FB4 engines (continued)

Piston rings

Ring end gap (installed)

Standard	0.24 mm
Service limit (max)	0.26 mm

Connecting rod

Small-end inside diameter	15 mm
Big-end side clearance	0.5 mm

Crankshaft

Runout (max)	0.12 mm
Diameter at main bearings	20 mm

Torque settings

Alternator rotor nut	40 Nm
Crankcase bolts	12 Nm
Cylinder head bolts	15 Nm
Drive belt cover bolts	10 Nm
Engine cover bolts	10 Nm
Engine mountings	
Crankcase-to-front bracket bolt	60 Nm
Front bracket-to-frame bolt	60 Nm
Engine/transmission case-to-rear shock bolt	25 Nm
Inlet manifold bolts	10 Nm
Oil pump mounting bolts	8 Nm
Starter motor mounting bolts	10 Nm

100 cc FB6 engine

General

Type	Single cylinder two-stroke
Capacity	99.9 cc
Bore	50.6 mm
Stroke	49.7 mm
Compression ratio	11 to 1

Piston

Piston diameter (measured 25 mm down from lower ring groove,
at 90° to piston pin axis)

Standard	50.45 mm
Piston pin diameter	14 mm

Piston rings

Ring end gap (installed)

Standard	0.30 mm
Service limit (max)	0.45 mm

Connecting rod

Small-end inside diameter	18 mm
Big-end side clearance	0.5 mm

Crankshaft

Runout (max)	0.12 mm
Diameter at main bearings	25 mm

Torque settings

Alternator rotor nut	40 Nm
Crankcase bolts	12 Nm
Cylinder head bolts	15 Nm
Drive belt cover bolts	10 Nm
Engine cover bolts	10 Nm
Engine mountings	
Crankcase-to-front bracket bolt	60 Nm
Front bracket-to-frame bolt	60 Nm
Engine/transmission case-to-rear shock bolt	25 Nm
Inlet manifold bolts	10 Nm
Oil pump mounting bolts	8 Nm
Starter motor mounting bolts	10 Nm

1 General information

The engine unit is a single cylinder two-stroke, with fan assisted air cooling. The fan is mounted on the alternator rotor, which is on the right-hand end of the crankshaft. The crankshaft assembly is pressed together, incorporating the connecting rod, with the big-end running on the crankpin on a needle roller bearing. The piston also runs on a needle roller bearing fitted in the small-end of the connecting rod. The crankshaft runs in caged ball main bearings. The crankcase divides vertically.

2 Operations possible with the engine in the frame

All components and assemblies, with the exception of the crankshaft assembly and its bearings, can be worked on without having to remove the engine/transmission unit from the frame. If however, a number of areas require attention at the same time, removal of the engine is recommended, as it is an easy task to undertake.

3 Operations requiring engine removal

To access the crankshaft assembly and the engine main bearings, the engine must be removed from the frame and the crankcase halves must be separated.

4 Major engine repair – general note

1 It is not always easy to determine when or if an engine should be completely overhauled, as a number of factors must be considered.
2 High mileage is not necessarily an indication that an overhaul is needed, while low mileage, on the other hand, does not preclude the need for an overhaul. Frequency of servicing is probably the single most important consideration. An engine that has regular and frequent maintenance will most likely give many miles of reliable service. Conversely, a neglected engine, or one which has not been run in properly, may require an overhaul very early in its life.
3 If the engine is making obvious knocking or rumbling noises, the connecting rod and/or main bearings are probably at fault.
4 Loss of power, rough running, excessive noise and high fuel consumption rates may also point to the need for an overhaul, especially if they are all present at the same

time. If a complete tune-up does not remedy the situation, major mechanical work is the only solution.
5 An engine overhaul generally involves restoring the internal parts to the specifications of a new engine. This may require fitting new piston rings and crankcase seals, or, after a high mileage, renewing the crankshaft and connecting rod assembly. The end result should be a like-new engine that will give as many trouble-free miles as the original.
6 Before beginning the engine overhaul, read through the related procedures to familiarise yourself with the scope and requirements of the job. Overhauling an engine is not all that difficult, but it is time consuming. Check on the availability of parts and make sure that any necessary special tools and materials are obtained in advance.
7 Most work can be done with typical workshop hand tools, although Peugeot produce a number of service tools for specific purposes such as separating the crankcase halves. Precision measuring tools are required for inspecting parts to determine if they must be renewed. Alternatively, a Peugeot dealer will handle the inspection of parts and offer advice concerning reconditioning and replacement. As a general rule, time is the primary cost of an overhaul so it does not pay to install worn or substandard parts.
8 As a final note, to ensure maximum life and minimum trouble from a rebuilt engine, everything must be assembled with care in a spotlessly clean environment.

5 Engine – removal and installation

Caution: *The engine is not heavy, however engine removal and installation should be carried out with the aid of an assistant; personal injury or damage could occur if the engine falls or is dropped.*

Removal

1 Support the machine securely in an upright position. Work can be made easier by raising the machine to a convenient working height on an hydraulic ramp or a suitable platform. Make sure it is secure and will not topple over.
2 Remove body panels as necessary according to model (see Chapter 7).
3 Remove the exhaust system (see Chapter 4).
4 If the engine is dirty, particularly around its mountings, wash it thoroughly before starting any major dismantling work. This will make work much easier and rule out the possibility of dirt falling into some vital component.
5 Disconnect the battery negative terminal (see Chapter 9) and pull the spark plug cap off the plug.
6 Trace the wiring from the alternator/ignition pulse generator coil and the starter motor on the right-hand side of the engine and

5.10 Remove the oil pump cable and bracket

disconnect it at the connectors. Free the wiring from any clips on the frame.
7 Remove the air filter housing and the air intake duct (see Chapter 4).
8 Disconnect the fuel pipe and fuel tap vacuum pipe from their unions on the carburettor and inlet manifold respectively. Release the clip securing the oil outlet hose to the carburettor and wrap a clean plastic bag around the end to prevent dirt entering the system, then displace the carburettor (see Chapter 4).
9 Undo the bolts securing the engine and fan cowlings and remove the cowlings (see Chapter 3).
10 Where fitted, detach the oil pump control cable from the pump pulley (see Section 13), then unscrew the bolts securing the oil pump control cable bracket and remove the bracket with the cable attached **(see illustration)**. Refit the bolts to secure the nuts on the underside of the pump mounting and to retain the pump in place.
11 Release the clip securing the oil inlet hose from the oil tank to the union on the oil pump and detach the hose (see Section 13). Clamp the hose and secure it in an upright position to minimise oil loss. Wrap a clean plastic bag around the end to prevent dirt entering the system.
12 On models fitted with a drum rear brake, disconnect the brake cable from the brake arm (see Chapter 8). Undo the screw securing the cable clip to the underside of the drive belt casing and detach the cable **(see illustration)**.
13 On models fitted with a disc rear brake, remove the rear wheel and displace the brake

5.12 Undo the clip (arrowed) to detach the brake cable

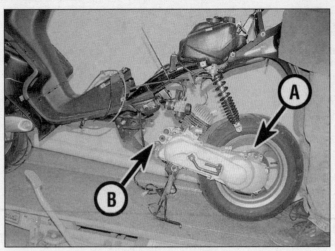

5.14 Remove the bolts securing the rear shock (A) and the frame (B) to the engine unit

7.2a The engine cowling is secured by a bolt on the cooling fan cowling . . .

caliper, then temporarily refit the rear wheel (see Chapter 8). Unclip the brake hose from the underside of the drive belt casing **(see illustration 5.12)** .

14 Check that all wiring, cables and hoses are clear of the engine/transmission unit. With the aid of an assistant, support the weight of the machine on the rear grab handle. Remove the bolt securing the rear shock absorber to the transmission casing, then remove the front engine mounting bolt and lift the frame away from the engine/transmission unit **(see illustration)**.

15 If required, remove the stand (see Chapter 6) and the rear wheel (see Chapter 8) .

Installation

16 Installation is the reverse of removal, noting the following points:
• Make sure no wires, cables or hoses become trapped between the engine and the frame when installing the engine.
• Tighten the engine mounting bolts to the torque settings specified at the beginning of this Chapter.
• Make sure all wires, cables and hoses are correctly routed and connected, and secured by any clips or ties.
• Bleed the oil pump (see Section 13) and check the adjustment of the oil pump cable where fitted (see Chapter 1).
• Check the operation of the rear brake before riding the machine (see Chapter 8).

6 Disassembly and reassembly –
general information

Disassembly

1 Before disassembling the engine, the external surfaces of the unit should be thoroughly cleaned and degreased. This will prevent contamination of the engine internals, and will also make working a lot easier and

cleaner. A high flash-point solvent, such as paraffin can be used, or better still, a proprietary engine degreaser such as Gunk. Use an old paintbrush to work the solvent into the various recesses of the engine casings. Take care to exclude solvent or water from the electrical components and inlet and exhaust ports.

⚠️ *Warning: The use of petrol (gasoline) as a cleaning agent should be avoided because of the risk of fire.*

2 When clean and dry, arrange the unit on the workbench, leaving suitable clear area for working. Gather a selection of small containers and plastic bags so that parts can be grouped together in an easily identifiable manner. Some paper and a pen should be on hand to permit notes to be made and labels attached where necessary. A supply of clean rag is also required.

3 Before commencing work, read through the appropriate section so that some idea of the necessary procedure can be gained. When removing components it should be noted that great force is seldom required, unless specified. In many cases, a component's reluctance to be removed is indicative of an incorrect approach or removal method – if in any doubt, re-check with the text.

4 When disassembling the engine, keep 'mated' parts that have been in contact with each other during engine operation together. These 'mated' parts must be reused or renewed as an assembly.

5 Complete engine disassembly should be done in the following general order with reference to the appropriate Sections. Refer to Chapter 2C for details of transmission components disassembly.

Remove the cooling fan (see Section 11)
Remove the alternator (see Chapter 9)
Remove the variator (see Chapter 2C)
Remove the cylinder head (see Section 7)
Remove the cylinder (see Section 8)
Remove the piston (see Section 9)

Remove the oil pump (see Section 13)
Remove the reed valve (see Chapter 4)
Remove the starter motor (see Chapter 9)
Separate the crankcase halves (see Section 14)

Reassembly

6 Reassembly is accomplished by reversing the general disassembly sequence.

7 Cylinder head –
removal, inspection
and installation

Note: *This procedure can be carried out with the engine in the frame. If the engine has been removed, ignore the steps that do not apply.*
Caution: The engine must be completely cool before beginning this procedure or the cylinder head may become warped.

Removal

1 Remove the body panels as necessary according to model (see Chapter 7).
2 Pull the spark plug cap off the spark plug, then remove the bolts securing the engine cowling and remove the cowling, noting how it fits **(see illustrations)**.
3 Remove the spark plug, then unscrew the

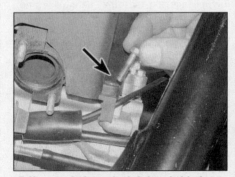

7.2b . . . a bolt on the left-hand side front of the cowling . . .

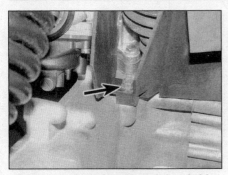

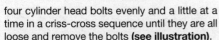

7.2c . . . and a bolt on the left-hand side rear of the cowling

7.3 Unscrew the cylinder head bolts evenly in a criss-cross sequence

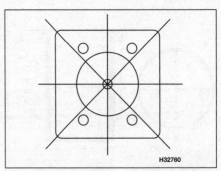

7.10 Check the cylinder head for warpage with a straight-edge in the directions shown

four cylinder head bolts evenly and a little at a time in a criss-cross sequence until they are all loose and remove the bolts **(see illustration)**.

4 Lift the head off the cylinder. If the head is stuck, tap around the joint face between the head and cylinder with a soft-faced mallet to free it. Do not attempt to free the head by inserting a screwdriver between the head and cylinder – you'll damage the sealing surfaces. *Caution: The cylinder head bolts also secure the cylinder to the crankcase. If the cylinder base gasket seal is broken when removing the head, a new gasket will have to be fitted on reassembly (see Section 8).*

5 Remove the cylinder head gasket and discard it as a new one must be fitted on reassembly.

Inspection

6 Refer to Chapter 1 and decarbonise the cylinder head.

7 Inspect the head very carefully for cracks and other damage. If cracks are found, a new head will be required.

8 Inspect the threads in the spark plug hole. Damaged or worn threads can be reclaimed using a thread insert; consult a Peugeot dealer or scooter engineer.

9 Check the mating surfaces on the cylinder head and cylinder for signs of leakage, which could indicate that the head is warped.

10 Using a precision straight-edge, check the head mating surface for warpage. Check vertically, horizontally and diagonally across the head, making four checks in all **(see illustration)**.

Installation

11 Ensure both cylinder head and cylinder mating surfaces are clean, and lubricate the cylinder bore with the specified type of two-stroke oil.

12 Install the new head gasket with the raised centre section uppermost, then carefully fit the cylinder head onto the cylinder **(see illustration)**.

13 Install the four bolts; ensure the bolt threads locate in the crankcase, then tighten them finger-tight **(see illustration)**. Now tighten them evenly and a little at a time in a criss-cross pattern to the torque setting specified at the beginning of this Chapter.

7.12 Install the new gasket with the raised section (arrowed) uppermost

14 Install the spark plug, then fit the engine cowling, making sure it locates correctly against the fan cowling **(see illustration 7.2a)**.

15 Install the remaining components in the reverse order of removal.

8 Cylinder – removal, inspection and installation

Note: This procedure can be carried out with the engine in the frame.

⚠ *Warning: The cylinder is Nicosil coated – under no circumstances should the cylinder be rebored or honed. No oversize pistons are available.*

Removal

1 Remove the exhaust system (see Chapter 4) and the cylinder head (see Section 7). Position the piston so that it is at the top of the bore.

2 Lift the cylinder up off the crankcase, supporting the piston as it becomes accessible to prevent it hitting the crankcase opening **(see illustration)**. If the cylinder is stuck, tap around the joint face between the cylinder and the crankcase with a soft-faced mallet to free it. Don't attempt to free the cylinder by inserting a screwdriver between it and the crankcase – you'll damage the sealing surfaces. When the cylinder is partway removed, stuff a clean rag into the crankcase opening around the piston to prevent anything falling inside, such as pieces of broken ring.

3 Remove the cylinder gasket and discard it as a new one must be fitted on reassembly.

7.13 The head bolts (arrowed) pass all the way through the cylinder

Inspection

4 Check the cylinder bore carefully for scratches and score marks. The bore's hard wearing Nicosil coating should prevent wear, and unless catastrophic engine damage has occurred, significant wear of the surface is unlikely.

5 The manufacturer does not supply a service limit for cylinder bore diameter, only the nominal diameter for a new bore given in the Specifications at the beginning of this Chapter. It is, however, possible to gain an indication of the bore's condition by using telescoping gauges and a micrometer to measure the bore diameter, and to calculate any taper or ovality. Measure near the top (but below the level of the top piston ring at TDC), centre and bottom (but above the level of the bottom ring at BDC) of the bore both parallel to and across the crankshaft axis **(see**

8.2 Support the piston as the cylinder is lifted off

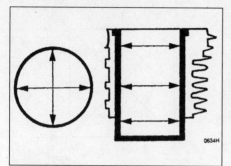

8.5 Measure the cylinder bore in the directions shown

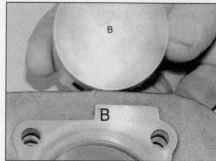

8.6 Cylinders and pistons are size coded and should always match

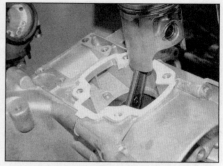

8.9 Ensure the new gasket is positioned correctly on the crankcase

8.10 Ring locating pins (arrowed) must be between the ring ends

8.12 Lower the cylinder carefully over the piston

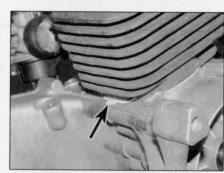

8.13 Check that the cylinder base gasket (arrowed) has not been displaced

illustration). Calculate any differences between the measurements taken to determine any taper and ovality in the bore.

6 If the bore is tapered, oval, or worn excessively, or badly scratched, scuffed or scored, the cylinder and piston will have to be renewed. Peugeot supply cylinders and pistons as matching sets. The cylinder and piston are size coded during manufacture and it is important that new parts are matched. The size codes are marked on the top of the cylinder and the piston **(see illustration)**.

7 If there is any doubt about the serviceability of the cylinder, consult a Peugeot dealer.

8 Inspect the cylinder head bolt threads in the crankcase (see Section 14).

Installation

9 Remove any rag from the crankcase opening. Lay the new base gasket in place on the crankcase making sure it is the correct

way round **(see illustration)**.

10 Check that the piston rings are correctly positioned so that the ring locating pins in the piston grooves are between the ring ends **(see illustration)**.

11 Lubricate the cylinder bore, piston and piston rings, and the connecting rod big and small ends, with the specified type of two-stroke oil, then locate the cylinder over the top of the piston **(see illustration 8.2)**.

12 Ensure the piston enters the bore squarely and does not get cocked sideways. Carefully compress and feed each ring into the bore as the cylinder is lowered, taking care that the ring end gaps remain correctly aligned with the pins **(see illustration)**. Do not use force if the cylinder appears to be stuck as the piston and/or rings will be damaged.

13 When the piston is correctly installed in the cylinder, check that the base gasket has not been displaced **(see illustration)**.

14 Install the remaining components in the reverse order of removal.

9 Piston – removal, inspection and installation

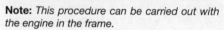

Note: *This procedure can be carried out with the engine in the frame.*

Removal

1 Remove the cylinder (see Section 8).

2 Before removing the piston from the connecting rod, stuff a clean rag into the hole around the rod to prevent the circlips or anything else from falling into the crankcase. The piston top should be marked with an arrow which faces towards the exhaust (forwards). If this is not visible, mark the piston accordingly so that it can be installed the correct way round. Note that the arrow may not be visible until the carbon deposits have been scraped off and the piston cleaned.

3 Carefully prise the circlip out from one side of the piston using needle-nose pliers or a small flat-bladed screwdriver inserted into the notch **(see illustration)**. Check for burring around the circlip groove and remove any with a very fine file or penknife blade, then push the piston pin out from the other side and remove the piston from the connecting rod **(see illustration)**. Use a socket extension to push the piston pin out if required. Remove the other circlip and discard them both as new ones must be used on reassembly.

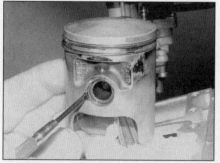

9.3a Remove the circlip . . .

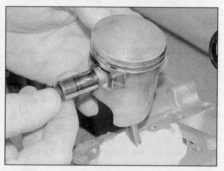

9.3b . . . then push out the piston pin

HAYNES HiNT *If a piston pin is a tight fit in the piston, soak a rag in boiling water then wring it out and wrap it around the piston – this will expand the alloy piston sufficiently to release its grip on the pin.*

4 The connecting rod small-end bearing is a loose fit in the rod; remove it for safekeeping, noting which way round it fits **(see illustration)**.

5 Using your thumbs or a piston ring removal and installation tool, carefully remove the rings from the piston. Do not nick or gouge the piston in the process. Note which way up each ring fits and in which groove as they must be installed in their original positions if being re-used. The upper surface of each ring should be marked at one end (see Section 10). Some pistons have an expander fitted behind the second ring. **Note:** *It is good practice to renew the piston rings when an engine is being overhauled. Ensure that the piston and bore are serviceable before purchasing new rings.*

6 Clean all traces of carbon from the top of the piston. A hand-held wire brush or a piece of fine emery cloth can be used once most of the deposits have been scraped away. Do not, under any circumstances, use a wire brush mounted in a drill motor; the piston material is soft and is easily damaged.

7 Use a piston ring groove cleaning tool to remove any carbon deposits from the ring grooves. If a tool is not available, a piece broken off an old ring will do the job. Be very careful to remove only the carbon deposits. Do not remove any metal and do not nick or gouge the sides of the ring grooves.

8 Once the carbon has been removed, clean the piston with a suitable solvent and dry it thoroughly. If the identification previously marked on the piston is cleaned off, be sure to re-mark it correctly.

Inspection

9 Inspect the piston for cracks around the skirt, at the pin bosses and at the ring lands. Normal piston wear appears as even, vertical wear on the thrust surfaces of the piston and slight looseness of the top ring in its groove. If the skirt is scored or scuffed, the engine may have been suffering from overheating and/or abnormal combustion, resulting in excessively high operating temperatures. Also check that the ring locating pins are securely fitted in the piston grooves.

10 A hole in the top of the piston, in one extreme, or burned areas around the edge of the piston crown, indicate that pre-ignition or knocking under load have occurred. If you find evidence of any problems the cause must be corrected or the damage will occur again. Refer to Chapter 4 for carburation checks and Chapter 5 for ignition checks.

11 Check the piston-to-bore clearance by

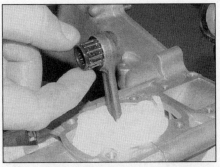

9.4 Remove the small end bearing

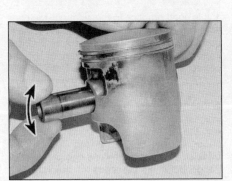

9.13a Check for freeplay between the piston and the piston pin

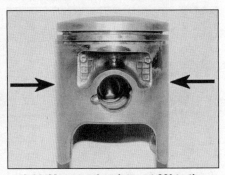

9.11 Measure the piston at 90° to the piston pin axis

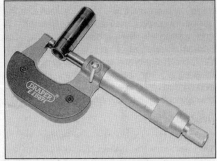

9.13b Measuring the piston pin where it runs in the piston

measuring the cylinder bore (see Section 8) and the piston diameter. Measure the piston 25 mm down from the bottom of the lower piston ring groove and at 90° to the piston pin axis **(see illustration)**. Subtract the piston diameter from the bore diameter to obtain the clearance. Peugeot do not specify a service limit for the piston-to-bore clearance, although anything greater than 0.1 mm should be considered worn. If the clearance is excessive, the piston is most likely to be worn, or in an extreme case the cylinder bore may also be worn. Note that the manufacturer does not supply a service limit for piston diameter, only the nominal diameter for a new piston given in the Specifications at the beginning of this Chapter. **Note:** *Cylinders and pistons are size coded during manufacture and it is important that new parts have matching codes, as marked on the top of the cylinder and the piston. Depending on the capacity and age of the engine, there are either two or three sizes of piston available. It is essential to supply the size code when purchasing a new piston.*

12 If the bore is worn, a new cylinder and piston set must be fitted.

13 Apply clean two-stroke oil to the piston pin, insert it into the piston and check for any freeplay between the two **(see illustration)**. If there is freeplay, measure the pin external diameter and compare the measurement to the specifications at the beginning of this Chapter **(see illustration)**. If the pin is worn, replace it with a new one, otherwise fit a new piston.

14 Check the condition of the connecting rod small-end bearing. A worn small-end bearing will produce a metallic rattle, most audible when the engine is under load, and increasing as engine speed rises. This should not be confused with big-end bearing wear, which produces a pronounced knocking noise. Inspect the bearing rollers for flat spots and pitting. Note that it is good practice to fit a new small-end bearing as a matter of course.

15 Measure the piston pin where it runs in the small-end bearing and compare the measurement to the specifications at the beginning of this Chapter **(see illustration)**. If the pin is good, install the bearing in the connecting rod, then slide the piston pin into the bearing and check for freeplay **(see illustration)**. There should only be slightly discernible freeplay between the piston pin,

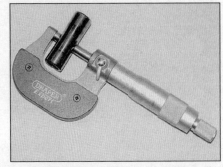

9.15a Measuring the piston pin where it runs in the small end bearing

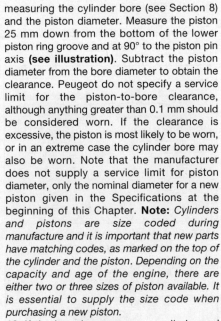

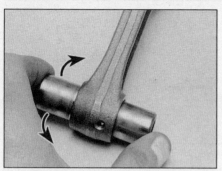

9.15b Rock the piston pin back and forth to check for freeplay

the bearing and the connecting rod. If there is freeplay, measure the internal diameter of the connecting rod small-end (see Section 14) and compare the measurement to the specifications at the beginning of this Chapter. If the small-end is good, renew the bearing. If the small-end has worn, the connecting rod and crankshaft assembly must be replaced with a new one (see Section 14).

Installation

16 Install the piston rings (see Section 10).
17 Lubricate the piston pin, the piston pin bore in the piston and the small-end bearing with the specified two-stroke oil and install the bearing in the connecting rod. Stuff clean rag into the crankcase mouth to prevent the circlips falling in.
18 Install a new circlip in one side of the piston, line up the piston on the connecting rod, making sure the arrow on the piston top faces towards the front of the engine (exhaust), and insert the piston pin from the other side. Secure the pin with the other new circlip. When installing the circlips, compress them only just enough to fit them in the piston, and make sure they are properly seated in their grooves with the open end away from the removal notch.
19 Install the cylinder (see Section 8).

10 Piston rings – inspection and installation

1 It is good practice to renew the piston rings when an engine is being overhauled. Pistons are size coded during manufacture and it is important that you get new rings of the correct size for your piston (see **Note** Section 9, Step 11). Before installing the new rings, the ring end gaps must be checked.
2 Insert the top ring into the top of the cylinder bore and square it up by pushing it in with the top of the piston. The ring should be about 20 mm below the top edge of the cylinder. To measure the end gap, slip a feeler gauge between the ends of the ring and compare the measurement to the specification at the beginning of this Chapter **(see illustration)**.
3 If the gap is larger or smaller than specified, check to make sure that you have the correct rings before proceeding.
4 If the gap is larger than specified it is likely the cylinder bore is worn. If the gap is too small the ring will not compress sufficiently to allow you to fit the piston into the cylinder.
5 Repeat the procedure for the other ring.
6 Once the ring end gaps have been checked, the rings can be installed on the piston. First identify the ring locating pin in each piston ring groove – the ring must be positioned so that the pin is in between the ends of the ring **(see illustration)**.
7 If the piston has an expander fitted behind the lower ring, fit that first, ensuring that the ends of the expander do not overlap the ring locating pin **(see illustration)**.
8 The upper surface of each ring should be marked at one end; make sure you fit the rings the right way up. Install the lower ring first. Do not expand the ring any more than is necessary to slide it into place, positioning the locating pin between the ends of the ring **(see illustration)**.
9 Install the top ring. Always ensure that the ring end gaps are positioned each side of the locating pins before fitting the piston into the cylinder.

11 Cooling fan – removal and installation

Note: *This procedure can be carried out with the engine in the frame.*

Removal

1 Remove the exhaust as required according to model (see Chapter 4).
2 Undo the bolts securing the fan cowling to the crankcase and remove the cowling **(see illustration)**.
3 If loose, remove the sleeve between the fan cowling and the engine cowling **(see illustration 7.2a)**.
4 Undo the bolts securing the cooling fan to the alternator rotor and remove the fan **(see illustration)**.

Installation

5 Installation is the reverse of removal. **Note:** *The holes for the fixing bolts in the cooling fan are oversize and it is important to centralise the fan on the bolts before tightening them, otherwise the fan will run out of true and*

10.2 Measuring installed ring end gap

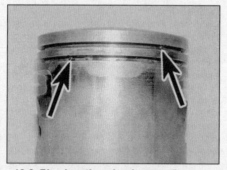

10.6 Ring locating pins (arrowed) are on the rear face of the piston

10.7 Fit the lower ring expander first . . .

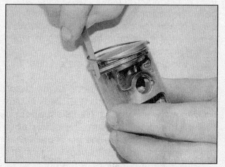

10.8 . . . followed by the lower and top rings

11.2 Remove the fan cowling . . .

11.4 . . . then the fan mounting bolts

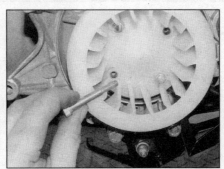

11.5 Use shouldered bolts to centralise the fan

cause engine vibration. Use two shouldered bolts, or wrap a short length of electrical tape tightly around two bolts, and fit them in opposite holes to centralise the fan, then install two fixing bolts **(see illustration)**. Remove the centralising bolts and install the two remaining fixing bolts.

12 Starter pinion assembly –
removal, inspection and installation

Note: *This procedure can be carried out with the engine in the frame.*

Removal

1 Remove the drive belt cover (see Chapter 2C).
2 Withdraw the starter pinion assembly **(see illustration)**.

12.2 Starter pinion assembly is located at the front of the casing

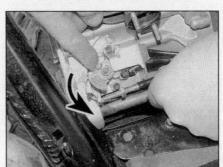

12.7 Engage inner pinion with starter motor shaft (arrowed)

Inspection

3 Some pinion assemblies are fitted with a rubber boot. If the boot shows signs of damage or deterioration, remove it. Peugeot do not list the boot as a separate item, but your Peugeot dealer may be able to supply a suitable replacement.
4 Check the starter pinion assembly for any signs of damage or wear, particularly for chipped or broken teeth on either of the pinions **(see illustration)**. Check the corresponding teeth on the starter motor pinion and the starter driven gear.
5 Rotate the outer pinion and check that it moves smoothly up and down the shaft, and that it returns easily to its rest position.
6 The starter pinion assembly is supplied as a complete unit; if any of the component parts is worn or damaged, the unit will have to be replaced with a new one.

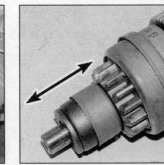

12.4 Check the pinion teeth. Outer pinion should move smoothly on shaft.

Installation

7 Installation is the reverse of removal. Apply a smear of grease to each end of the pinion shaft, then install the pinion assembly, ensuring the inner pinion engages with the starter motor shaft **(see illustration)**.

13 Oil pump –
removal, inspection, installation and bleeding

Note 1: *Generally speaking, all 100 cc models and 50 cc models manufactured before 2000 are fitted with a cable operated pump; all other models are fitted with a centrifugal pump. A quick visual check will confirm which pump is fitted to your machine.*
Note 2: *This procedure can be carried out with the engine in the frame.*

Removal

1 Remove the exhaust system (see Chapter 4).
2 On models fitted with a cable operated pump, detach the cable from the pump pulley **(see illustration)**, then unscrew the bolts securing the cable bracket and remove the bracket with the cable attached **(see illustration 5.10)**. **Note:** *Early 50 cc models were fitted with a Keihin oil pump which is retained by a single bolt.*
3 On all models, release the clip securing the oil inlet hose from the oil tank to the union on the pump and detach the hose **(see illustration)**. Clamp the hose and secure it in an upright position to minimise oil loss. Release the clip securing the oil outlet hose to the union on the pump and detach the hose. Wrap clean plastic bags around the hose ends to prevent dirt entering the system. **Note:** *The inlet and outlet hoses are protected from the exhaust pipe by a heat-proof sheath. Remove the sheath if necessary but don't forget to refit it on reassembly.*
4 On models fitted with a centrifugal pump (without cable operation), unscrew the pump mounting bolts and remove the bolts.
5 Withdraw the pump from the crankcase and remove the wave washer **(see illustration)**. Note how the tab on the back of the pump locates in the slot in the pump drive shaft.

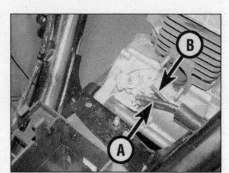

13.3 Detach the oil inlet hose (A) and outlet hose (B)

13.2 Rotate pulley to detach the oil pump cable

13.5 Remove the wave washer

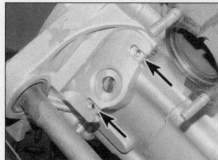

13.8 Mounting nuts (arrowed) locate in slots in casing

6 Stuff a clean rag into the crankcase opening to prevent dirt falling inside.

7 Remove the O-ring from the pump body and discard it as a new one must be fitted on reassembly.

8 If required, remove the two nuts from the underside of the pump mounting on the crankcase for safekeeping (see illustration).

9 Ensure no dirt enters the pump body and clean it using a suitable solvent, then dry the pump thoroughly.

Inspection

10 Check the pump body for obvious signs of damage especially around the mounting bolt holes. Turn the drive tab by hand and check that the pump rotates smoothly. Where fitted, check that the cable pulley turns freely and returns to rest under pressure of the return spring.

11 No individual components are available

for the pump. If it is damaged, or, if after bleeding the operation of the pump is suspect, replace it with a new one.

Installation

12 If removed, install the two nuts on the underside of the pump mounting (see illustration 13.8).

13 Install a new O-ring on the pump body and lubricate it with a smear of grease (see illustration).

14 Remove any rag from the crankcase opening and apply a smear of suitable sealant around the chamfered outer edge. Install the wave washer, then install the pump, ensuring the tab on the back of the pump engages with the slot in the drive shaft (see illustration).

15 If removed, fit the heat-proof sheath over the oil inlet and outlet hoses, then connect the hoses to the pump unions and secure them with the clips (see illustration).

16 On models fitted with a cable operated pump, bleed the pump (see Step 18), then install the cable bracket and the pump mounting bolts, and tighten the bolts to the torque setting specified at the beginning of this Chapter. Connect the cable to the pump pulley and check the operation of the cable (see Chapter 1).

Caution: Accurate cable adjustment is important to ensure that the oil pump delivers the correct amount of oil to the engine and is correctly synchronised with the throttle.

17 On models fitted with a centrifugal pump, install the pump mounting bolts and tighten them to the specified torque setting, then bleed the pump.

Bleeding

18 Bleeding the pump is the process of removing air from it and allowing it to be filled with oil. First ensure that the inlet hose from the oil tank and the oil filter are completely filled with oil. If necessary, detach the hose from the pump and wait until oil flows from the hose, then reconnect it.

19 Loosen the bleed screw on the pump and wait until oil, without any air mixed with it, flows out the hole, then tighten the screw (see illustrations).

20 Ensure the ignition switch is OFF. Disconnect the oil outlet hose from the carburettor and crank the engine with the kickstarter until oil, without any air mixed with it, flows out the hose, then reconnect the hose and secure it with the clip. Alternatively, fill an auxiliary fuel tank with a 2% petrol/two-stroke oil mix and connect it to the carburettor. Disconnect the oil outlet hose from the carburettor, start the engine and run it until oil, without any air mixed with it, flows out the hose, then reconnect the hose and secure it with the clip.

⚠ *Warning: Never run the engine without an oil supply or crank the engine on the electric starter without an oil supply. Never crank the engine with the ignition ON and the spark plug cap disconnected from the spark plug as the ignition system may be damaged.*

13.13 Fit a new pump body O-ring

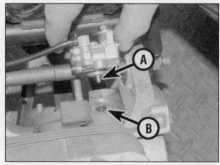

13.14 Ensure tab (A) locates in slot (B)

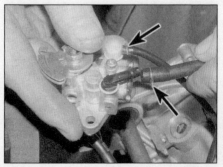

13.15 Oil hoses must be secured by clips (arrowed)

13.19a Bleed screw on centrifugal oil pump

13.19b Bleeding a cable operated oil pump

14.3 Undo the crankcase bolts evenly in a criss-cross sequence

14.4 Drawing the right-hand crankcase half off the crankshaft

14.5 Pressing the crankshaft out of the left-hand crankcase half

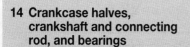

14 Crankcase halves, crankshaft and connecting rod, and bearings

Note: *To separate the crankcase halves, the engine must be removed from the frame.*

Separation

1 To access the crankshaft and its bearings, the crankcase must be split into two parts.

2 To enable the crankcase halves to be separated, the engine must be removed from the frame (see Section 5) and the following components must be removed:

• Cooling fan (see Section 11)
• Alternator (see Chapter 9)
• Variator (see Chapter 2C)
• Cylinder head (see Section 7)
• Cylinder (see Section 8)
• Piston (see Section 9)
• Oil pump (see Section 13)
• Reed valve (see Chapter 4)
• Starter motor (see Chapter 9)

3 Tape some rag around the connecting rod to prevent it knocking against the cases, then loosen the crankcase bolts evenly, a little at a time and in a criss-cross sequence until they are all finger-tight, then remove them **(see illustration)**.

4 Carefully remove the right-hand crankcase half from the left-hand half by drawing it off the right-hand end of the crankshaft. Peugeot produce a service tool (Pt. No. 750807) to do this. Before fitting the tool, place the end cap

(Pt. No. 68007) onto the end of the crankshaft to prevent it being damaged. Alternatively, use the set-up shown; thread the old alternator nut onto the end of the crankshaft to protect the threads and apply equal pressure to both sides of the puller at all times **(see illustration)**.

5 Now press the crank assembly out of the left-hand crankcase half. Peugeot produce a service tool (Pt. No. 64706) and pressure plate (Pt. No. 752168) to do this. Before fitting the tool, place the end cap (Pt. No. 69098) onto the end of the crankshaft to prevent it being damaged. Alternatively, use the set-up shown; thread the old variator nut onto the end of the crankshaft to protect the threads **(see illustration)**.

Note: *If the crankcase halves do not separate easily, first ensure all fasteners have been removed. Apply steady pressure with the tools described and heat the bearing housings with a hot air gun. Do not try and separate the halves by levering against the mating surfaces as they are easily scored and will not seal correctly afterwards. Do not strike the ends of the crankshaft with a hammer as damage to the end threads or the shaft itself will result.*

6 Remove the oil pump drive shaft and the shaft bush from the right-hand crankcase half. If necessary, heat the crankcase around the bush while applying pressure to the shaft.

7 Remove the crankcase gasket and discard it as a new one must be fitted on reassembly. Remove the dowels from either crankcase half for safekeeping if they are loose.

8 Note the position of the crankshaft oil seals

and measure any inset before removing them **(see illustration)**. Note which way round the seals are fitted. Remove the seals by tapping them gently on one side and then pulling them out with pliers **(see illustration)**. Discard the seals as new ones must be fitted on reassembly.

9 The main bearings will either remain in place in the crankcase halves during disassembly or come out with the crank assembly. To remove them from the crankcase halves, heat the bearing housings with a hot air gun and tap them out using a bearing driver or suitable socket **(see illustration)**. Note which way round the bearings are fitted. If the bearings are stuck on the crankshaft, check their condition (see Step 19) and only remove them if they are unserviceable. The bearings must be removed from the crankshaft with an external bearing puller to avoid damaging the crank assembly.

10 If required, remove the transmission assembly from the left-hand crankcase half (see Chapter 2C).

Inspection

11 Remove all traces of old gasket from the crankcase mating surfaces, taking care not to nick or gouge the soft aluminium if a scraper is used. Wash all the components in a suitable solvent and dry them with compressed air.

Caution: Be very careful not to nick or gouge the crankcase mating surfaces or oil leaks will result. Check both crankcase halves very carefully for cracks and other damage.

14.8a Measuring crankshaft oil seal inset

14.8b Tap the seals with a punch to displace them

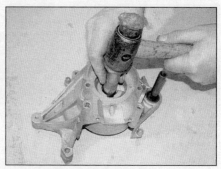

14.9 Driving a main bearing out of the crankcase

14.16 Inspect the mounting bushes (A) and the main bearing housings (B)

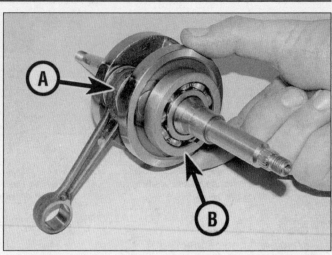

14.18 The crank assembly big-end (A) and main bearings (B)

12 Small cracks or holes in aluminium castings may be repaired with an epoxy resin adhesive as a temporary measure. Permanent repairs can only be effected by welding, and only a specialist in this process is in a position to advise on the economy or practical aspect of such a repair. If the right-hand crankcase half is damaged beyond repair it can be replaced individually; the left-hand crankcase half is only available as part of a complete crankcase assembly.

13 Damaged threads can be economically reclaimed by using a diamond section wire insert, of the Heli-Coil type, which is easily fitted after drilling and re-tapping the affected thread. Most motorcycle dealers and small engineering firms offer a service of this kind.

14 Sheared screws can usually be removed with screw extractors, which consist of a tapered, left thread screw of very hard steel. These are inserted into a pre-drilled hole in the stud, and usually succeed in dislodging the most stubborn screw. If you are in any doubt about removing a sheared screw, consult a Peugeot dealer or a specialist motorcycle engineer.

15 Always wash the crankcases thoroughly after any repair work to ensure no dirt or metal swarf is trapped inside when the engine is rebuilt.

16 Inspect the engine mounting bushes (see illustration). If they show signs of deterioration replace all three at the same time. To remove a bush, first note its position in the casing. Heat the casing with a hot air gun, then support the casing and drive the bush out with a hammer and a suitably sized socket. Clean the bush housing with steel wool to remove any corrosion, then reheat the casing and fit the new bush. Note: *Always support the casing when removing or fitting bushes to avoid breaking the casing.*

17 Inspect the housings for the main bearings (see illustration 14.16). If a bearing outer race has spun in its housing, the inside of the housing will be damaged. A bearing locking compound can be used to fix the outer race in place on reassembly if the damage is not too severe.

18 The crank assembly should give many thousands of miles of service. The most likely problems to occur will be worn main bearings or a worn big-end bearing due to poor lubrication (see illustration). If the main bearings have failed, excessive rumbling and vibration will be felt when the engine is running. Sometimes this may cause the oil seals to fail, resulting in poor running.

19 Wash the bearings with a suitable solvent and dry them with compressed air, then apply a few drops of light oil inside each bearing. A bearing should be almost silent when spun; if it grates or rattles it is worn and must be replaced with a new one (see illustration). Always renew both main bearings at the same time, never individually. Note that it is good practice to renew the main bearings in the course of an engine overhaul.

20 A worn big-end bearing will produce a pronounced knocking noise, most audible when the engine is under load, and increasing as engine speed rises. This should not be confused with small-end bearing wear, which produces a lighter, metallic rattle. To assess the condition of the big-end bearing, hold the crank assembly firmly and push and pull on the connecting rod, checking for any freeplay between the two (see illustration). If any freeplay is noted, the bearing is worn and the crank assembly will have to be replaced with a new one.

21 Measure the big-end side clearance with a feeler gauge (see illustration). If the clearance is greater than the service limit specified at the beginning of this Chapter, renew the crank assembly.

22 Measure the internal diameter of the connecting rod small end with a telescoping gauge and compare the measurement to the specifications at the beginning of this Chapter

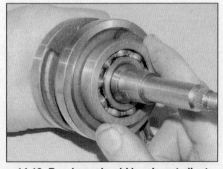

14.19 Bearings should be almost silent when spun

14.20 Any freeplay indicates a worn big-end bearing

14.21 Measuring big-end side clearance

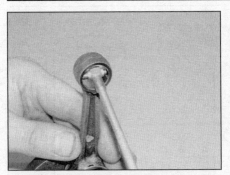

14.22 Measuring the internal diameter of the connecting rod small-end

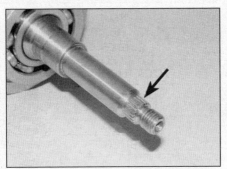

14.23a Inspect the shaft end threads and the variator pulley splines (arrowed)

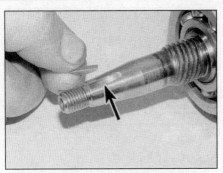

14.23b Inspect the shaft taper and slot (arrowed) for the Woodruff key

14.24 Inspect the oil pump drive gear teeth

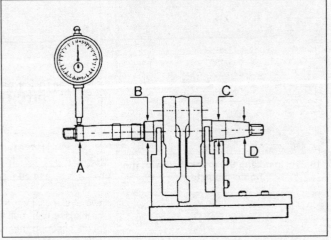

14.26 Check crankshaft runout at points A, B, C and D

(see illustration). If the small-end has worn, the connecting rod and crankshaft assembly must be replaced with a new one.

23 Inspect the threads on each end of the crankshaft and ensure that the retaining nuts for the alternator rotor and the variator are a good fit (see illustration). Inspect the splines for the variator pulley on the left-hand end of the shaft. Inspect the taper and the slot in the right-hand end of the shaft for the alternator Woodruff key (see illustration). Damage or wear that prevents the rotor from being fitted securely will require a new crankshaft.

24 Inspect the oil pump drive gear teeth on the crankshaft and on the pump drive shaft for damage or wear, and inspect the ends of pump drive shaft where it runs in its bearings (see illustration). Renew any components that are worn or damaged.

25 Inspect both sides of the crankshaft where it passes through the main bearings for wear and scoring. Measure the shaft with a micrometer and compare the results with the measurements specified at the beginning of this Chapter. If the crankshaft is worn it must be renewed. Evidence of extreme heat, such as discoloration or blueing, indicates that lubrication failure has occurred. Be sure to check the oil pump and lubrication system before reassembling the engine.

26 Place the crank assembly on V-blocks and check the crankshaft runout at either end using a dial gauge (see illustration). Compare the reading to the maximum specified at the beginning of this Chapter. If the runout exceeds the limit, the crank assembly must be replaced, although it may be possible to have it trued by an engineer.

Reassembly

27 If removed, fit the main bearings into the crankcase halves. Heat the bearing housings with a hot air gun and carefully tap the bearings in using a bearing driver or suitable

socket which bears only on the bearing's outer race.

28 Fit the new crankshaft oil seals into the crankcase halves and drive them to the previously measured inset (see Step 8) using a seal driver or socket which bears on the seal's hard outer edge. Ensure the seals are fitted the right way round and that they enter the cases squarely (see illustration).

29 Tape some rag around the connecting rod to prevent it knocking against the cases, then fit the crank assembly into the left-hand crankcase half first (see illustration). Lubricate the shaft, seal and bearing with the specified

14.28 Ensure the new oil seals are installed correctly

14.29a Fit the crankshaft into the left-hand crankcase half first

14.29b Installing the crankshaft with the Peugeot service tools

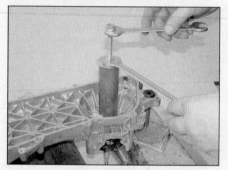

14.29c Installing the crankshaft with the home-made tool

14.29e Heating the crankcase with a hot air gun

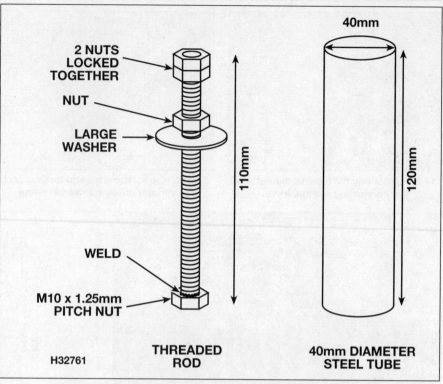

14.29d Details of the home-made tool for installing the crankshaft

two-stroke oil, then, if the main bearing is in the crankcase half, pull the crank assembly into place ensuring the connecting rod is aligned with the crankcase mouth. Peugeot produce five individual service tools (Pt. Nos. 752168, 64706, 750069, 64710 and 69104) to do this **(see illustration)**. Alternatively, use the set-up shown **(see illustrations)**. If the main bearing is on the crankshaft, heat the bearing housing in the crankcase with a hot air gun before fitting the crank assembly **(see illustration)**. **Note:** *Avoid applying direct heat onto the crankshaft oil seal.*

30 Wipe the mating surfaces of both crankcase halves with a rag soaked in a suitable solvent and fit the dowels and new gasket to the left-hand half **(see illustration)**.
31 Now fit the right-hand crankcase half. Lubricate the shaft, seal and bearing with the specified two-stroke oil, then, if the main bearing is in the crankcase half, press the crankcase half into place. Peugeot produce five individual service tools (Pt. Nos. 750808, 64706, 750069, 64710 and 69104) to do this **(see illustration)**. Alternatively, place a thick washer over the centre of the crankcase to

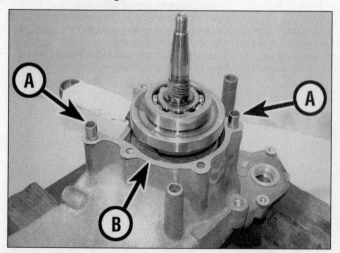

14.30 Install the crankcase dowels (A) and gasket (B)

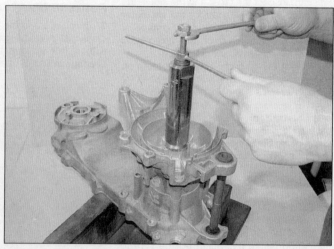

14.31 Installing the right-hand crankcase half with the Peugeot service tools

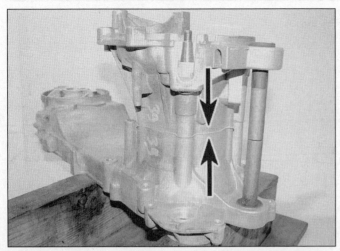
14.32a Ensure crankcase halves are seated on the gasket

14.32b Position of main bearings can be checked through oilways (arrowed)

protect the aluminium and use the set-up shown in Step 29 (see illustration 14.29c). If the main bearing is on the crankshaft, heat the bearing housing with a hot air gun before fitting the crankcase half. **Note:** *Avoid applying direct heat onto the crankshaft oil seal.*
32 Check that the crankcase halves are seated on the gasket and that the main bearings are pressed fully into their housings (see illustrations). If the casings are not correctly seated, heat the bearing housings while applying firm pressure with the assembly tools used previously. **Note:** *Do not attempt to pull the crankcase halves together using the crankcase bolts as the casing will crack and be ruined.*
33 Clean the threads of the crankcase bolts and install them finger-tight, then tighten them evenly a little at a time in a criss-cross sequence to the torque setting specified at the beginning of this Chapter (see illustration 14.3). Rotate the crankshaft by hand – if there are any signs of undue stiffness, tight or rough spots, or of any other problem, the fault must be rectified before proceeding further.
34 Trim the crankcase gasket flush with the mating surface for the cylinder (see illustration).

35 Lubricate the oil pump drive shaft and install the shaft and the shaft bush; tap the bush into its seat with a hammer and suitable sized socket (see illustrations). Rotate the crankshaft to ensure the oil pump drive gears are correctly engaged.
36 Install all other assemblies in the reverse order of removal.

15 Initial start-up after overhaul

1 Make sure the oil tank is at least partly full and the pump is correctly adjusted (see Chapter 1) and bled of air (see Section 13).
2 Make sure there is fuel in the tank.
3 With the ignition OFF, operate the kickstart to check that the engine turns over easily.
4 Turn the ignition ON, start the engine and allow it to run at a slow idle until it reaches operating temperature. Do not be alarmed if there is more than the usual amount of smoke from the exhaust – this will be due to the oil used to lubricate the engine components during assembly and should subside after a while.

5 If the engine proves reluctant to start, remove the spark plug and check that it has not become wet and oily. If it has, clean it and try again. If the engine refuses to start, go through the fault finding charts at the end of this manual to identify the problem.

16 Recommended running-in procedure

1 Treat the engine gently for the first few miles to allow any new parts to bed in.
2 If a new piston, rings or cylinder has been fitted, the engine will have to be run in as when new. This means a restraining hand on the throttle until at least 300 miles (500 km) have been covered. There's no point in keeping to any set speed limit – the main idea is to keep from labouring the engine and to gradually increase performance up to the 600 mile (1000 km) mark. Make sure that the throttle position is varied to vary engine speed, and use full throttle only for short bursts. Experience is the best guide, since it's easy to tell when an engine is running freely.

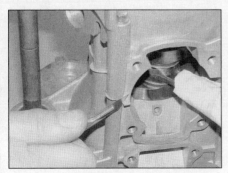
14.34 Trim off any excess gasket

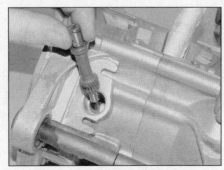
14.35a Install the oil pump shaft . . .

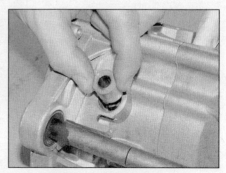
14.35b . . . and shaft bush

Chapter 2 Part B:
Liquid-cooled two-stroke engine

Refer to Chapter 1 for model identification details

Contents

Degrees of difficulty

| Easy, suitable for novice with little experience | | Fairly easy, suitable for beginner with some experience | | Fairly difficult, suitable for competent DIY mechanic | | Difficult, suitable for experienced DIY mechanic | | Very difficult, suitable for expert DIY or professional | |

Specifications

50 cc FL1 engine

General

Type	Single cylinder two-stroke
Capacity	49.13 cc
Bore	40.0 mm
Stroke	39.1 mm
Compression ratio	6.6 to 1

Piston

Piston diameter (measured 25 mm down from lower ring groove, at 90° to piston pin axis)	
Standard	39.85 mm
Piston pin diameter	12 mm

Piston rings

Ring end gap (installed)	
Standard	0.24 mm
Service limit (max)	0.26 mm

Connecting rod

Small end inside diameter	15 mm
Big end side clearance	0.5 mm

Crankshaft

Runout (max)	0.12 mm
Diameter at main bearings	20 mm

Torque settings

Alternator rotor nut . . . . 40 Nm
Crankcase bolts . . . . 12 Nm
Cylinder head bolts . . . . 15 Nm
Drive belt cover bolts . . . . 10 Nm
Engine cover bolts . . . . 10 Nm
Engine mountings
  Crankcase-to-front bracket bolt . . . . 60 Nm
  Front bracket-to-frame bolt . . . . 60 Nm
  Engine/transmission case-to-rear shock bolt . . . . 25 Nm
Inlet manifold bolts . . . . 10 Nm
Oil pump mounting bolts . . . . 8 Nm
Starter motor mounting bolts . . . . 10 Nm

1 General information

The engine unit is a single cylinder two-stroke with liquid cooling. The water pump is driven by the alternator rotor, which is on the right-hand end of the crankshaft. The crankshaft assembly is pressed, incorporating the connecting rod, with the big-end running on the crankpin on a needle roller bearing. The piston also runs on a needle roller bearing fitted in the small-end of the connecting rod. The crankshaft runs in caged ball main bearings. The crankcase divides vertically.

2 Operations possible with the engine in the frame

All components and assemblies, with the exception of the crankshaft/connecting rod and its bearings, can be worked on without having to remove the engine/transmission unit from the frame. If however, a number of areas require attention at the same time, removal of the engine is recommended, as it is easy to do so.

3 Operations requiring engine removal

To access the crankshaft and connecting rod and its bearings, the engine must be removed from the frame and the crankcase halves must be separated.

4 Major engine repair –
general note

1 It is not always easy to determine when or if an engine should be completely overhauled, as a number of factors must be considered.
2 High mileage is not necessarily an indication that an overhaul is needed, while low mileage, on the other hand, does not preclude the need for an overhaul. Frequency

of servicing is probably the single most important consideration. An engine that has regular and frequent maintenance will most likely give many miles of reliable service. Conversely, a neglected engine, or one which has not been run in properly, may require an overhaul very early in its life.
3 If the engine is making obvious knocking or rumbling noises, the connecting rod and/or main bearings are probably at fault.
4 Loss of power, rough running, excessive noise and high fuel consumption rates may also point to the need for an overhaul, especially if they are all present at the same time. If a complete tune-up does not remedy the situation, major mechanical work is the only solution.
5 An engine overhaul generally involves restoring the internal parts to the specifications of a new engine. This may require fitting new piston rings and crankcase seals, or, after a high mileage, renewing the crankshaft and connecting rod assembly. The end result should be a like-new engine that will give as many trouble-free miles as the original.
6 Before beginning the engine overhaul, read through the related procedures to familiarise yourself with the scope and requirements of the job. Overhauling an engine is not all that difficult, but it is time consuming. Check on the availability of parts and make sure that any necessary special tools and materials are obtained in advance.
7 Most work can be done with typical workshop hand tools, although Peugeot produce a number of service tools for specific

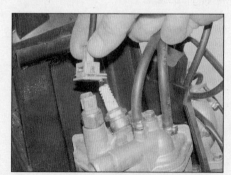

5.4 Disconnect the temperature sender wiring connector

purposes such as separating the crankcase halves. Precision measuring tools are required for inspecting parts to determine if they must be renewed. Alternatively, a Peugeot dealer will handle the inspection of parts and offer advice concerning reconditioning and replacement. As a general rule, time is the primary cost of an overhaul so it does not pay to install worn or substandard parts.
8 As a final note, to ensure maximum life and minimum trouble from a rebuilt engine, everything must be assembled with care in a spotlessly clean environment.

5 Engine –
removal and installation

Caution: The engine is not heavy, however engine removal and installation should be carried out with the aid of an assistant; personal injury or damage could occur if the engine falls or is dropped.

Removal

1 Support the machine securely in an upright position. Work can be made easier by raising the machine to a convenient working height on an hydraulic ramp or a suitable platform. Make sure it is secure and will not topple over.
2 Remove the body panels as necessary according to model (see Chapter 7).
3 If the engine is dirty, particularly around its mountings, wash it thoroughly before starting any major dismantling work. This will make work much easier and rule out the possibility of dirt falling into some vital component.
4 Disconnect the battery negative terminal (see Chapter 9). Pull the spark plug cap off the plug and disconnect the wire to the temperature sender on the cylinder head **(see illustration)**.
5 Drain the cooling system and disconnect the coolant hoses from the unions on the water pump and cylinder head (see Chapter 3).
6 Trace the wiring from the alternator/ignition pulse generator and the starter motor on the right-hand side of the engine and disconnect it a the connectors. Free the wiring from any clips on the frame.
7 Remove the air filter housing and the air intake duct (see Chapter 4).

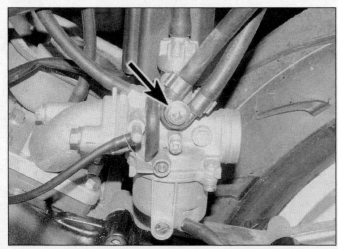

5.8 Detach the carburettor heater union

5.9 Remove the engine heat shield

8 Disconnect the fuel pipe and fuel tap vacuum pipe from their unions on the carburettor and inlet manifold respectively, then undo the screw securing the carburettor heater union to the carburettor **(see illustration)**. Release the clip securing the oil outlet hose to the carburettor and wrap a clean plastic bag around the end to prevent dirt entering the system, then displace the carburettor (see Chapter 4).

9 Undo the bolts securing the engine heat shield and remove the shield **(see illustration)**.

10 Where fitted, detach the oil pump control cable from the pump pulley (see Chapter 2A, Section 13), then unscrew the bolts securing the oil pump control cable bracket and remove the bracket with the cable attached (see Chapter 2A). Refit the bolts to secure the nuts on the underside of the pump mounting and to retain the pump in place.

11 Release the clip securing the oil inlet hose from the oil tank to the union on the oil pump and detach the hose (see Section 13). Clamp the hose and secure it in an upright position to minimise oil loss. Wrap a clean plastic bag around the end to prevent dirt entering the system.

12 On models fitted with a drum rear brake, disconnect the brake cable from the brake arm (see Chapter 8). Undo the screw securing the cable clip to the underside of the drive belt casing and detach the cable (see Chapter 2A).

13 On models fitted with a disc rear brake, remove the rear wheel and displace the brake caliper, then temporarily refit the rear wheel (see Chapter 8). Unclip the brake hose from the underside of the drive belt casing (see Chapter 2A).

14 Check that all wiring, cables and hoses are clear of the engine/transmission unit. With the aid of an assistant, support the weight of the machine on the rear grab handle. Remove the bolt securing the rear shock absorber to the transmission casing, then remove the front

engine mounting bolt and lift the frame away from the engine/transmission unit.

15 If required, remove the stand (see Chapter 6) and the rear wheel (see Chapter 8) .

Installation

16 Installation is the reverse of removal, noting the following points:
• Make sure no wires, cables or hoses become trapped between the engine and the frame when installing the engine.
• Tighten the engine mounting bolt and shock absorber bolt to the torque settings specified at the beginning of this Chapter.
• Make sure all wires, cables and hoses are correctly routed and connected, and secured by any clips or ties.
• Fill the cooling system (see Chapter 3).
• Bleed the oil pump (see Chapter 2A, Section 13) and check the adjustment of the oil pump cable where fitted (see Chapter 1).
• Check the operation of the rear brake before riding the machine (see Chapter 8).

6 Disassembly and reassembly – general information

Disassembly

1 Before disassembling the engine, the external surfaces of the unit should be thoroughly cleaned and degreased. This will prevent contamination of the engine internals, and will also make working a lot easier and cleaner. A high flash-point solvent, such as paraffin can be used, or better still, a proprietary engine degreaser such as Gunk. Use an old paintbrush to work the solvent into the various recesses of the engine casings. Take care to exclude solvent or water from the electrical components and inlet and exhaust ports.

 Warning: The use of petrol (gasoline) as a cleaning agent should be avoided because of the risk of fire.

2 When clean and dry, arrange the unit on the workbench, leaving suitable clear area for working. Gather a selection of small containers and plastic bags so that parts can be grouped together in an easily identifiable manner. Some paper and a pen should be on hand to permit notes to be made and labels attached where necessary. A supply of clean rag is also required.

3 Before commencing work, read through the appropriate section so that some idea of the necessary procedure can be gained. When removing components it should be noted that great force is seldom required, unless specified. In many cases, a component's reluctance to be removed is indicative of an incorrect approach or removal method – if in any doubt, re-check with the text.

4 When disassembling the engine, keep 'mated' parts that have been in contact with each other during engine operation together. These 'mated' parts must be reused or replaced as an assembly.

5 Complete engine disassembly should be done in the following general order with reference to the appropriate Sections. Refer to Chapter 2C for details of transmission components disassembly.

Remove the water pump (see Chapter 3)
Remove the alternator (see Chapter 9)
Remove the variator
Remove the cylinder head
Remove the cylinder
Remove the piston
Remove the oil pump
Remove the reed valve (see Chapter 4)
Remove the starter motor (see Chapter 9)
Separate the crankcase halves

Reassembly

6 Reassembly is accomplished by reversing the general disassembly sequence.

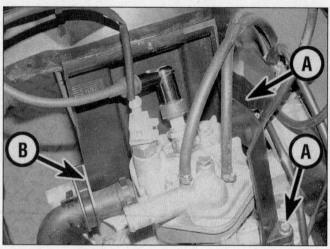

7.1 Shield is retained by bolts (A) and clip (B) on coolant hose

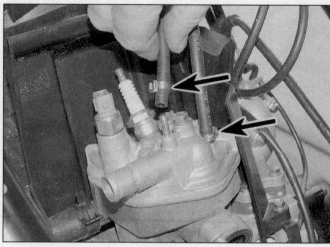

7.3 Disconnect the carburettor heater hoses (arrowed)

7 Cylinder head – removal, inspection and installation

Note: *This procedure can be carried out with the engine in the frame. If the engine has been removed, ignore the steps that do not apply.*
Caution: The engine must be completely cool before beginning this procedure or the cylinder head may become warped.

Removal

1 Remove the body panels as necessary according to model (see Chapter 7). Undo the bolts and remove the shield from the rear of the cylinder **(see illustration)**. Note how the shield clips to the cylinder coolant hose.
2 Disconnect the battery negative terminal (see Chapter 9). Pull the spark plug cap off the plug and disconnect the wire to the temperature sender on the cylinder head **(see illustration 5.4)**.
3 Drain the cooling system and disconnect the coolant hose from the union on the cylinder head, then disconnect the carburettor heater hoses **(see illustration)**.
4 If required, remove the spark plug, then unscrew the four cylinder head bolts evenly and a little at a time in a criss-cross sequence until they are all loose and remove the bolts **(see illustration)**.
5 Lift the head off the cylinder, taking care to retrieve the thermostat and thermostat spring **(see illustration)**. If the head is stuck, tap around the joint face between the head and cylinder with a soft-faced mallet to free it. Do not attempt to free the head by inserting a screwdriver between the head and cylinder – you'll damage the sealing surfaces.
Caution: The cylinder head bolts also secure the cylinder to the crankcase. If the cylinder base gasket seal is broken when removing the head, a new gasket will have to be fitted on reassembly (see Section 8).
6 If the thermostat is stuck in the cylinder head, remove it.
7 Remove the cylinder head gaskets and discard them as new ones must be fitted on reassembly.
8 If required, unscrew the temperature sender and coolant bleed valve from the cylinder head **(see illustration)**.

Inspection

9 Refer to Chapter 1 and decarbonise the cylinder head.
10 Inspect the head very carefully for cracks and other damage. If cracks are found, a new head will be required.
11 Inspect the threads in the spark plug hole. Damaged or worn threads can be reclaimed using a thread insert; consult a Peugeot dealer or scooter engineer.
12 Check the mating surfaces on the cylinder head and cylinder for signs of leakage, which could indicate that the head is warped.
13 Using a precision straight-edge, check the head mating surface for warpage. Check vertically, horizontally and diagonally across the head, making four checks in all (see Chapter 2A).
14 Ensure that the thermostat bypass passage is clear **(see illustration)**.
15 Check the condition of the thermostat (see Chapter 3).

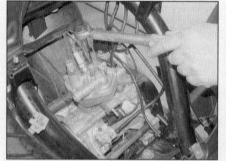

7.4 Undo the cylinder head bolts . . .

7.5 . . . and remove the head with the thermostat and spring (arrowed)

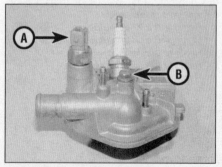

7.8 Temperature sender (A) and coolant bleed valve (B)

7.14 Thermostat bypass passage must be clear

Installation

16 If removed, smear the threads of the temperature sender with a suitable non-permanent sealant and screw it into the head. Tighten the sender securely. Check the condition of the coolant bleed valve washer and replace it with a new one if it is damaged. It is good practice to renew the washer if the valve is removed. Install the valve finger tight.

17 Ensure both cylinder head and cylinder mating surfaces are clean, and lubricate the cylinder bore with the specified two-stroke oil. Ensure the grooves for the head gaskets are clean and install the gaskets, pressing them firmly into place **(see illustrations)**.

18 Install the thermostat into its recess in the head and fit the spring over the thermostat. Hold the spring and thermostat in place with a small screwdriver and fit the head onto the cylinder **(see illustrations)**.

19 Install the four bolts and tighten them finger-tight, then tighten them evenly and a little at a time in a criss-cross pattern to the torque setting specified at the beginning of this Chapter **(see illustration 7.4)**.

20 If removed, install the spark plug, then connect the wire to the temperature sender.

21 Fit the carburettor heater hoses and coolant hose onto their unions and secure them with the clips, then refill the cooling system (see Chapter 3).

22 Install the remaining components in the reverse order of removal.

8 Cylinder – removal, inspection and installation

Note: *This procedure can be carried out with the engine in the frame. If the engine has been removed, ignore the steps that do not apply.*

 **Warning: The cylinder is Nicosil coated – under no circumstances should the cylinder be rebored or honed. No oversize pistons are available.**

Removal

1 Remove the exhaust system (see Chapter 4) and the cylinder head (see Section 7).

2 Loosen the clip securing the coolant hose to the cylinder and detach the hose **(see illustration)**.

3 Lift the cylinder up off the crankcase, supporting the piston as it becomes accessible to prevent it hitting the crankcase opening (see Chapter 2A). Take care that no residual coolant in the cylinder water jacket spills into the crankcase opening. If the cylinder is stuck, tap around the joint face between the cylinder and the crankcase with a soft-faced mallet to free it. Don't attempt to free the cylinder by inserting a screwdriver between it and the crankcase – you'll damage the sealing surfaces. When the cylinder is partway removed, stuff a clean rag into the crankcase opening around the piston to prevent anything falling inside, such as pieces of broken ring.

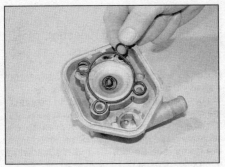

7.17a Press the centre head gasket . . .

4 Remove the cylinder gasket and discard it as a new one must be fitted on reassembly.

Inspection

5 The procedure for inspecting and measuring the cylinder bore is the same as for the air-cooled engine (see Chapter 2A, Section 8). If the cylinder is excessively worn or damaged and has to be renewed, ensure that the new cylinder and piston have matching size codes, as marked on the top of the cylinder and the piston.

6 In addition, clean any corrosion out of the cylinder water jacket and inspect the cylinder to cylinder head gasket surfaces for corrosion which will cause coolant leakage and loss of compression.

7 If there is any doubt about the serviceability of the cylinder, consult a Peugeot dealer.

8 Inspect the cylinder head bolt threads in the crankcase (see Chapter 2A, Section 14).

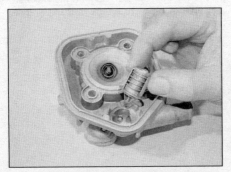

7.18a Install the thermostat . . .

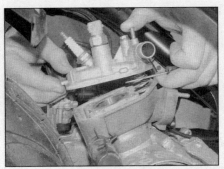

7.18c . . . then hold them in place while the head is installed

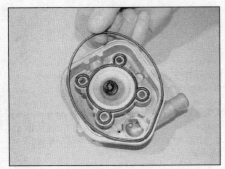

7.17b . . . and the outer gasket firmly into their grooves

Installation

9 The procedure for installing the cylinder is the same as for the air-cooled engine (see Chapter 2A, Section 8).

10 Fit the coolant hose to the cylinder and secure it with the clip after installing the cylinder head to avoid damaging the cylinder base gasket, then install the exhaust system (see Chapter 4).

9 Piston – removal, inspection and installation

Note: *This procedure can be carried out with the engine in the frame. If the engine has been removed, ignore the steps that do not apply.*

1 The procedure for removal, inspection and installation of the piston is the same as for the air-cooled engine (see Chapter 2A, Section 9).

7.18b . . . and the thermostat spring . . .

8.2 Detach the coolant hose (arrowed) from the cylinder

10 Piston rings – inspection and installation

Note: *This procedure can be carried out with the engine in the frame. If the engine has been removed, ignore the steps that do not apply.*
1 The procedure for removal, inspection and installation of the piston rings is the same as for the air-cooled engine (see Chapter 2A, Section 10).

11 Starter pinion assembly – removal, inspection and installation

Note: *This procedure can be carried out with the engine in the frame. If the engine has been removed, ignore the steps that do not apply.*
1 The procedure for removal, inspection and installation of the starter pinion assembly is the same as for the air-cooled engine (see Chapter 2A, Section 12).

12 Oil pump – removal, inspection, installation and bleeding

Note: *This procedure can be carried out with the engine in the frame. If the engine has been removed, ignore the steps that do not apply.*
1 The procedure for removal, inspection and installation and bleeding of the oil pump is the same as for the air-cooled engine (see Chapter 2A, Section 13).

13 Crankcase halves, crankshaft and connecting rod, and bearings

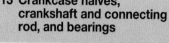

Note: *To separate the crankcase halves, the engine must be removed from the frame.*
1 To access the crankshaft and its bearings, the crankcase must be split into two parts.
2 To enable the crankcase halves to be separated, the engine must be removed from the frame (see Section 5) and the following components must be removed:
• Water pump (see Chapter 3)
• Alternator (see Chapter 9)
• Variator (see Chapter 2C)
• Cylinder head (see Section 7)
• Cylinder (see Section 8)
• Piston (see Section 9)
• Oil pump (see Section 12)
• Reed valve (see Chapter 4)
• Starter motor (see Chapter 9)
3 The remainder of the procedure is the same as for air-cooled models. Refer to Chapter 2A, Section 14 for details.

14 Initial start-up after overhaul

1 Make sure the oil tank is at least partly full and the pump is correctly adjusted (see Chapter 1) and bled of air (see Chapter 2A, Section 13).
2 Make sure there is fuel in the tank.
3 With the ignition OFF, operate the kickstart a couple of times to check that the engine turns over easily.

4 Turn the ignition ON, start the engine and allow it to run at a slow idle until it reaches operating temperature. Do not be alarmed if there is a little smoke from the exhaust – this will be due to the oil used to lubricate the piston and bore during assembly and should subside after a while.
5 Check the coolant level and bleed any trapped air from the coolant system (see Chapter 3, Section 2).
6 If the engine proves reluctant to start, remove the spark plug and check that it has not become wet and oily. If it has, clean it and try again. If the engine refuses to start, go through the fault finding charts at the end of this manual to identify the problem.

15 Recommended running-in procedure

1 Treat the engine gently for the first few miles to allow any new parts to bed in.
2 If a new piston, rings or cylinder have been fitted, the engine will have to be run in as when new. This means a restraining hand on the throttle until at least 300 miles (500 km) have been covered. There's no point in keeping to any set speed limit – the main idea is to keep from labouring the engine and to gradually increase performance up to the 600 mile (1000 km) mark. Make sure that the throttle position is varied to vary engine speed, and use full throttle for only short bursts. Experience is the best guide, since it's easy to tell when an engine is running freely.

Chapter 2 Part C:
Transmission

Refer to Chapter 1 for model identification details

Contents

Degrees of difficulty

Easy, suitable for novice with little experience	Fairly easy, suitable for beginner with some experience	Fairly difficult, suitable for competent DIY mechanic 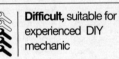	Difficult, suitable for experienced DIY mechanic	Very difficult, suitable for expert DIY or professional

Specifications

Variator

Centre sleeve length	38 mm
Roller colour code and diameter – 50 cc engines	
Speedfight/Speedfight 2 (black)	16 mm
Trekker (black)	16 mm
Vivacity (black)	16 mm
Roller colour code and diameter – 100 cc engines	
Speedfight (yellow)	19 mm
Speedfight 2 (brown)	18 mm
Trekker (yellow)	19 mm
Vivacity – up to 1999 (yellow)	19 mm
Vivacity – from 2000 (brown)	18 mm

Clutch

50 cc engines	
Centre spring free length	103.5 mm
Shoe spring free length	32 mm
100 cc engines	
Centre spring free length	105.5 mm
Shoe spring free length	31.8 mm

Torque settings

Clutch assembly nut	50 Nm
Clutch centre nut	45 Nm
Drive belt cover bolts	10 Nm
Relay box cover bolts	10 Nm
Relay box drain plug	12 Nm
Relay box filler plug	12 Nm
Variator nut	40 Nm

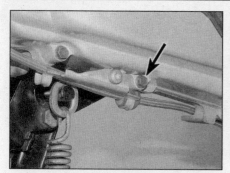

2.1a Undo the screw and remove the brake cable/hose bracket . . .

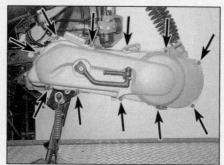

2.1b . . . then remove the cover retaining bolts

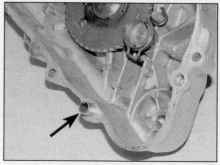

2.2 Remove any dowels for safekeeping if they are loose

1   General information

The transmission on all models is fully automatic in operation. Power is transmitted from the engine to the rear wheel by belt, via a variable size drive pulley (the variator), an automatic clutch on the driven pulley, and a reduction relay box. The variator and the automatic clutch both work on the principal of centrifugal force.

The transmission can be worked on with the engine in the frame.

2   Drive belt cover –
removal and installation

Removal

1 Undo the screw securing the rear brake cable or hose bracket to the underside of the transmission casing and remove the bracket **(see illustration)**. Working in a criss-cross pattern, loosen the drive belt cover retaining bolts and remove the bolts **(see illustration)**. On some machines the bolts are different

lengths; note where they fit **Note:** *It is not necessary to remove the kickstart lever before removing the cover.*

2 Remove the cover and note the position of any locating dowels **(see illustration)**. Remove the dowels for safekeeping if they are loose. **Note:** *Sealant should not be used on the cover, but if it will not lift away easily, tap it gently around the edge with a soft-faced hammer.* On Vivacity 50 models fitted with a cover manufactured from composite material, remove the gasket. If the gasket is damaged, discard it and fit a new one on reassembly.

3 Note the position of the kickstart quadrant and the engaging pinion, and how the outer end of the starter motor pinion assembly locates in the cover **(see illustration)**.

4 If fitted, undo the retaining bolt for the air cooling duct and remove the duct. Inspect the duct filter element. If it is dirty, the element should be washed in soapy water and refitted when dry. If the element is damaged or has deteriorated, replace it with a new one.

5 On Vivacity 50 models with a composite cover, check the condition of the rubber stop for the kickstart quadrant inside the cover. If the stop is damaged or excessively worn, replace it with a new one.

6 Clean any dust or dirt from the inside of the casing with a suitable solvent, taking care to

avoid contact with the belt and the drive faces of the pulleys. Any evidence of oil inside the casing suggests a worn seal either on the crankshaft or the relay box input shaft which must be rectified. Evidence of grease inside the casing suggests worn seals either in the variator or the clutch centre which should also be rectified.

Installation

7 If fitted, install the air cooling duct and tighten its retaining bolt securely.

8 If removed, fit the dowels in the cover and apply a smear of grease to the end of the starter motor pinion and to the threads of the cover bolts. On Vivacity 50 models with a composite cover, install the cover gasket.

9 Ensure the kickstart quadrant and engaging pinion are correctly located in the cover (see Section 3), then fit the cover. Make sure the starter motor pinion locates correctly inside the cover **(see illustration)**, then install the bolts finger tight. On machines fitted with bolts of different lengths, ensure the bolts are installed in their original locations (see Step 1).

10 Working in a criss-cross pattern, tighten the cover bolts to the torque setting specified at the beginning of this Chapter, then crank the kickstart lever to ensure the mechanism engages correctly with the kickstart driven

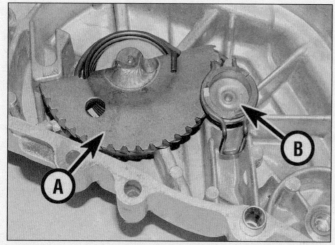

2.3 Kickstart quadrant (A) and engaging pinion (B) are located in the cover

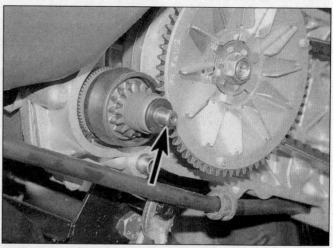

2.9 Ensure end of starter motor pinion locates correctly inside the cover

3.3 Kickstart lever rest position

3.4a Remove the circlip . . .

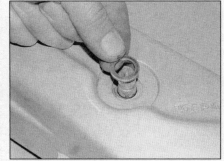

3.4b . . . and washer from the kickstart shaft

3.5 Release the tension in the spring and unhook it from the quadrant

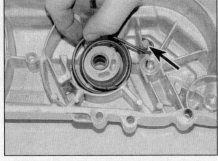

3.6a Unhook the spring from the post (arrowed) . . .

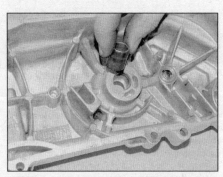

3.6b . . . and remove the kickstart bush

gear and that the lever returns to its proper rest position afterwards. Fit the bracket over the rear brake cable or hose and secure it to the underside of the drive belt cover with the screw.

3 Kickstart mechanism – removal, inspection and installation

Removal

1 Remove the drive belt cover (see Section 2).

2 Pull the engaging pinion out of its recess in the cover, noting how the spring locates **(see illustration 2.3)**. Remove the washer from behind the pinion.

3 Note the rest position of the kickstart lever, then undo the lever pinch bolt and pull the lever off the shaft **(see illustration)**.

4 Remove the circlip and washer (if fitted) from the kickstart shaft on the outside of the cover **(see illustrations)**.

5 Ease the kickstart shaft out of the cover and release the tension on the kickstart return spring. Unhook the spring from the kickstart quadrant and remove the shaft **(see illustration)**.

6 Note how the return spring locates inside the cover and remove the spring and kickstart bush **(see illustrations)**.

7 Clean all the components with a suitable solvent.

Inspection

8 Check the dogs on the end of the engaging pinion and the corresponding dogs on the kickstart driven gear **(see illustrations)**. Inspect the teeth on the engaging pinion and the teeth on the kickstart quadrant **(see illustrations)**. Check the shafts of the engaging pinion and the kickstart quadrant,

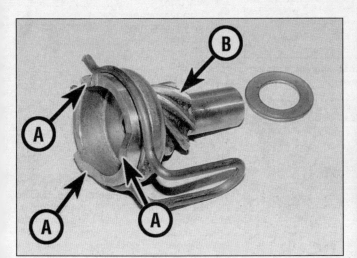

3.8a Inspect the dogs (A) and teeth (B) on the engaging pinion

3.8b Inspect the dogs on the kickstart driven gear (arrowed)

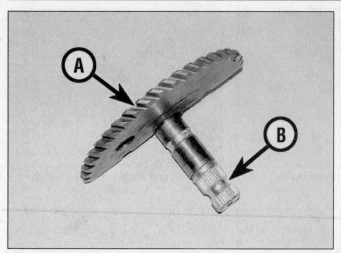

3.8c Inspect the teeth (A) and the splines (B) on the kickstart quadrant

3.11 Quadrant should butt against stop (arrowed) on inside of case

and the quadrant bush, for signs of wear, and inspect the splines on the end of the quadrant shaft for damage **(see illustration 3.8c)**. Replace any components that are worn or damaged with new ones. **Note:** *The kickstart driven gear is an integral part of the outer half of the variator pulley. Peugeot list two types of outer pulley halves which are not interchangeable. Consult a Peugeot dealer to ensure you obtain the correct new part.*

9 Ensure the spring on the engaging pinion is a firm fit and inspect the kickstart return spring for cracks and wear at each end. When fitted, the return spring should return the

kickstart lever to the rest position and hold it there; if not, it has worn and should be renewed.

Installation

10 Press the kickstart bush into the cover, then install the return spring with its long end innermost. Hook the long end around the post on the inside of the cover **(see illustration 3.6a)**.
11 Lubricate the kickstart shaft with a smear of molybdenum disulphide grease and insert it through the bush, then hook the outer end of the return spring onto the quadrant. Rotate the shaft anti-clockwise against the spring

tension until the quadrant can be butted against the stop on the inside of the case **(see illustration)**. Ensure the shaft is pressed all the way into the case, then install the washer (if fitted) and circlip **(see illustrations 3.4a and 3.4b)**.
12 Fit the kickstart lever in the rest position and tighten the pinch bolt securely. Operate the lever to check that it turns smoothly and returns to its rest position under spring pressure.
13 Lubricate the shaft of the engaging pinion with a smear of grease and install the washer, then fit the pinion into the case. Align the spring with the detent in the case, then operate the kickstart lever to engage the pinion with the kickstart quadrant and draw the pinion into the case **(see illustration)**.
14 Check the operation of the mechanism, then refit the cover (see Section 2).

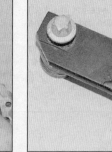

3.13 Operate kickstart lever to draw kickstart pinion into the case

4.2 Variator pulley teeth engage in notch (arrowed)

4 Variator –
removal, inspection and installation

Removal

1 Remove the drive belt cover (see Section 2).
2 To remove the variator centre nut, the crankshaft must be locked to stop it turning. Peugeot produce a service tool (Pt. No. 752370) which bolts onto the engine case and locates between the teeth on the variator pulley. Alternatively a similar tool can be made **(see illustration)**.
3 Undo the nut and remove the outer half of the variator pulley **(see illustrations)**. Discard the nut as a new one must be fitted on reassembly. Move the drive belt aside. **Note:** *Unless you are removing the clutch assembly, leave the belt on the clutch pulley. Mark the belt with a directional arrow if it is removed so that it can be refitted the correct way round* **(see illustration)**.

4.3a Lock the crankshaft with the tool (A) and undo the nut (B) . . .

4.3b . . . then remove the outer half of the pulley

4.3c Mark the belt with a directional arrow

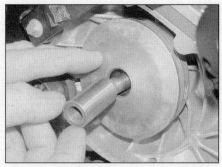

4.4 Withdraw the variator centre sleeve . . .

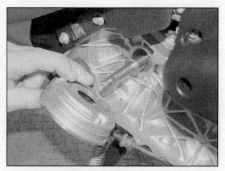

4.5 . . . and pull off the variator assembly . . .

4.6 . . . and the washer (if fitted)

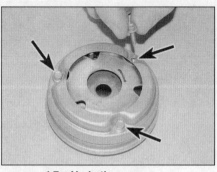

4.7a Undo the screws . . .

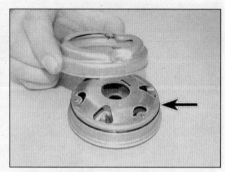

4.7b . . . and lift off the cover. Discard the O-ring (arrowed) if fitted

4 Hold the variator assembly and withdraw the centre sleeve **(see illustration)**.
5 Pull the variator assembly off the crankshaft **(see illustration)**. **Note:** *If the variator is just being displaced, grip the assembly so that the*

ramp plate at the back is held into the variator body as you remove it, otherwise the rollers inside will fall out off their ramps and the variator will have to be disassembled to reposition them.

6 Remove the washer (if fitted) from the crankshaft **(see illustration)**.
7 To disassemble the variator, remove the three screws or bolts and lift off the cover. On models fitted with greased rollers, remove the O-ring and discard it as a new one must be fitted on reassembly **(see illustrations)**.
8 On restricted 50 cc machines, lift out the restrictor plate **(see illustration)**.
9 Lift out the ramp plate, noting how it fits, and remove the ramp guides, then lift out the rollers **(see illustrations)**.
10 Clean all the components using a suitable solvent.

Inspection

11 Measure the diameter of each roller; they should all be the same size. Inspect the surface of each roller for flat spots **(see illustration)**. If any rollers are worn below the nominal diameter for new rollers specified at the

4.8 Lift out the restrictor plate (if fitted)

4.9a Lift out the ramp plate . . .

4.9b . . . and remove the ramp guides . . .

4.9c . . . then lift out the rollers

4.11 Measure the rollers and check them for flat spots

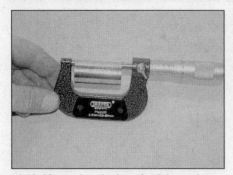
4.13 Measuring the length of the variator sleeve

4.14 Check the splines (arrowed) for wear and the surface of the pulley for blueing

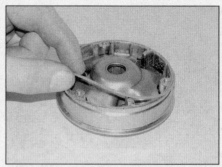
4.18 Fit a new O-ring to the variator body if applicable

4.21a Clean the inner faces of the variator pulley . . .

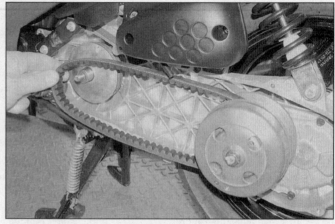
4.21b . . . then press the belt into the clutch pulley and fit it onto the variator pulley

beginning of this Chapter, or have worn flat, renew all the rollers as a set. **Note:** *Variator rollers are not interchangeable between different models in the Peugeot range. Always specify the year and model of your scooter when buying new rollers. Greased-type variator rollers cannot be replaced by the later non-greased type unless a completely new variator assembly is being fitted.*

12 Inspect the surface of the ramps in the variator body and the ramp plate for wear or damage and check the slots in the ramp guides where they fit in the variator body and fit new components as necessary.

13 Measure the length of the variator sleeve and compare the result with the nominal length for a new sleeve specified at the beginning of this Chapter **(see illustration)**. Replace the sleeve with a new one if necessary.

14 Check the condition of the splines in the centre of the outer half of the variator pulley and inspect the inner face of the pulley for signs of overheating or blueing, caused by the pulley running out of alignment **(see illustration)**. Renew the pulley half if it is damaged.

Installation

15 Fit the rollers into the variator body **(see illustration 4.9c)**. If applicable, lubricate the rollers and the ramps with high melting point grease before installation. **Note:** *Too much grease in the variator will make it run out of balance and cause vibration.*

16 Check that the ramp guides are correctly fitted on the ramp plate and install the plate **(see illustration 4.9b)**.

17 On restricted 50 cc machines, fit the restrictor plate.

18 If applicable, fit a new O-ring in the groove around the variator body **(see illustration)**. Install the cover, and tighten the cover screws or bolts securely. **Note:** *Take care not to dislodge the O-ring when the cover is installed.*

19 Install the washer (if fitted) on the crankshaft. Grip the variator so that the ramp plate is held into the body and install the assembly **(see illustration 4.5)**. **Note:** *If the ramp plate moves and the rollers are dislodged, disassemble the variator and reposition them correctly.*

20 Clean the outer surface of the sleeve with a suitable solvent and slide it into the centre of the variator.

21 Clean both inner faces of the variator pulley with a suitable solvent, then compress the clutch pulley centre spring and press the drive belt into the clutch pulley to facilitate fitting it over the variator pulley **(see illustrations)**.

22 Install the outer half of the variator pulley, ensuring the splines align with the crankshaft, and fit the new centre nut finger-tight **(see illustrations)**. Make sure the outer pulley half

4.22a Install the outer pulley half . . .

4.22b . . . and tighten the centre nut finger-tight

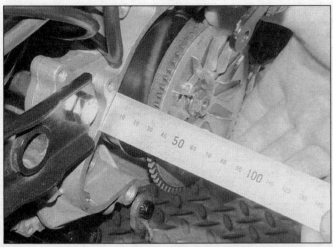

4.24 Check by measuring that the pulley is not skewed

4.25 Ease the belt into place between the two pulleys

butts against the sleeve and is not skewed by the belt. **Note:** *Do not use a thread locking compound on the centre nut.*

23 Install the locking tool used on removal (see Step 2) and tighten the centre nut to the specified torque setting.

24 Measure the distance between the crankcase face and the edge of the outer pulley half, then rotate the crankshaft and repeat the measuring procedure several times to ensure the outer pulley half is not skewed **(see illustration)**.

25 Ease the drive belt out of the clutch pulley to reduce the slack in the belt **(see illustration)**, then fit the cover (see Section 2).

5 Drive belt – inspection and renewal

Inspection

1 Peugeot specify that the belt should be checked every 3000 miles (5000 km) and renewed every 6000 miles (10,000 km), but it is good practice to check the condition of the belt whenever the cover is removed (see Section 2).

2 Check along the entire length of the belt for cracks, splits, fraying and damage and renew the belt if any such damage is found. The belt will wear during the normal course of use and dust will accumulate inside the cover. However, a large amount of dust or debris inside the cover is an indication of abnormal wear and the cause, such as high spots on the pulleys or the pulleys running out of alignment, should be investigated. **Note:** *Drive belts are not interchangeable between different models in the Peugeot range. Always specify the year and model of your scooter when buying a new belt. If in doubt, check the part number marked on the belt with a Peugeot dealer.*

3 Oil or grease inside the casing will contaminate the belt and prevent it gripping the pulleys (see Section 2).

Renewal

4 The drive belt must be replaced with a new one at the specified service interval, or earlier dependant on belt condition (see Step 2). Remove the outer half of the variator pulley (see Section 4) and lift the belt off the crankshaft and the clutch pulley without disturbing the variator assembly.

5 Fit the new belt, making sure any directional arrows point in the direction of normal rotation, then install the variator outer pulley half (see Section 4).

6 Clutch and clutch pulley – removal, inspection and installation

Removal

1 Remove the drive belt (see Section 5).

2 To remove the clutch centre nut it is necessary to hold the clutch to prevent it turning. Peugeot produce a service tool (Pt. No. 752237) which locates in the holes in the clutch drum. Alternatively a similar tool can be made (see *Tool Tip*) or you can use a strap wrench **(see illustrations)**.

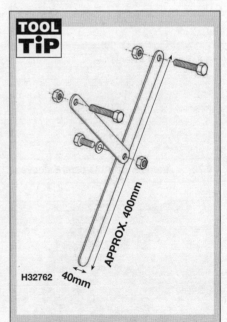

A clutch holding tool can be made using two strips of steel bolted together in the middle, and with a nut and bolt through each end which locate into the holes in the rotor.

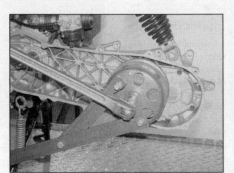

6.2a Prevent the clutch from turning with a home-made tool ...

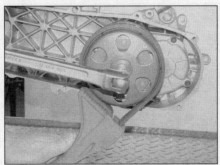

6.2b ... or a strap wrench

6.3 Remove the clutch drum . . .

6.4 . . . then pull the clutch and pulley off the shaft

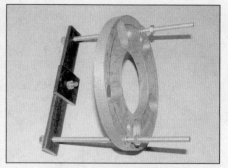

6.5a A home-made clamp for disassembling the clutch

6.5b Ensure the clamp does not rest on the rim (arrowed) of the pulley

6.6 Hold the clutch with a strap wrench and undo the nut

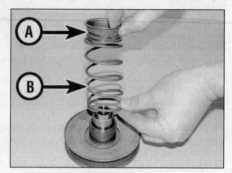

6.7a Lift off the spring seat (A) and spring (B) . . .

3 Undo the nut and remove the clutch drum **(see illustration)**. Discard the nut as a new one must be fitted on reassembly.
4 Draw the clutch and pulley assembly off the relay box input shaft **(see illustration)**.

5 To disassemble the clutch and pulley assembly, first clamp the assembly together to hold the pressure of the centre spring while the assembly nut is undone. Peugeot produce a service tool (Pt. No. 752127) to do this.

Alternatively, use the set-up shown, ensuring no pressure is applied to the rim of the pulley and that there is adequate room to undo the nut **(see illustrations)**.
6 Fit a strap wrench around the clutch shoes to hold the assembly while the nut is undone, then release the spring pressure by undoing the clamp **(see illustration)**.
7 Remove the clutch, then remove the spring seat, the spring and the centre sleeve **(see illustrations)**.
8 Two O-rings are fitted to the pulley outer half **(see illustration)**. Peugeot do not list the O-rings as separate items, so remove them with care. **Note:** *If the O-rings are damaged, consult a Peugeot dealer or automotive parts supplier who may be able to supply suitable replacements.*
9 Withdraw the guide pins and separate the pulley halves **(see illustrations)**.
10 Clean all the components with a suitable solvent.

Inspection

11 Check the inner surface of the clutch drum for damage and scoring and inspect the splines in the centre; replace it if necessary **(see illustration)**. Measure the internal diameter of the drum at several points to determine if it is worn or out-of-round. If it is worn or out-of-round, replace it with a new one.
12 Check the amount of friction material remaining on the clutch shoes **(see illustration)**. If the friction material has worn down to the shoe, or the shoes are worn unevenly, fit a new clutch.

6.7b . . . then remove the centre sleeve

6.8 Remove the O-rings carefully

6.9a Withdraw the guide pins . . .

6.9b . . . and separate the pulley halves

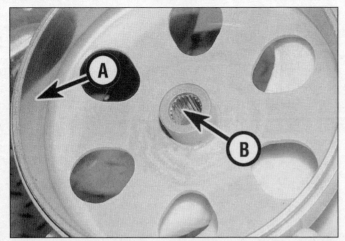

6.11 Check the inner surface of the drum (A) for scoring and the splines (B) for wear

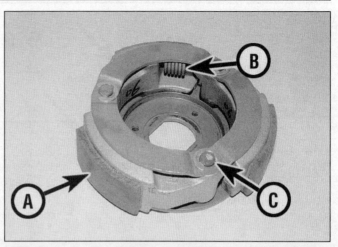

6.12 Check the clutch friction material (A), shoe springs (B) and retaining clips (C)

13 Inspect the shoe springs for wear, cracks and stretching. Measure the free length of the springs and compare the result with the nominal values for new components given Specifications at the beginning of this Chapter. Ensure that the shoes are not seized on their pivot pins and that the retaining circlips are secure on the ends of the pins (see illustration 6.12). Clutch components are not available as individual items; if any parts are worn or damaged, fit a new clutch.

14 Inspect the inner faces of the clutch pulley for signs of overheating or blueing, caused by the pulley running out of alignment. Check the seals inside the pulley outer half (see illustration). If the seals are worn or damaged, grease will pass onto the face of the pulley. Inspect the guide pins and the pin slots for wear. Two bearings are fitted in the hub of the pulley inner half; inspect the rollers of the inner bearing for flat spots and ensure the outer sealed ball bearing turns smoothly (see illustrations). Clutch pulley components are not available as individual items; if any parts are worn or damaged, a complete new clutch and clutch pulley assembly will have to be fitted.

15 Check the condition of the spring (see illustration 6.7). If it is bent or appears weak, renew it. Measure the free length of the spring and compare it with the figure for a new spring given in the Specifications. Renew the spring if it has worn to less than the limit.

Installation

16 Assemble the two halves of the clutch pulley and install the guide pins and the O-rings. Lubricate the pin slots with molybdenum disulphide grease, then fit the centre sleeve, the spring and the spring seat.

17 Position the clutch on the spring seat and compress the assembly using the same method as for disassembly (see Step 5). Ensure the flats on the clutch are aligned with the pulley hub and install the assembly nut finger tight. Hold the assembly around the clutch shoes with a strap wrench and tighten

the nut to the specified torque setting, then release the clamp (see illustration 6.6).

18 Lubricate the needle bearing in the hub of the pulley inner half with molybdenum disulphide grease and install the clutch and pulley assembly on the input shaft. Install the clutch drum, ensuring the splines align with the shaft, and fit the new centre nut finger tight. Use the method employed on removal to prevent the clutch turning and tighten the centre nut to the specified torque setting. Note: Do not use a thread locking compound on the centre nut.

19 Clean both inner faces of the clutch pulley with a suitable solvent and install the drive belt (see Section 5).

6.14a Inspect the pulley internal seals (arrowed) . . .

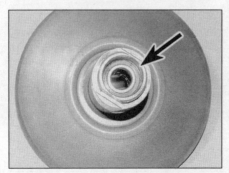

6.14c . . . and the sealed ball bearing

7 Relay box – removal, inspection and installation

Removal

1 Remove the clutch and clutch pulley (see Section 6). On machines fitted with a drum rear brake, remove the rear wheel; on machines fitted with a disc rear brake, remove the rear wheel, hub and brake disc (see Chapter 8).

2 If a drain plug is fitted to the machine, drain the relay box oil (see illustration).

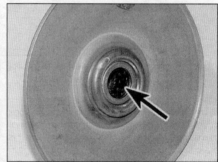

6.14b . . . the needle roller bearing . . .

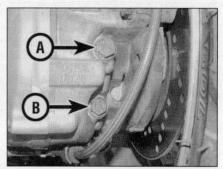

7.2 Relay box filler plug (A) and drain plug (B)

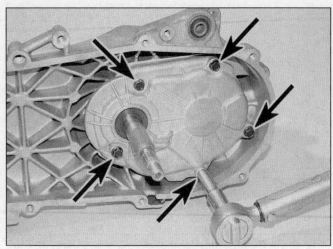

7.3a Undo the cover retaining bolts . . .

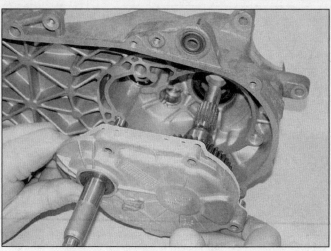

7.3b . . . and lift out the cover and shafts

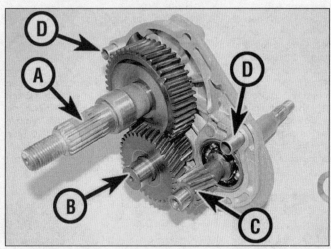

7.3c Output shaft (A), intermediate shaft (B), input shaft (C) and cover dowels (D)

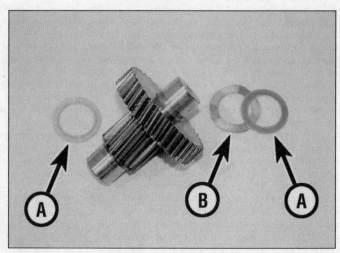

7.4 Intermediate shaft, thrust washers (A) and wave washer (B)

3 Unscrew the bolts securing the relay box cover and remove the cover, taking care not to damage the output shaft seal as the shaft is pulled through it. The output shaft, intermediate shaft and input shaft will come out with the cover **(see illustrations)**. The cover is fitted with two dowels; note their position and remove them for safekeeping if they are loose. Discard the gasket as a new one must be fitted on reassembly. **Note:** *On machines not fitted with a drain plug, position a tray beneath the case to catch the oil when the cover is removed.*

4 Remove the thrust washer and wave washer (if fitted) from the intermediate shaft, then lift out the shaft and remove the inner thrust washer **(see illustration)**. The large and small pinions are an integral part of the shaft.

5 Lift out the output shaft. The pinion is a press fit on the shaft and should not be removed.

6 The input shaft is a press fit in its bearing; only remove the shaft if a new one is being fitted, or if a new bearing or seal is being fitted. Support the cover on blocks of wood and drive the shaft out using a soft-faced mallet on the clutch end. If the shaft is being reused, fit the clutch centre nut to protect the threads. The pinion is an integral part of the shaft.

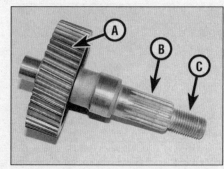

7.8 Check the pinion teeth (A), splines (B) and threads (C) for wear and damage

Inspection

7 Remove all traces of old gasket from the case and cover mating surfaces, taking care not to nick or gouge the soft aluminium if a scraper is used. Wash all the components in a suitable solvent and dry them with compressed air.

8 Check the pinion teeth for cracking, chipping, pitting and other obvious wear or damage, then check for signs of scoring or blueing on the pinions and shafts caused by overheating due to inadequate lubrication **(see illustration)**. Replace any damaged components. **Note:** *The input shaft and intermediate shaft are supplied as paired items and are not available individually. The pinion on the output shaft should be a tight fit; if it is loose, fit a new shaft and pinion assembly.*

9 Inspect the splines and threads on the input and output shafts **(see illustration 7.8)**.

10 Check the intermediate shaft thrust

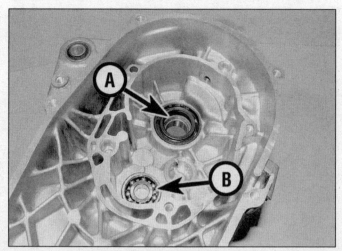

7.11a Check the condition of the oil seals (A) and bearings (B)

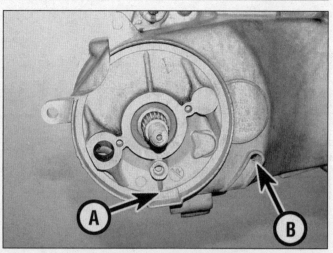

7.11b If the output shaft seal fails oil will drain at (A), if the input shaft seal fails oil will drain at (B)

washers and replace them if they are damaged or worn. Fit new ones if in any doubt.

11 Check the condition of the oil seals. If the input shaft oil seal fails, oil will run out of the drain hole in the back of the case or into the drive belt case behind the clutch. If the output shaft seal fails, oil will run out of the drain in the bottom of the case **(see illustrations)**. If either of the shafts has been removed, it is good practice to fit a new seal (see Steps 13 to 14).

12 Inspect the bearings; ensure each bearing is clean and dry, then apply a few drops of oil inside and check that it turns smoothly. If it grates or rattles it is worn and must be replaced with a new one (see Steps 15 to 16). The bearings should be a tight fit in their housings; if a bearing is loose and the housing is not damaged, use a suitable bearing locking compound to hold it in place.

13 To remove an oil seal, first note the position of the seal and which way round it is fitted, then lever it out with a flat bladed

screwdriver or seal extractor **(see illustration)**. Take care not to damage the case.

14 Smear the new seal with grease and press it into place with a suitably sized socket which bears only on the hard outer edge of the seal. Check that the seal is correctly positioned and square in the case **(see illustration)**.

15 To remove the outer bearing on each shaft, first lever out the seal. Note the position of the bearing, then support the casing on blocks of wood, heat the bearing housing with a hot air gun and drive the bearing out with a bearing driver or suitably sized socket from the seal side **(see illustration)**. Install the new bearing with a bearing driver or socket large enough to contact the outer race of the bearing (do not allow it to contact the inner race), then fit the new seal.

16 The inner bearings on each shaft are fitted in blind holes and require an internal bearing puller to extract them without damaging the case; consult a Peugeot dealer or a specialist motorcycle engineer if they need removing.

7.13 Lever out the old oil seal . . .

The new bearings should be installed with a bearing driver or socket large enough to contact the outer race of the bearing.

Installation

17 If removed, fit the input shaft through its bearing in the cover. Smear the inside of the seal with grease and support the cover on

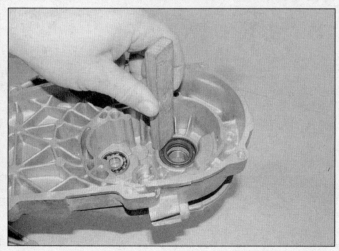

7.14 . . . and ensure the new seal is fitted square with the case

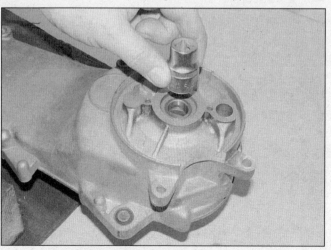

7.15 Removing the output shaft outer bearing

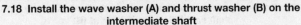

7.18 Install the wave washer (A) and thrust washer (B) on the intermediate shaft

7.19 Fit the new gasket over the cover dowels

blocks of wood, then drive the shaft into the bearing with a soft-faced mallet.

18 Fit the output shaft into its bearing in the cover. Lubricate both ends of the intermediate shaft with molybdenum disulphide grease, then install the thrust washer on the shaft against the small gear pinion and fit the shaft into the cover. Install the wave washer and then the thrust washer on the intermediate shaft against the large gear pinion **(see illustration)**.

19 If removed, fit the two dowels into the cover then fit a new gasket over the dowels **(see illustration)**.

20 Smear the inside of the output shaft oil seal with grease, then install the cover and relay shafts into the case, taking care not to damage the output shaft seal as the shaft is pushed through it **(see illustration 7.3b)**. Ensure the dowels locate correctly and install the cover bolts. Tighten the bolts evenly and in a criss-cross pattern to the torque setting specified at the beginning of this Chapter.

21 Install the remaining components in the reverse order of removal. Note that from mid-2002 the relay box oil level/filler plug was relocated on the gearbox cover outer plate – on these models the oil must be added before the drive belt cover is installed.

22 If a drain plug is fitted to the relay box, ensure it is tightened to the specified torque setting. Fill the relay box with the specified amount and type of oil (see Chapter 1). **Note:** *Peugeot do not recommend the use of hypoid oil in the relay box.*

Chapter 3
Cooling system (liquid-cooled engine)

Refer to Chapter 1 for model identification details

Contents

Degrees of difficulty

Easy, suitable for novice with little experience	**Fairly easy,** suitable for beginner with some experience	**Fairly difficult,** suitable for competent DIY mechanic
Difficult, suitable for experienced DIY mechanic	**Very difficult,** suitable for expert DIY or professional	

Specifications

Coolant
Type and mixture . . . .   50% distilled water and 50% Procor 3000 anti-freeze is needed. Peugeot state that other anti-freeze products will not mix with Procor 3000.

Temperature sender
Resistance
@ 20°C . . . .   1.91 to 2.58 K-ohms
@ 90°C . . . .   92 to 124 ohms

Torque settings
Water pump mounting bolts . . . .   10 Nm

---

1 General information

The cooling system uses a water/antifreeze coolant to carry excess energy away from the engine in the form of heat. The coolant is contained within a water jacket inside the cylinder and cylinder head which is connected to the radiator and the water pump by the coolant hoses.

Coolant heated by the engine is circulated by thermo-syphonic action, and the action of the pump, to the radiator. It flows across the radiator core, where it is cooled by the passing air, then through the water pump and back to the engine where the cycle is repeated.

A thermostat is fitted in the cylinder head to prevent the coolant flowing to the radiator when the engine is cold, therefore accelerating the speed at which the engine reaches normal operating temperature. A coolant temperature sender mounted in the cylinder head is connected to the temperature gauge on the instrument panel.

⚠ **Warning: Do not remove the reservoir cap when the engine is hot. Scalding hot coolant and steam may be blown out under pressure, which could cause serious injury.**

⚠ **Warning: Do not allow antifreeze to come in contact with your skin or painted or plastic surfaces of the scooter. Rinse off any spills immediately with plenty of water. Antifreeze is highly toxic if ingested. Never leave antifreeze lying around in an open container or in puddles on the floor; children and pets are** *attracted by its sweet smell and may drink it. Check with the local authorities about disposing of used antifreeze. Many communities will have collection centres which will see that antifreeze is disposed of safely. Antifreeze is also combustible, so don't store it near open flames.*

Caution: At all times use the specified type of antifreeze, and always mix it with distilled water in the correct proportion. The antifreeze contains corrosion inhibitors which are essential to avoid damage to the cooling system. A lack of these inhibitors could lead to a build-up of corrosion which would block the coolant passages, resulting in overheating and severe engine damage. Distilled water must be used as opposed to tap water to avoid a build-up of scale which would also block the passages.

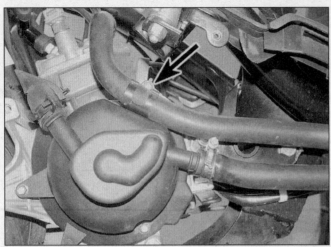

2.3a Undo the bolt (arrowed) and release the hose from the guide

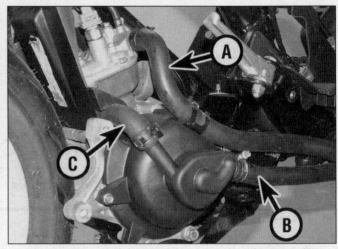

2.3b Coolant hose from the cylinder head to the radiator (A), radiator to the pump (B) and pump to cylinder (C)

2 Cooling system –
draining, flushing and refilling

 Warning: Allow the engine to cool completely before performing this maintenance operation. Also, don't allow antifreeze to come into contact with your skin or the painted or plastic surfaces of the scooter. Rinse off spills immediately with plenty of water.

Draining

1 Remove the headlight panel, the right-hand side panel, the right-hand belly panel and the storage compartment (see Chapter 7).
2 Remove the cap from the coolant reservoir. If you hear a hissing sound as you unscrew it (indicating there is still pressure in the system), wait until it stops.
3 Release the hose from the cylinder head to the radiator from the guide on the upper water pump mounting bolt **(see illustration)**.

Position a suitable container beneath the water pump. Loosen the clips securing the coolant hoses from the radiator to the pump and the cylinder head to the radiator, then detach the hoses and allow the coolant to drain from the system **(see illustrations)**.
4 Loosen the clip securing the coolant hose from the cylinder to the pump and drain any residual coolant, then reconnect the hose and secure it with the clip **(see illustration 2.3b)**.

Flushing

5 Flush the system with clean tap water by connecting a garden hose to the lower radiator hose and back-filling the system. Allow the water to run through the system until it is clear and flows cleanly out of the detached hose. If the radiator is extremely corroded it should be renewed.
6 Attach the coolant hoses to the pump and the cylinder head and secure them with the clips.
7 Fill the system through the coolant reservoir with clean water mixed with a flushing

compound. **Note:** *Make sure the flushing compound is compatible with aluminium components and follow the manufacturer's instructions carefully.* Loosen the bleed valve on the cylinder head to release any trapped air, then tighten the valve securely **(see illustration)**.
8 If necessary, top-up the reservoir (see *Daily (pre-ride) checks*) and fit the cap.
9 Start the engine and allow it to reach normal operating temperature. Let it run for about five minutes.
10 Stop the engine. Let it cool for a while, then remove the reservoir cap (see Step 2) and drain the system (see Steps 3 and 4).
11 Reconnect the coolant hoses and secure them with the clips, then fill the system with clean water only and repeat the procedure in Steps 7 to 10.

Refilling

12 Ensure all the hoses are correctly attached and secured with their clips.
13 Fill the system through the reservoir with

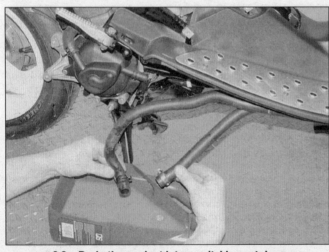

2.3c Drain the coolant into a suitable container

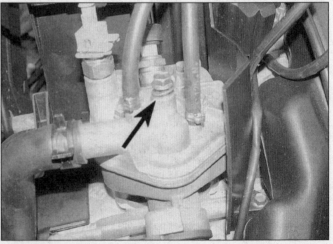

2.7 Release any trapped air through the bleed valve (arrowed)

the proper coolant mixture (see this Chapter's Specifications). **Note:** *Pour the coolant in slowly to minimise the amount of air entering the system.* Loosen the bleed valve on the cylinder head to release any trapped air, then tighten the valve securely **(see illustration 2.7).** If necessary, top-up the reservoir (see *Daily (pre-ride) checks)* and fit the cap.

14 Start the engine and allow it to idle for 2 to 3 minutes. Flick the throttle twistgrip part open 3 or 4 times, so that the engine speed rises, then stop the engine. Release any trapped air through the bleed valve, then tighten the valve securely. Check the system for leaks.

⚠️ **Warning: Make sure that the machine is on its centre stand and that the rear wheel is off the ground before bleeding the cooling system. If necessary, place a support under the stand to prevent the rear wheel contacting the ground.**

15 Let the engine cool and check the coolant level (see *Daily (pre-ride) checks)*, then install the bodywork (see Chapter 7).

16 Do not dispose of the old coolant by pouring it down the drain. Pour it into a heavy plastic container, cap it tightly and take it into an authorised disposal site or garage – see **Warning** in Section 1.

---

3   Temperature gauge and sender – check and replacement

Temperature gauge

Check

1 The circuit consists of the sender mounted in the cylinder head and the gauge assembly in the instrument panel. If the system malfunctions, first check the coolant level (see

Daily (pre-ride) checks). If the level is correct, check that the battery is fully charged and that the fuse is good (see Chapter 9).

2 If the gauge is still not working, open the engine access panel in the storage compartment, disconnect the wire from the sender and connect it to earth (ground) with a jumper wire **(see illustration).** Turn the ignition switch ON; the temperature gauge needle should swing over to the 'H' on the gauge. If the needle moves as described, check the operation of the sender (see Steps 5 to 7).

Caution: If the needle moves, turn the ignition OFF immediately to avoid damaging the gauge.

3 If the needle movement is still faulty, or if it does not move at all, the fault lies in the wiring or the gauge itself. Check all the relevant wiring and wiring connectors; if all appears to be well, the gauge is defective and must be renewed.

Replacement

4 Refer to Chapter 9 for instrument cluster removal and installation. **Note:** *The temperature gauge is an integral part of the instrument cluster and cannot be obtained as a separate item.*

Temperature gauge sender

Check

5 Disconnect the battery negative (-ve) lead, then disconnect the sender wiring connector **(see illustration 3.2).** Using a continuity tester, check for continuity between the sender body and earth (ground). There should be continuity. If there is no continuity, check that the sender mounting is secure, then recheck the operation of the gauge.

6 Remove the sender (see Steps 8 to 11 below). Fill a small heatproof container with water and place it on a stove. Set a multimeter to the ohms x 1 scale and connect the

positive (+ve) probe to the terminal on the sender and the negative (-ve) probe to the sender body. Using some wire or other support, suspend the sender in the water so that just the sensing portion and the threads are submerged **(see illustration).** Also place a thermometer capable of reading temperatures up to 90°C in the water so that its bulb is close to the sensor. **Note:** *None of the components should be allowed to directly touch the container.*

7 Check the resistance of the sender at approximately 20°C and keep the water temperature constant at 20°C for 3 minutes before continuing the test. Then increase the heat gradually, stirring the water gently.

⚠️ **Warning: This must be done very carefully to avoid the risk of personal injury.**

As the temperature of the water rises, the resistance of the sender should fall. Check that the correct resistance is obtained at the temperatures specified at the beginning of this Chapter. If the meter readings obtained are different, or they are obtained at different temperatures, then the sender is faulty and must be renewed.

Replacement

⚠️ **Warning: The engine must be completely cool before carrying out this procedure.**

8 Disconnect the battery negative (-ve) lead and drain the cooling system (see Section 2).

9 Disconnect the sender wiring connector **(see illustration 3.2).** Unscrew the sender and remove it from the cylinder head.

10 Apply a smear of a suitable non-permanent sealant to the threads of the new sender, then install it into the cylinder head and tighten it securely. Connect the sender wiring.

11 Refill the cooling system (see Section 2) and reconnect the battery negative (-ve) lead.

3.2 Temperature sender wiring connector

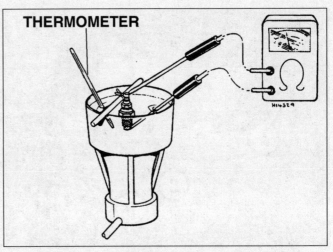

3.6 Set-up for testing the temperature gauge sender

4 Thermostat –
removal, check and installation

Removal

⚠️ **Warning: The engine must be completely cool before carrying out this procedure.**

1 The thermostat is automatic in operation and should give many years service without requiring attention. In the event of a failure, the thermostat valve will probably jam open, in which case the engine will take much longer to reach its normal operating temperature, resulting in increased fuel consumption. If the valve jams shut, the coolant will be unable to circulate and the engine will overheat with the risk of seizure. In either case, if the thermostat is found to be faulty, a new unit should be fitted immediately.

2 The thermostat is located in the front of the cylinder head. Remove the head, the thermostat and the thermostat spring (see Chapter 2B, Section 7).

3 Examine the thermostat visually before carrying out the test. If it remains in the open position at room temperature (20°C approximately), it should be renewed.

Check

4 Fill a small, heatproof container with cold water and place it on a stove. Using a piece of wire, suspend the thermostat in the water **(see illustration)**. Heat the water and see whether the thermostat opens. Peugeot do not specify the temperature at which the thermostat should open. If it has not opened by the time the water starts to boil, it is faulty and must be replaced.

5 Inspect the thermostat spring and replace it with a new one if it is corroded or damaged.

Installation

6 Install the thermostat, its spring and the cylinder head as described in Chapter 2B,

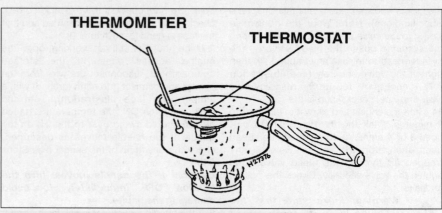

THERMOMETER   **THERMOSTAT**

4.4 Set-up for testing the thermostat

Section 7. On completion, refill the cooling system as described in Section 2.

5 Coolant reservoir –
removal and installation

Removal

⚠️ **Warning: Ensure that the engine is cold before working on the coolant reservoir.**

1 The coolant reservoir is located behind the headlight panel. Remove the panel for access (see Chapter 7).

2 Remove the reservoir cap and position a suitable container beneath the water pump on the right-hand side of the engine. Loosen the clip securing the coolant hose from the radiator to the pump, then detach the hose and drain enough coolant to empty the reservoir (see Section 2). Reconnect the hose and secure it with the clip.

3 Loosen the clips securing the hoses to the reservoir and detach the hoses, then undo the reservoir mounting screw and remove the reservoir **(see illustration)**.

Installation

4 Installation is the reverse of removal. Make sure the hoses are correctly installed and secured with their clips. On completion, refill the reservoir with the proper coolant mixture (see *Daily (pre-ride) checks*) , fit the cap and the panel.

6 Radiator –
removal and installation

Removal

⚠️ **Warning: Ensure that the engine is cold before working on the radiator.**

1 The radiator is located behind the headlight panel. Remove the panel for access and remove the right-hand side panel (see Chapter 7).

2 Drain the cooling system (see Section 2).

3 Loosen the clips securing the coolant hoses to the radiator and detach the hoses **(see illustration)**. Loosen the clips securing the coolant reservoir hoses to the radiator and detach the hoses **(see illustration 5.3)**.

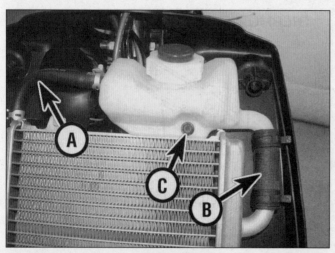

5.3 Detach the hoses (A) and (B) from the reservoir then undo the mounting screw (C)

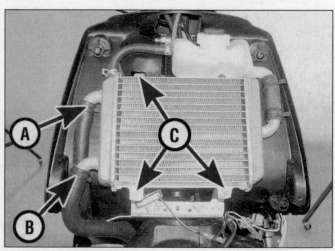

6.3 Radiator coolant hoses (A) and (B) and mounting bolts (C)

Caution: The radiator unions are fragile. Do not use excessive force when attempting to remove the hoses.

4 Undo the reservoir mounting screw and remove the reservoir **(see illustration 5.3)**.

5 Undo the radiator mounting bolts and remove the radiator **(see illustration 6.3)**. **Note:** *Some of the bolts have captive nuts, some do not.*

6 A heat shield is mounted behind the radiator; remove the heat shield if required **(see illustration)**.

7 Check the radiator for signs of damage and clear any dirt or debris that might obstruct air flow and inhibit cooling (see Chapter 1, Section 19). If the radiator fins are badly damaged or broken the radiator must be renewed.

 HAYNES HiNT *If a radiator hose is corroded in place on its union, cut the hose with a sharp knife then slit it lengthways and peel it off the union. Whilst this means renewing the hose, it is preferable to buying a new radiator.*

Installation

8 Installation is the reverse of removal, noting the following:
• Align the heatshield with the holes for the headlight panel fixing screws.
• Tighten the mounting bolts securely.
• Ensure the coolant hoses are in good condition (see Chapter 1, Section 19), and are securely retained by their clips, using new ones if necessary.
• Refill the cooling system and bleed it correctly (see Section 2).

7 Water pump – check, removal and installation

1 The water pump is located on the right-hand side of the engine **(see illustration 2.3b)**. The pump is driven by the alternator rotor.

2 An internal seal prevents leakage of coolant from the pump; if the seal fails coolant will drain out of the bottom of the pump housing. Individual components are not available for the pump; if it is leaking coolant a new unit must be fitted. **Note:** *Leaks leave tell-tale scale deposits or coolant stains. Ensure the coolant is leaking from inside the pump and not from a hose connection or damaged hose.*

Removal

3 Drain the coolant and leave the hoses detached from the pump (see Section 2).

4 Undo the pump mounting bolts and remove the bolts and the guide for the upper coolant hose **(see illustration)**.

5 Lift the pump away from the engine, noting how the pump drive dampers are attached to

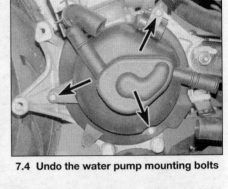

6.6 Heat shield fits behind the radiator

7.4 Undo the water pump mounting bolts

7.5a Water pump is driven by dampers on the alternator rotor . . .

7.5b . . . which engage in holes in the back of the pump

the alternator rotor and how the dampers locate into the back of the pump **(see illustrations)**.

6 If required, hold the alternator rotor to prevent it turning and unscrew the dampers. Renew the damper rubbers as a set if they are worn.

Installation

7 Installation is the reverse of removal, noting the following:
• Make sure the drive dampers fit correctly into the back of the pump.
• Tighten the pump mounting bolts to the specified torque setting.
• Ensure the coolant hoses are pushed fully onto the pump unions and secured with the clips.
• Refill the cooling system and bleed it correctly (see Section 2).

8 Coolant hoses – removal and installation

Removal

1 Before removing a hose, drain the coolant (see Section 2).

2 Loosen the hose clip, then slide it back along the hose clear of the union. Pull the hose off its union **(see illustrations)**.

3 If a hose proves stubborn, release it by rotating it on its union before working it off. If all else fails, slit the hose with a sharp knife at the union (see *Haynes Hint* in Section 6).

Caution: The radiator unions are fragile. Do not use excessive force when attempting to remove the hoses.

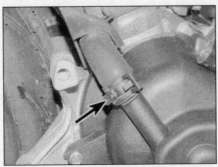
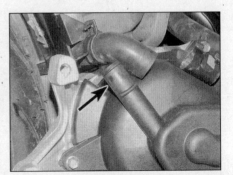

8.2a Loosen the hose clip (arrowed) and slide it back along the hose . . .

8.2b . . . then pull the hose off the union (arrowed)

8.5 Ensure the hose is pushed up to the index mark on the hose union

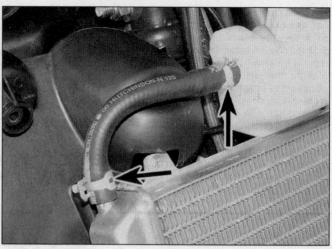

8.6 Clips must be in good condition to secure the hoses firmly

4 Check the condition of the hose clips; if they are corroded or have lost their tension, replace them with new ones.

Installation

5 Slide the clips onto the hose first, then work the hose all the way onto its unions as indicated by the index marks **(see illustration)**.

 HAYNES HiNT *If the hose is difficult to push on its union, it can be softened by soaking it in very hot water, or alternatively a little soapy water can be used as a lubricant.*

6 Rotate the hose on its unions to settle it in position before sliding the clips into place and tightening them securely **(see illustration)**.
7 Refill the cooling system and bleed it correctly (see Section 2).

Chapter 4
Fuel and exhaust systems

Refer to Chapter 1 for model identification details

Contents

Degrees of difficulty

Easy, suitable for novice with little experience	**Fairly easy,** suitable for beginner with some experience	**Fairly difficult,** suitable for competent DIY mechanic ⚒	**Difficult,** suitable for experienced DIY mechanic ⚒	**Very difficult,** suitable for expert DIY or professional ⚒

Specifications

Note: *Carburettor jet sizes may vary – always check the jets fitted to your machine before ordering new parts.*

Fuel

Fuel type	Unleaded petrol (gasoline) min 95 octane
Tank capacity	
Speedfight models	7.2 litres
50 cc Trekker models	6.0 litres
100 cc Trekker models	7.2 litres
Vivacity models	6.0 litres

Automatic choke mechanism

Choke unit resistance	
1996 to 2003 models (Gurtner)	approx. 36 ohms @ 20°C
1997 to 2003 models (Dell'Orto)	approx. 5.2 ohms @ 20°C
Choke resistor resistance	
1996 to 2003 models	approx. 6.7 ohms @ 20°C
Integral choke unit resistance	
2004-on models	approx. 56.5 ohms @ 20°C

Carburettor – 50 cc Speedfight and Speedfight 2 (air-cooled)

Type/ID no.	Gurtner PA360
Pilot screw initial setting	1⅛ turns out
Float height	not adjustable
Idle speed	1500 rpm
Starter jet	50
Pilot jet	36
Main jet	72
Needle (clip position)	L3035H (top notch)

Carburettor – 50 cc Speedfight and Speedfight 2 (liquid-cooled)

Type/ID no.	Gurtner PA370
Pilot screw initial setting	1⅛ turns out
Float height	not adjustable
Idle speed	1500 rpm
Starter jet	50
Pilot jet	36
Main jet	72
Needle (clip position)	L3035H (top notch)

Carburettor – 50 cc Trekker (air-cooled)

Type/ID no.	Gurtner PA360
Pilot screw initial setting	1⅛ turns out
Float height	not adjustable
Idle speed	1500 rpm
Starter jet	45
Pilot jet	42
Main jet	72
Needle (clip position)	L3035H (top notch)

Carburettor – 50 cc Vivacity (air-cooled)

Type/ID no.	Gurtner PA370
Pilot screw initial setting	1⅛ turns out
Float height	not adjustable
Idle speed	1500 rpm
Starter jet	45
Pilot jet	42
Main jet	72
Needle (clip position)	L3035H (top notch)

Carburettor – all 100 cc air-cooled engines

Type/ID no.	Dell'Orto PHVA 17.5
Pilot screw setting	1¾ turns out
Float height	not adjustable
Idle speed	1600 rpm
Starter jet	65
Pilot jet	30
Main jet	83
Needle (clip position)	A11 (2nd notch from top)

Torque settings

Carburettor mounting bolts	8 Nm
Exhaust downpipe bracket bolt	20 Nm
Exhaust system mounting bolts	25 Nm
Exhaust manifold-to-cylinder nuts	16 Nm
Inlet manifold-to-crankcase bolts	10 Nm

---

1 General information and precautions

General information

The fuel system consists of the fuel tank, fuel tap with integral filter, carburettor, fuel hose and control cables. In addition, oil for engine lubrication is fed from the oil tank, via the oil pump, into the carburettor where it is mixed with the fuel before entering the engine.

The fuel tap is automatic in operation and is opened by engine vacuum.

For cold starting, an electrically-operated automatic choke is fitted in the carburettor. Liquid-cooled models are fitted with an external carburettor heater.

Air is drawn into the carburettor through an intake duct and air filter on the left-had side of the machine.

The exhaust system is attached to the right-hand side of the machine.

Many of the fuel system service procedures are considered routine maintenance items and for that reason are included in Chapter 1.

Precautions

⚠ **Warning: Petrol (gasoline) is extremely flammable, so take extra precautions when you work on any part of the fuel system. Don't smoke or allow open flames or bare light bulbs near the work area, and don't work in a garage where a natural gas-type appliance is present. If you spill any fuel on your skin, rinse it off immediately with soap and water. When you perform any kind of work on the fuel system, wear safety glasses and have a fire extinguisher suitable for a class B type fire (flammable liquids) on hand.**

Always perform service procedures in a well-ventilated area to prevent a build-up of fumes.

Never work in a building containing a gas appliance with a pilot light, or any other form of naked flame. Ensure that there are no naked light bulbs or any sources of flame or sparks nearby.

Do not smoke (or allow anyone else to smoke) while in the vicinity of petrol or of components containing it. Remember the possible presence of vapour from these sources and move well clear before smoking.

Check all electrical equipment belonging to the house, garage or workshop where work is being undertaken (see the Safety first! section of this manual). Remember that certain electrical appliances such as drills, cutters etc. create sparks in the normal course of operation and must not be used near petrol or any component containing it. Again, remember the possible presence of fumes before using electrical equipment.

Always mop up any spilt fuel and safely dispose of the rag used.

Any stored fuel that is drained off during servicing work must be kept in sealed containers that are suitable for holding petrol, and clearly marked as such; the containers themselves should be kept in a safe place.

Read the Safety first! section of this manual carefully before starting work.

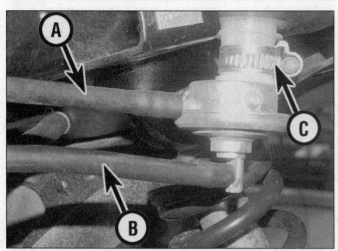

2.1 Fuel hose (A) to carburettor, vacuum hose (B) to inlet manifold and retaining clip (C)

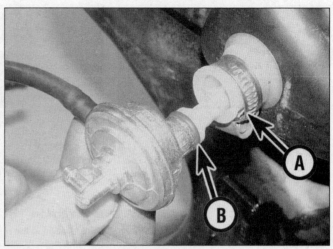

2.8 Loosen the clip (A) and withdraw the tap. Note the O-ring (B)

2 Fuel tap and filter –
check, removal and installation

Warning: Refer to the precautions given in Section 1 before starting work.

Check

1 The fuel tap is located on the underside of the fuel tank on the left-hand side. Remove any body panels as required for access (see Chapter 7). The tap is automatic, operated by a vacuum drawn through the vacuum hose from the inlet manifold when the engine is turned over **(see illustration)**.

2 The tap should not be removed from the tank unnecessarily to avoid the possibility of damaging the tap body O-ring or the filter. If the fuel tap-to-tank joint is leaking, first ensure that the tap retaining clip is tight **(see illustration 2.1)**. If leakage persists, drain the tank, remove the tap and fit a new O-ring (see Step 8).

3 If fuel flow problems are experienced, first check that the breather hole in the tank cap is clear and that the tap vacuum hose is in good condition and its connections are air tight,

then remove the tap and check the tap filter (see Step 9).

4 If the filter is clean and in good condition, check the operation of the tap diaphragm. Disconnect the fuel and vacuum hoses from the carburettor and place the free end of the fuel hose in a suitable container below the level of fuel in the tank. When vacuum is drawn in the vacuum hose, the diaphragm should open and fuel should flow from the tank.

5 If there is no fuel flow the tap is blocked internally; the tap is a sealed unit and must be replaced with a new one.

6 If fuel flows from the tap with no vacuum in the vacuum hose, the diaphragm is faulty and the tap must be replaced with a new one.

Removal

7 Disconnect the fuel and vacuum hoses from the carburettor and place the free end of the fuel hose in a suitable container below the level of fuel in the tank. Create a vacuum in the vacuum hose and drain the tank. If the tap is blocked, remove the tank to drain the fuel (see Section 3).

8 Loosen the clip securing the tap and withdraw the tap assembly **(see illustration)**. Check the condition of the O-ring and replace it with a new one if it is damaged. **Note:** *The O-ring is not*

listed as a separate item; consult a Peugeot dealer or automotive parts supplier who may be able to supply a suitable alternative.

9 Allow the filter gauze to dry, then clean it with a soft brush or compressed air to remove all traces of dirt and sediment. Check the gauze for holes **(see illustration)**. If any are found, a new tap should be fitted as the filter is not available as a separate item.

Installation

10 If removed, install the fuel tank. Ensure the O-ring is correctly positioned on the tap, then push the tap into the tank with the fuel union facing towards the front of the machine and tighten the clip securely.

11 Connect the fuel and vacuum hoses onto their respective unions.

3 Fuel tank –
removal and installation

Removal

1 Remove the storage compartment (see Chapter 7).

2 Disconnect the battery negative (-ve) lead and disconnect the fuel gauge sender wiring connector (see Chapter 9).

3 Disconnect the fuel and vacuum hoses from the unions on the fuel tap **(see illustration 2.1)**.

4 Lift the tank off the frame noting how it is retained by the storage compartment fixings **(see illustration)**.

Warning: If the fuel tank is removed from the scooter, it should not be placed in an area where sparks or open flames could ignite the fumes coming out of the tank. Be especially careful inside garages where a natural gas-type appliance is located, because the pilot light could cause an explosion.

2.9 Clean the filter and check it for holes

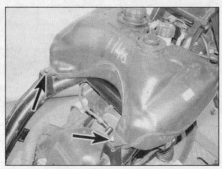

3.4 Tank is held in place by the storage compartment fixings (arrowed)

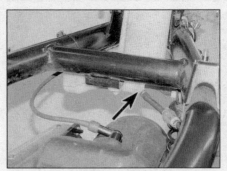

4.3 Release the clip and detach the hose

4.4a Undo the tank front mounting nut . . .

4.4b . . . and the rear mounting nut

Installation

5 Installation is the reverse of removal, noting the following:
• Ensure no wiring is trapped between the tank and the frame.
• Tighten the fixing nuts securely.
• Ensure the fuel and vacuum hoses are a tight fit on the tap unions.

4 Oil tank –
removal and installation

Removal

1 Remove the storage compartment (see Chapter 7) and the fuel tank (see Section 3).
2 Disconnect the oil level warning light sensor wiring connector (see Chapter 9).
3 Release the clip securing the oil hose from the tank to the oil filter and detach the hose **(see illustration)**. Clamp the hose to prevent oil loss. Wrap a clean plastic bag around the oil filter to prevent dirt entering the system and secure the filter in an upright position to minimise oil loss.
4 Undo the tank mounting nuts and lower the tank out of the frame **(see illustrations)**.

Installation

5 Installation is the reverse of removal, noting the following:
• Ensure no wiring is trapped between the tank and the frame.
• Tighten the fixing nuts securely.
• Ensure the oil hose is pushed fully onto the union on the filter and secure it with the clip.
• Bleed any air trapped in the filter (see Chapter 1, Section 11).

5 Idle fuel/air mixture adjustment –
general information

⚠ *Warning: Adjustment of the fuel/air mixture is made with the engine running. To prevent accidents caused by the rear wheel contacting the ground, ensure that the scooter is on its stand and if necessary place a support under the stand to prevent the rear wheel contacting the ground.*

1 Idle fuel/air mixture is set using the pilot screw **(see illustrations)**. Adjustment of the pilot screw is not normally necessary and should only be performed if the engine is

running roughly, stalls continually, or when fitting a new pilot screw.
2 If a new pilot screw is being fitted, screw it in until it seats lightly, then back it out the number of turns specified at the beginning of this Chapter. Adjust the pilot screw as described below.
3 Before adjusting the pilot screw, ensure the throttle cable is correctly adjusted (see Chapter 1, Section 10). With the engine at normal operating temperature, stop the engine and screw the pilot screw in until it seats lightly, then back it out the number of turns specified at the beginning of this Chapter. Start the engine and check the idle speed (see Chapter 1, Section 15).
4 With the idle speed correctly adjusted, try turning the pilot screw inwards by about a _ turn, noting its effect on the idle speed, then open the throttle gently to ensure the engine does not stall. Repeat the process, this time turning the screw outwards.
5 The pilot screw should be set in the position which gives the steadiest idle speed with the smoothest pick-up when the throttle is opened. Snap the throttle open and shut a few times and ensure the idle speed is still steady. Readjust the idle speed if necessary and stop the engine.

5.1a Pilot screw location on Gurtner carburettor

5.1b Pilot screw location on Dell'Orto carburettor

6 Air filter housing –
removal and installation

Removal

1 Remove the cover from the air filter housing and remove the filter element (see Chapter 1).
2 Unscrew the bolts securing the air filter housing to the transmission casing and manoeuvre the housing away, noting how it fits **(see illustrations)**.
3 Unscrew the bolt securing the air intake duct to the transmission casing and remove the duct **(see illustrations)**.

Installation

4 Installation is the reverse of removal. Ensure the filter housing is a firm fit over the carburettor intake.

7 Choke mechanism –
check

1 Poor starting or poor engine performance and an increase in fuel consumption are possible signs that the automatic choke mechanism is not working properly.
2 The resistance of the automatic choke unit should be checked with a multimeter when the engine is cold. Remove the storage compartment (see Chapter 7) and trace the wiring from the automatic choke unit on the carburettor and disconnect it at the connectors **(see illustrations)**.
3 Measure the resistance between the terminals on the choke unit side of the connector with the multimeter set to the ohms x 1 scale. If the result is not as specified at the beginning of this Chapter, the choke unit is probably faulty. Renew the choke unit (see Section 10).
4 On 1996 to 2003 models, if the automatic choke unit appears to be functioning correctly, check the resistance in the choke resistor **(see illustration)**. Remove the headlight panel (see Chapter 7) and disconnect the resistor wiring connector (see *Wiring Diagrams*, Chapter 9). Measure the

6.2a Fixings for air filter housing on Speedfight

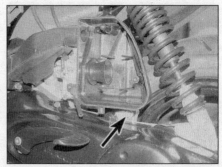

6.2b Fixing for air filter housing on Trekker and Vivacity

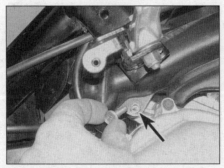

6.3a Fixing for air intake duct on Speedfight

6.3b Fixing for air intake duct on Trekker and Vivacity

resistance between the terminal on the resistor side of the connector and earth (ground). If the result is not as specified at the beginning of this Chapter, the resistor is probably faulty.

8 Carburettor overhaul –
general information

1 Poor engine performance, hesitation, hard starting, stalling, flooding and backfiring are all signs that major carburettor maintenance may be required.
2 Keep in mind that many so-called carburettor problems are really not carburettor problems at all, but mechanical problems within the engine or ignition system malfunctions. Try to establish for certain that the carburettor is in need of maintenance

before beginning a major overhaul.
3 Check the fuel tap and filter, the fuel and vacuum hoses, the air filter, the ignition system and the spark plug before assuming that a carburettor overhaul is required.
4 Most carburettor problems are caused by dirt particles, varnish and other deposits which build up in and block the fuel and air passages. Also, in time, gaskets and O-rings shrink or deteriorate and cause fuel and air leaks which lead to poor performance.
5 When overhauling the carburettor, disassemble it completely and clean the parts thoroughly with a carburettor cleaning solvent, then dry them with filtered compressed air. Blow through the fuel and air passages with compressed air to force out any dirt that may have been loosened but not removed by the solvent. Once the cleaning process is complete, reassemble the carburettor using new gaskets and O-rings.

7.2a Trace the wiring from the automatic choke unit . . .

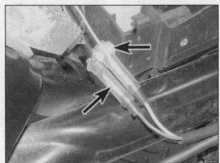

7.2b . . . and disconnect it at the connectors

7.4 Choke resistor is mounted behind the front panel

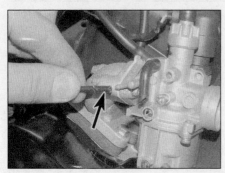

9.5 Detach the oil hose from the carburettor . . .

9.6 . . . then detach the fuel hose

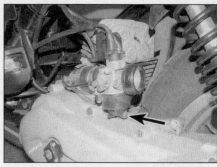

9.7 Loosen the drain screw and drain off any residual fuel

6 Before disassembling the carburettor, make sure you have all necessary gaskets, some carburettor cleaner, a supply of clean rags, some means of blowing out the carburettor passages and a clean place to work.

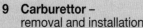
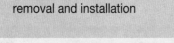

9 Carburettor –
removed and installation

Warning: Refer to the precautions given in Section 1 before starting work.

Removal

1 Remove the left-hand side panel and belly panel, and the storage compartment (see Chapter 7).
2 Remove the air filter housing (see Section 6).
3 Disconnect the battery negative (-ve) lead (see Chapter 9) then trace the wiring from the automatic choke unit and disconnect it at the connector (see Section 7). Free the wiring from any clips or ties and feed it back to the carburettor.
4 On liquid-cooled models, undo the screw securing the carburettor heater union to the carburettor and displace the heater and heater hoses (see Section 14).
5 Release the clip securing the oil hose to the

9.8a Unscrew the top of the Gurtner carburettor

carburettor and detach the hose **(see illustration)**. Clamp the hose to minimise oil loss and wrap a clean plastic bag around the end of the hose to prevent dirt entering the system.
6 Detach the fuel hose from the carburettor **(see illustration). Note:** *There will be a small amount of residual fuel in the hose but fuel should not leak from the hose once this has drained. If fuel continues to leak from the hose, check the operation of the fuel tap (see Section 2).*
7 Position a suitable container underneath the carburettor, then loosen the drain screw and drain any residual fuel from the float chamber **(see illustration)**.

9.8b Undo the retaining screw to remove the top of the Dell'Orto carburettor

8 On a Gurtner carburettor, unscrew the carburettor top and withdraw the throttle slide and needle **(see illustration)**. On a Dell'Orto carburettor, undo the screw retaining the carburettor top, then remove the top and withdraw the throttle slide and needle **(see illustration)**. Secure the throttle cable where the slide and needle will not be damaged. To detach the slide and needle from the cable see Section 9.
9 Either loosen the clip or undo the bolts securing the carburettor to the inlet manifold on the engine and remove the carburettor **(see illustrations)**. Note the position of the manifold gasket, where fitted, then discard it

9.9a Gurtner carburettor is retained by two bolts

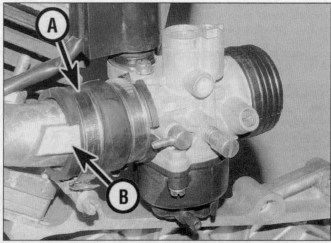

9.9b Dell'Orto carburettor is retained by a clip (A). Note the locator for the mounting sleeve (B)

as a new gasket should be fitted on reassembly **(see illustration)**.
10 Where fitted, loosen the clip and remove the mounting sleeve from the carburettor **(see illustration)**. Check the condition of the mounting sleeve and replace it with a new one if it is cracked or perished.
Caution: Stuff clean rag into the intake manifold to prevent dirt falling inside.

Installation

11 Installation is the reverse of removal, noting the following.
• Depending on the fitting, ensure the carburettor is fully engaged with the mounting sleeve and the sleeve is fully engaged with the inlet manifold before tightening the clips securely, or that the manifold gasket is correctly positioned and the mounting bolts are tightened to the torque setting specified at the beginning of this Chapter.
• When fitting the carburettor top ensure that the needle is correctly aligned with the main jet.
• Make sure the hoses are correctly routed and secured.
• Check the operation of the throttle cable and adjust it as necessary (see Chapter 1).
• Check the idle speed and adjust as necessary (see Chapter 1).

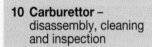

10 Carburettor –
disassembly, cleaning and inspection

Warning: Refer to the precautions given in Section 1 before starting work.

Disassembly

1 Remove the carburettor (see Section 9).
2 Remove the cover on the automatic choke unit, then undo the screws retaining the choke unit clamp and remove the clamp **(see illustrations)**. Withdraw the choke, noting how it fits **(see illustration)**. Remove the O-ring from the choke body and discard it as a new one must be fitted on reassembly.
3 Undo the screws securing the float chamber to the base of the carburettor and remove it **(see illustration)**. Remove the

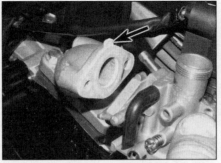
9.9c Note the tab on the top edge of the manifold gasket

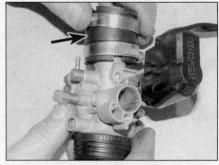
9.10 Remove the carburettor mounting sleeve

gasket and discard it as a new one must be fitted on reassembly **(see illustrations)**.
4 On a Gurtner carburettor, undo the screw retaining the float pin and remove the float and pin **(see illustrations)**. If loose, remove

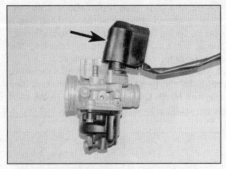
10.2a Remove the choke unit cover . . .

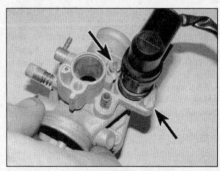
10.2b . . . then undo the clamp screws (arrowed) . . .

the pin from the float. On a Dell'Orto carburettor, carefully withdraw the float pin and remove the float **(see illustration)**.
5 Remove the float valve, noting how it fits onto the tab on the float **(see illustration)**.

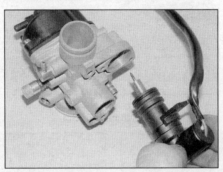
10.2c . . . and pull out the choke unit

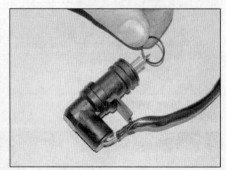
10.2d Discard the O-ring

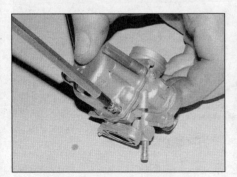
10.3a Undo the float chamber screws on the underside of the carburettor

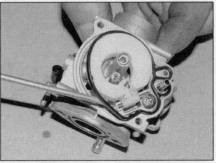
10.3b Float chamber gasket is in the body of the Gurtner carburettor . . .

10.3c . . . and in the rim of the float bowl of the Dell'Orto carburettor

10.4a Undo the fixing screw . . .

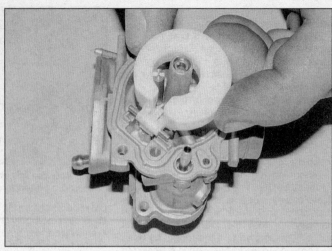

10.4b . . . and remove the float on the Gurtner carburettor

6 Unscrew and remove the pilot jet and the main jet **(see illustrations)**.
7 On a Dell'Orto carburettor, unscrew and remove the starter jet **(see illustration 10.6a)**. On a Gurtner carburettor the starter jet is a press fit in the carburettor body and should not be removed.
8 The idle speed adjuster screw projects into the carburettor body to limit the movement of

the throttle slide **(see illustration)**. Unscrew the idle speed adjuster screw and remove it and its spring **(see illustration)**. **Note:** *Record the screw's current setting by counting the number of turns required to remove it.*
9 The pilot screw can be removed if required, but note that its setting will be disturbed (see *Haynes Hint*). Unscrew and remove the pilot screw along with its spring (see Section 5).

HAYNES HINT *To record the pilot screw's current setting, turn it in until it seats lightly, counting the number of turns necessary to achieve this, then unscrew it fully . On reassembly, turn the screw in until it seats lightly, then back it out the number of turns you've recorded.*

10.4c Withdraw the pin . . .

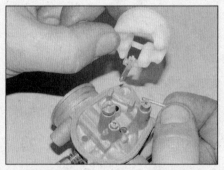

10.4d . . . and remove the float on a Dell'Orto carburettor

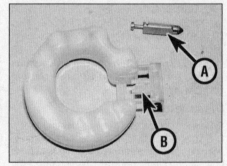

10.5 Note how the float valve (A) fits into the tab (B)

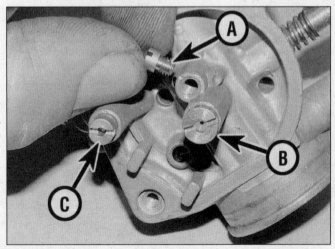

10.6a Dell'Orto carburettor pilot jet (A), main jet (B) and starter jet (C)

10.6b Gurtner carburettor pilot jet (A) and main jet (B)

10.8a Adjuster screw limits movement of throttle slide

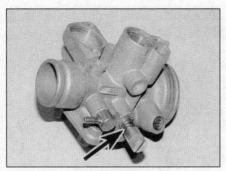

10.8b Remove the adjuster screw and spring

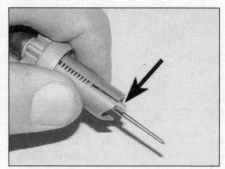

10.10a Compress the spring until the cable nipple (arrowed) is free from the bottom of the slide

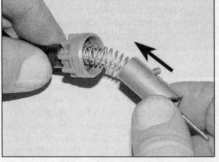

10.10b Gurtner carburettor: slot the nipple up through the slide

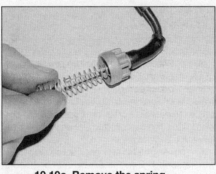

10.10c Remove the spring . . .

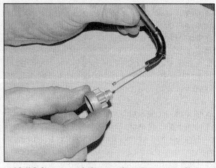

10.10d . . . and the carburettor top from the cable

10 On a Gurtner carburettor, to remove the throttle slide and needle from the throttle cable, compress the slide spring to release the cable nipple from the recess at the bottom of the slide, then slot the cable nipple up through the side of the slide **(see illustrations)**. Remove the spring from the cable, then pull back the boot on the end of the cable elbow and remove the carburettor top **(see illustrations)**. The needle is retained in the slide by a spring strip; withdraw the spring strip and lift the needle out of the slide **(see illustration)**. Note the position of the needle clip **(see illustration)**.

11 On a Dell'Orto carburettor, to remove the throttle slide and needle from the throttle cable, compress the slide spring and slot the cable nipple out of its recess and through the hole in the bottom of the slide **(see illustration)**. Detach the slide and needle, then detach the spring seat and spring from the cable **(see illustrations)**. Note which way round the spring seat fits. Lift the needle out of the slide and note the position of the needle clip **(see illustration)**. If required, pull back the boot on the cable adjuster in the carburettor top and pull the top off the cable.

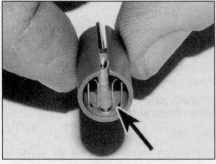

10.10e Spring strip (arrowed) retains the carburettor needle

10.10f Components of the Gurtner carburettor throttle slide assembly

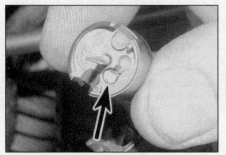

10.11a Dell'Orto carburettor: slot the nipple through the hole (arrowed) in the bottom of the slide

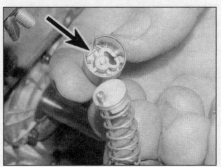

10.11b Remove the slide and needle (arrowed) . . .

10.11c . . . then remove the spring seat (arrowed) and spring

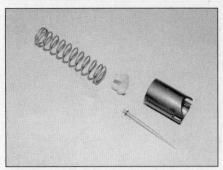

10.11d Components of the Dell'Orto carburettor throttle slide assembly

Cleaning

Caution: Use only a dedicated carburettor cleaner or petroleum-based solvent for carburettor cleaning. Do not use caustic cleaners.

12 Soak the carburettor body and individual components in the cleaner to loosen and dissolve the varnish and other deposits (always check the directions for use of solvent products, especially when applying them to non-metallic items). Use a nylon-bristle brush to remove the stubborn deposits, then rinse and dry the components with compressed air.
13 Use compressed air to blow out all the fuel and air passages in the carburettor body and the jets.

Caution: Never clean the jets or passages with a piece of wire or a drill bit, as they will be enlarged, causing the fuel and air metering rates to be upset.

Inspection

14 Check the carburettor body, float chamber and top for cracks, distorted sealing surfaces and other damage. If any defects are found, renew the faulty component.
15 Insert the slide in the carburettor body and check that it moves up-and-down smoothly. Check the surface of the slide for wear. If it's worn excessively or doesn't move smoothly, fit a new one.
16 Check the needle for straightness by rolling it on a flat surface such as a piece of glass. Renew it if it's bent or if the tip is worn. Ensure the needle clip is a firm fit on the needle.
17 If removed, check the tapered portion of the pilot screw and the spring for wear or damage. Renew them if necessary.
18 Check the tip of the float valve for grooves or scratches or other signs of wear. Gently push down on the plunger on the top of the valve then release it – it should spring back immediately. If any defects are found, replace the valve with a new one.
19 Check the float for damage. This will usually be apparent by the presence of fuel inside the float. If the float is damaged, replace it with a new one.
20 Check the automatic choke unit needle for signs of wear or damage and fit a new unit it if necessary.

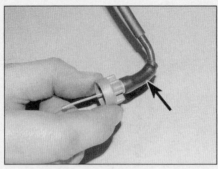

11.8 Install the boot on the carburettor top

11 Carburettor – reassembly

⚠ **Warning: Refer to the precautions given in Section 1 before proceeding.**

Note: *When reassembling the carburettors, be sure to use new O-rings and gaskets. Do not overtighten the carburettor jets and screws as they are easily damaged.*

1 If removed, install the pilot screw together with its spring. Turn the screw in until it seats lightly, then back it out the number of turns recorded on disassembly.
2 Install the idle speed adjuster screw together with its spring. Turn the screw in the number of turns recorded on disassembly.
3 On a Dell'Orto carburettor, install the starter jet (see illustration 10.6a).
4 Install the pilot jet and the main jet (see illustrations 10.6a and 10.6b).
5 Hook the float valve onto the float tab, then position the float assembly in the carburettor, making sure the needle valve enters its seat. On a Gurtner carburettor, install the pin and secure it with the retaining screw (see illustration 10.4a). On a Dell'Orto carburettor, install the pin (see illustration 10.4c).
6 Fit a new gasket, either to the carburettor body or the float chamber as applicable, making sure it is seated properly in its groove (see illustrations 10.3b and 10.3c). Install the chamber onto the carburettor and tighten the screws securely.

12.3 Release the cable from the grommet

7 Install a new O-ring on the automatic choke unit and carefully press the choke body into place to avoid damaging the O-ring, ensuring the wires face towards the front of the machine. Install the clamp and secure it with the screws (see illustration 10.2b), then install the cover.
8 On a Gurtner carburettor, ensure the needle clip is correctly positioned on the needle, then install the needle in the slide and secure it with the spring strip (see illustration 10.10f). Thread the carburettor top onto the throttle cable and ensure the cable outer is pressed into the recess in the top, then install the boot (see illustration). Thread the slide spring over the end of the cable, then compress the spring against the underside of the top and slot the cable nipple down through the side of the slide until it locates in the recess at the bottom of the slide (see illustrations 10.10b and 10.10a).
9 On a Dell'Orto carburettor, ensure the needle clip is correctly positioned on the needle, then install the needle in the slide. Thread the carburettor top onto the throttle cable and ensure the cable outer is pressed into the adjuster in the top, then install the boot. Thread the slide spring over the end of the cable, then compress the spring and install the spring seat (see illustration 10.11c). Compress the spring with the spring seat and thread the cable nipple through the hole in the bottom of the slide and into its recess. Rotate the spring seat so that the button on the seat blocks the hole in the bottom of the slide (see illustration 10.11a).

12 Throttle cable – removal and installation

Note: *Generally speaking, all 100 cc models and 50 cc models manufactured before 2000 are fitted with cable operated pumps. A quick visual check will confirm which pump is fitted to your machine.*

Models not fitted with a cable-operated oil pump

Removal

1 To access the cable remove the upper or front handlebar cover, front panel, floor panel and storage compartment (see Chapter 7).
2 On liquid-cooled models, undo the radiator mounting bolts and displace the radiator and coolant reservoir assembly and secure it to the machine with cable ties while removing and installing the throttle cable (see Chapter 3).
3 Release the cable from the grommet where it passes through the lower handlebar cover (see illustration).
4 Undo the twistgrip housing screws and pull off the rear half of the housing, then slide the twistgrip and front half of the housing off the handlebar (see illustrations).
5 Detach the twistgrip from the housing and release the cable nipple from the twistgrip (see illustration). Withdraw the cable from the housing (see illustration).

12.4a Twistgrip housing screws are on the front of the assembly

12.4b Slide the twistgrip off the handlebar

12.5a Release the cable nipple from the twistgrip . . .

12.5b . . . and withdraw the cable from the housing

12.10 Cable splitter is clipped to the frame behind the kick panel

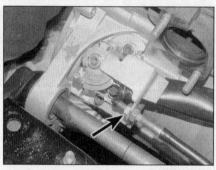

12.14 Unscrew the locknut (arrowed) to release cable from the bracket

6 Feed the cable back towards the battery location, noting its route and how it is retained by the guides on the frame.
7 Remove the carburettor top (see Section 9) and detach the cable from the throttle slide (see Section 10).
8 Withdraw the cable from the machine, noting the correct routing.

Installation

9 Installation is the reverse of removal, noting the following:
• Make sure the cable is correctly routed and secured. It must not interfere with any other component and should not be kinked or bent sharply.
• Lubricate the throttle cable nipple with multi-purpose grease before connecting it to the twistgrip.
• Check the throttle cable adjustment (see Chapter 1).
• Start the engine and check that the idle speed does not rise as the handlebars are turned. If it does, the cable is routed incorrectly. Correct the problem before riding the machine.

Models fitted with a cable operated oil pump

Removal

10 The throttle cable consists of three sections **(see illustration 10.6 in Chapter 1)** – the main cable from the throttle twistgrip goes into a splitter located behind the kick panel, with separate cables going from the splitter to the carburettor and oil pump **(see illustration)**. Individual cables are not

available, so if a cable problem is diagnosed, the complete cable assembly will have to be replaced with a new one. Before removing the cables, make a careful note of their routing to ensure correct installation.
11 To access the cable assembly, remove the upper or front handlebar cover, front panel, floor panel and storage compartment (see Chapter 7). If required, remove the exhaust system (see Section 15).
12 On liquid-cooled models, undo the radiator mounting bolts and displace the radiator and coolant reservoir assembly; secure it to the machine with cable ties while removing and installing the throttle cable (see Chapter 3).
13 Release the cable from the grommet where it passes through the lower handlebar cover, then remove the twistgrip housing and release the cable (see Steps 3 to 6).
14 Unscrew the locknut on the lower end of the oil pump cable adjuster, detach the cable nipple from the pump pulley and withdraw the cable from its bracket **(see illustration)**.
15 Remove the carburettor top (see Section 9) and detach the cable from the throttle slide (see Section 10).
16 Withdraw the cable from the machine, noting the correct routing.

Installation

17 Installation is the reverse of removal, noting the following:
• Make sure the cables are correctly routed and secured. They must not interfere with any other component and should not be kinked or bent sharply.

• Lubricate the throttle cable nipple with multi-purpose grease before connecting it to the twistgrip.
• Check the throttle cable adjustment and the oil pump setting (see Chapter 1, Sections 10 and 13).
• Start the engine and check that the idle speed does not rise as the handlebars are turned. If it does, a cable is routed incorrectly. Correct the problem before riding the scooter.

13 Reed valve – removal, inspection and installation

Removal

1 Remove the carburettor (see Section 9).
2 Detach the fuel tap vacuum hose from the union on the inlet manifold **(see illustration)**.

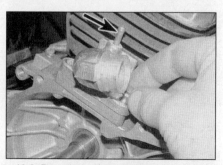

13.2 Detach the vacuum hose from the union (arrowed) and unscrew the mounting bolts

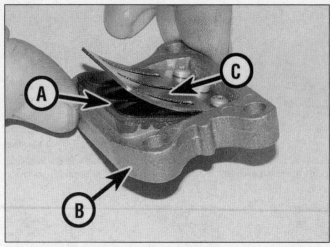
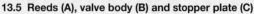

13.5 Reeds (A), valve body (B) and stopper plate (C)

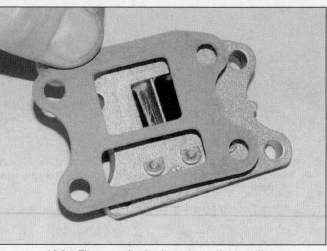

13.8a Fit new valve body and manifold gaskets

3 Undo the bolts securing the carburettor inlet manifold to the crankcase and remove the manifold, the manifold gasket, the reed valve and the reed valve gasket. Note which way round the reed valve is fitted. Discard the gaskets as new ones must be fitted on reassembly.

Inspection

4 Check the reed valve body closely for cracks, distortion and any other damage, particularly around the mating surfaces between the crankcase and the intake manifold – a good seal must be maintained between the components, otherwise crankcase pressure will be lost and engine performance will be affected.

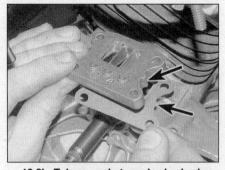

13.8b Tab on gaskets and valve body should face to the rear

5 Check the reeds themselves for cracks and any other damage. Ensure there are no dirt particles trapped between the reeds and the valve body. The reeds should sit flat against the valve body so that a good seal is obtained when the crankcase is under pressure (see illustration). After prolonged use, the reeds tend to become bent and will not seal properly, in which case a new reed valve should be fitted. A good way to check is to hold the valve up to the light – if light is visible between the reeds and the body they are not sealing properly. If the engine is difficult to start or idles erratically, this could be the problem.
6 Check that the stopper plate retaining screws are tight; do not disassemble the valve unnecessarily as individual components are not available.

Installation

7 Ensure that the mating surfaces between the crankcase, the reed valve and the inlet manifold are clean and perfectly smooth.
8 Install a new gasket on the crankcase (see illustration). The reed valve will only fit one way round so ensure the gasket is fitted correctly, then install the valve (see illustration).
9 Install the new manifold gasket and the manifold, then install the inlet manifold-to-

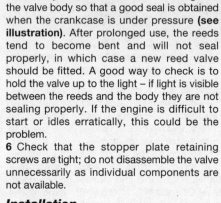

crankcase bolts and tighten them to the torque setting specified at the beginning of this Chapter.
10 Securely reconnect the fuel tap vacuum hose, then refit the carburettor (see Section 9).

14 Carburettor heater – removal and installation (liquid-cooled engines)

Removal

1 Remove the storage compartment (see Chapter 7).
2 Undo the screw securing the carburettor heater union to the carburettor (see illustration).
3 Release the clips securing the carburettor heater hoses to the unions on the cylinder head and detach the hoses (see illustration).
4 Withdraw the heater assembly from the machine and drain out any residual coolant.
5 Check the condition of the heater hose clips and discard them if they are damaged and fit new clips on reassembly.

Installation

6 Installation is the reverse of removal. Ensure the hose clips secure the hoses firmly on the cylinder head unions (see illustration).

14.2 Detach the carburettor heater union

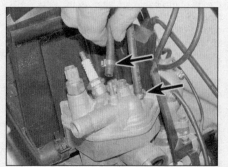

14.3 Detach the heater hoses from the cylinder head

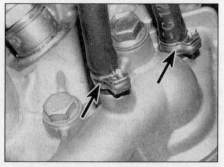

14.6 Hoses must be clipped securely to the unions

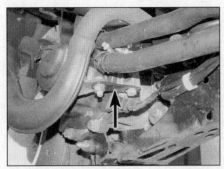

15.2 Detach the exhaust from the small bracket

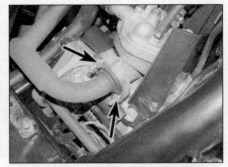

15.3 Undo the exhaust manifold nuts

15.4 Mounting bolts for the exhaust on 50 cc machines

7 Check the coolant level and top-up if necessary (see *Daily (pre-ride) checks*).

15 Exhaust system –
removal and installation

 Warning: *If the engine has been running the exhaust system will be very hot. Allow the system to cool before carrying out any work.*

Removal

1 Remove the storage compartment and the right-hand side belly panel (see Chapter 7).
2 Where fitted, undo the nut and bolt securing the exhaust to the small exhaust bracket **(see illustration)**.
3 Undo the two nuts securing the exhaust manifold to the cylinder **(see illustration)**.
4 On 50 cc machines, loosen the bolts securing the exhaust to the lugs on the crankcase, then support the exhaust and remove the bolts and lift the system away from the machine **(see illustration)**.
5 On 100 cc machines, loosen the nuts and bolts securing the exhaust to the large bracket, then support the exhaust and remove the bolts and lift it off the scooter **(see illustration)**. If required, undo the bolts securing the large bracket to the lugs on the crankcase **(see illustration)**.
6 Inspect the crankcase lugs for cracks; if the machine falls on its right-hand side they are prone to break. If the lugs are damaged they

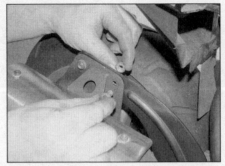

15.5a Mountings for the exhaust on 100 cc machines

can be repaired or the crankcase half renewed (see Chapter 2A, Section 14).
7 Remove the gasket from the port in the cylinder and discard it as a new gasket must be fitted on reassembly **(see illustration)**.
8 The exhaust fitted to restricted 50 cc machines is fitted with a resonator tube **(see illustration)**. If your machine has been de-restricted and the resonator tube has been removed, check around the welded patch on the exhaust for gas leaks. De-restricting requires a number of modifications to the machine and should only be undertaken by a Peugeot dealer.
9 On later models, fitted with a two-part exhaust system, the silencer section can be separated from the expansion chamber if required **(see illustration)**. Remove the three bolts securing the silence and lift it off, noting the gasket. If the gasket is damaged or deformed, fit a new one on reassembly.

15.5b Exhaust bracket is retained by two bolts

Installation

10 Installation is the reverse of removal, noting the following:

• Clean the cylinder studs and lubricate them with a suitable copper-based grease before reassembly.

• Clean the jointing surfaces of the exhaust manifold and cylinder port. Smear the gasket with grease to hold it in place while fitting the exhaust.

• Leave all fasteners finger-tight until the exhaust has been installed, making alignment easier. Tighten the mountings to the torque settings specified at the beginning of this Chapter. Tighten the manifold-to-cylinder nuts first.

• Run the engine and check that there are no exhaust gas leaks.

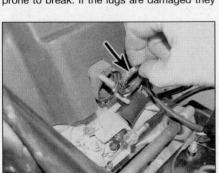

15.7 Remove the exhaust gasket

15.8 Resonator tube on restricted 50 cc exhaust system

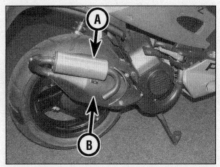

15.9 Silencer (A) and expansion chamber (B) on later exhaust system

Chapter 5
Ignition system

Refer to Chapter 1 for model identification details

Contents

Degrees of difficulty

Easy, suitable for novice with little experience		Fairly easy, suitable for beginner with some experience		Fairly difficult, suitable for competent DIY mechanic		Difficult, suitable for experienced DIY mechanic		Very difficult, suitable for expert DIY or professional	

Specifications

Spark plug
Type and gap .... see Chapter 1
Resistance .... 3.75 to 6.25 K-ohms

Source coil
Refer to Section 1 for details of the ignition system types
Basic CDI system/AEC 400 ignition system
  Coil resistance @ 20°C .... 0.44 to 0.66 K-ohms
ACI 100 ignition system
  Coil resistance @ 20°C .... 0.64 to 0.96 ohms

Pulse generator coil
Coil resistance @ 20°C .... 102 to 138 ohms

Ignition HT coil and spark plug cap
HT coil primary windings resistance .... 0.26 ohm ± 20%
HT coil secondary windings resistance .... 3.0 K-ohms ± 20%
Spark plug cap resistance .... 4.5 to 5.5 K-ohms

Immobiliser
Transponder aerial resistance .... 13.6 to 20.4 ohms

1 General information

All models are fitted with a fully transistorised electronic ignition system, which due to its lack of mechanical parts is totally maintenance-free. The system comprises the alternator rotor and source coil, pulse generator coil, CDI unit and ignition HT coil (refer to the wiring diagrams at the end of Chapter 9 for details).

The ignition trigger, which is on the outside surface of the alternator rotor, operates the pulse generator coil as the crankshaft rotates, sending a signal to the CDI unit which then supplies the HT coil with the power necessary to produce a spark at the plug.

The CDI unit incorporates an ignition advance system controlled by signals from the ignition pulse generator coil. There is no provision for adjusting the ignition timing.

Depending upon the model and specification, Peugeot scooters were originally fitted with either a basic CDI system or the AEC 400 ignition system with separate CDI unit and ignition immobiliser. On later models, including the Speedfight 2 range, the separate CDI unit and ignition immobiliser were replaced by the ACI 100 ignition system with a combined CDI and immobiliser unit. Some models were still available with the basic CDI system (see *Wiring Diagrams*, Chapter 9).

The ignition system incorporates a safety circuit and diode which prevent the engine from being started unless the rear brake lever is pulled in.

Because of their nature, the individual ignition system components can be checked but not repaired. If ignition system troubles occur, and the faulty component can be isolated, the only cure for the problem is to replace the part with a new one. Keep in mind that most electrical parts, once purchased, cannot be returned. To avoid unnecessary expense, make very sure the faulty component has been positively identified before buying a replacement part.

2.2 Ground (earth) the spark plug and operate the starter

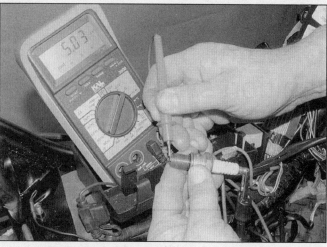

2.4 Measuring the resistance of the spark plug

2 Ignition system – check

⚠️ **Warning: The energy levels in electronic systems can be very high. On no account should the ignition be switched on whilst the plug or plug cap is being held – shocks from the HT circuit can be most unpleasant. Secondly, it is vital that the engine is not turned over with the plug cap removed, and that the plug is soundly earthed when the system is checked for sparking. The ignition system components can be seriously damaged if the HT circuit becomes isolated.**

1 As no means of adjustment is available, any failure of the system can be traced to failure of a system component or a simple wiring fault. Of the two possibilities, the latter is by far the most likely. In the event of failure, check the system in a logical fashion, as described below.

2 Disconnect the HT lead from the spark plug. Connect the lead to a new plug of the correct specification and lay the plug on the engine with the thread earthed (grounded) **(see illustration)**. If necessary, hold the spark plug with an insulated tool.

⚠️ **Warning: Do not remove the spark plug from the engine to perform this check – atomised fuel being pumped out of the open spark plug hole could ignite, causing severe injury!**

3 Having observed the above precautions, turn the ignition switch ON and turn the engine over on the starter motor. If the system is in good condition a regular, fat blue spark should be evident between the plug electrodes. If the spark appears thin or yellowish, or is non-existent, further investigation will be necessary. Before proceeding further, turn the ignition OFF.

Caution: The ignition system is designed for the combined resistance of the spark plug (5 K-ohms) and spark plug cap (5 K-ohms). Under no circumstances should a spark testing tool be used on this system.

4 Spark plug resistance can be checked with a multimeter. Remove the plug and clean the electrodes (see Chapter 1). Set the multimeter to the K-ohms scale and connect the meter probes to the terminal at the top of the plug and the central electrode **(see illustration)**. If the reading is not within the range shown in the Specifications, the plug is defective and must be replaced with a new one.

5 Ignition faults can be divided into two categories, namely those where the ignition system has failed completely, and those which are due to a partial failure. The likely faults are listed below, starting with the most probable source of failure. Work through the list systematically, referring to the subsequent sections for full details of the necessary checks and tests. **Note:** *Before checking the following items ensure that the battery is fully charged and that all fuses are in good condition.*

• Loose, corroded or damaged wiring connections, broken or shorted wiring between any of the component parts of the ignition system (see Chapter 9).
• Faulty spark plug with dirty, worn or corroded plug electrodes, or incorrect gap between electrodes (see Chapter 1).
• Faulty HT coil or spark plug cap.
• Faulty ignition (main) switch (see Chapter 9).
• Faulty immobiliser (where fitted).
• Faulty source coil.
• Faulty pulse generator coil.
• Faulty CDI unit.

6 If the above checks don't reveal the cause of the problem, have the ignition system tested by a Peugeot dealer.

3 HT coil and spark plug cap – check, removal and installation

Check

1 On Speedfight and Vivacity machines the HT coil is mounted on the right-hand side of the frame behind the seat cowling **(see illustration)**. On Trekker machines the HT coil is mounted alongside the battery **(see illustration)**. Remove any body panels as required for access (see Chapter 7). Disconnect the battery negative (-ve) lead (see Chapter 9).

2 Pull the spark plug cap off the plug and inspect the cap, HT lead and coil for cracks and other damage.

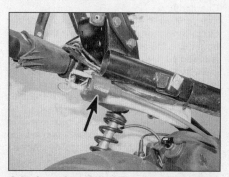

3.1a Location of the HT coil on Speedfight and Vivacity models

3.1b Location of the HT coil on Trekker models

3 Check the condition of the coil primary and secondary windings with a multimeter. Note the position of the primary circuit wiring connectors, then disconnect them **(see illustration)**. Set the multimeter to the ohms x 1 scale and connect the meter probes to the primary circuit wiring terminals. This will give a resistance reading for the coil primary windings which should be consistent with the Specifications at the beginning of this Chapter. If the reading is outside the specified range, it is likely the coil is defective.

4 Set the multimeter to the K-ohms scale and connect the meter probes between the green primary circuit wire terminal of the coil and the spark plug terminal inside the plug cap. This will give a combined resistance reading for the coil secondary windings and plug cap. If the reading is not within the range shown in the Specifications (secondary windings resistance plus plug cap resistance), unscrew the plug cap from the HT lead and connect the probes between the green primary circuit wire terminal of the coil and the core of the HT lead. If the reading is now as specified for the secondary coil windings, the plug cap is suspect. If the reading is still outside the specified range, it is likely that the coil is defective.

5 Should any of the above checks not produce the expected result, have your findings confirmed by a Peugeot dealer. If the coil is confirmed to be faulty, it must be renewed; the coil is a sealed unit and cannot be repaired.

6 To check the condition of the spark plug cap, set the multimeter to the K-ohms scale and connect the meter probes to the HT lead and plug terminals inside the cap **(see illustration)**. If the reading is outside the specified range, the cap is defective and a new one must be fitted. If the reading is as specified, the cap connection may have been faulty. Remake the connection between the cap and the HT lead and check again.

Removal and installation

7 Remove any body panels as required for access (see Chapter 7). Disconnect the battery negative (-ve) lead (see Chapter 9).
8 Note the position of the primary circuit wiring connectors, then disconnect them **(see illustration 3.3)**. Disconnect the HT lead from the spark plug.

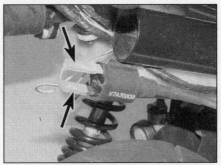

3.3 Disconnect the primary circuit connectors from the coil

9 Unscrew the bolt securing the coil to the frame and remove it.
10 Installation is the reverse of removal. Make sure the wiring connectors and HT lead are securely connected.

---

4 Immobiliser system –
  general information and check

General information

Note: *The AEC 400 ignition system has a separate immobiliser; the ACI 100 ignition system has a combined CDI unit and immobiliser.*

1 The system comprises a security coded ignition key with integral transponder, the immobiliser and transponder aerial. When the key is inserted into the ignition switch the security code is transmitted from the key to the immobiliser via the aerial which is located around the switch. The code deactivates the immobiliser and the warning LED on the instrument panel stops flashing. When the key is removed, the immobiliser is activated and the warning LED starts flashing. **Note:** *To minimise battery discharging, the warning LED goes out after 48 hours although the immobiliser system remains active. Disconnecting the battery does not deactivate the immobiliser system.*

2 One red master key and two black ignition keys are supplied with each machine from new. The keys and the immobiliser are encoded by the factory. The master key

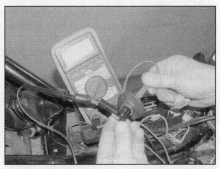

3.6 Measuring the resistance of the spark plug cap

should be kept in a safe place and not used on a day-to-day basis.

3 If a black ignition key is lost, obtain a replacement from a Peugeot dealer and have the system recoded. The dealer will require the red master key for this purpose. Once the system is recoded the lost key will not deactivate the immobiliser.

4 The black ignition keys can lose their code. If the machine will not start with the ignition switched ON, and the LED continues to flash, use the spare key or the red master key and have the system, including the key that has lost its code, recoded by a Peugeot dealer.

Check

5 Insert the ignition key into the switch and turn the switch ON. Once the LED stops flashing, the immobiliser has been deactivated; if the machine will not start, the problem lies elsewhere. If the LED continues to flash, and using another key does not deactivate the immobiliser (see Step 4), the immobiliser is suspect.

6 Remove the kick panel (see Chapter 7) and disconnect the battery negative (-ve) terminal. Trace the transponder aerial wiring from the ignition switch to the immobiliser and disconnect the wiring **(see illustrations)**. Check the resistance in the aerial with a multimeter set to the ohms x 1 scale. Connect the meter probes to the terminals in the connector and compare the result with the Specifications at the beginning of this Chapter **(see illustration)**. If the reading is not within the specification, fit a new aerial and try starting the machine again.

4.6a Transponder aerial is clipped to the ignition switch behind the kick panel

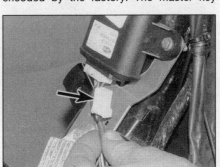

4.6b Disconnect the aerial wiring connector

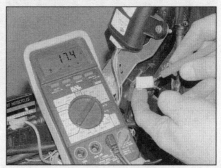

4.6c Measuring the resistance in the transponder aerial

7 If the machine still will not start, the immobiliser should be checked by a Peugeot dealer. **Note:** *It is not possible to substitute an immobiliser from another machine, or a second-hand immobiliser, as this will not recognise the security code from your ignition key.*

8 When a new (uncoded) immobiliser is fitted, check that it is working before encoding it. Turn the ignition ON and start the engine; the engine should run but will not rev above 2000 rpm. If the engine runs, the immobiliser can be encoded using the red master key. **Note:** *Encoding the immobiliser is irreversible – only encode a new immobiliser once you are sure the system is working correctly. If in any doubt, consult a Peugeot dealer before proceeding.*

9 If the engine does not start, the problem lies elsewhere.

10 To check the LED, remove the instrument cluster (see Chapter 9) and test for continuity between the LED terminals **(see illustration)**. There should be continuity in one direction only. If there is no continuity, or continuity in both directions, replace the LED with a new one.

5 Source coil and pulse generator coil – check and renewal

Check

1 Remove the belly panel (see Chapter 7) and disconnect the battery negative (-ve) lead.

2 Trace the wiring from the alternator/pulse generator coil and disconnect it at the connector **(see illustration)**.

3 Check the condition of the source coil and pulse generator coil with a multimeter. Make the tests on the alternator side of the connector.

4 To check the source coil on the basic CDI system or AEC 400 ignition system, set the multimeter to the K-ohms scale and connect

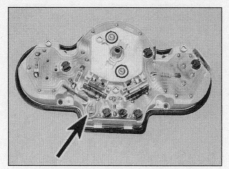

4.10 LED terminals (arrowed) on instrument cluster circuit

the meter probes between the red/black wire terminal in the connector and earth (ground).

5 To check the source coil on the ACI 100 ignition system, set the multimeter to the ohms x 1 scale and connect the meter probes between the white wire terminal in the connector and earth (ground).

6 This will give a resistance reading for the source coil which should be consistent with the Specifications at the beginning of this Chapter.

7 To check the pulse generator coil on the basic CDI system or ACI 100 system, set the multimeter to the ohms x 100 scale and connect the meter probes between the yellow/blue wire terminal in the connector and earth (ground) **(see illustration)**.

8 To check the pulse generator coil on the AEC 400 system, set the multimeter to the ohms x 100 scale and connect the meter probes between the black wire terminal in the connector and earth (ground).

9 This will give a resistance reading for the pulse generator coil which should be consistent with the Specifications at the beginning of this Chapter.

10 If the readings obtained differ greatly from those given, particularly if the meter indicates a short circuit (no measurable resistance) or an open circuit (infinite, or very high resistance), the entire alternator stator assembly must be renewed as no individual

components are available. However, first check that the fault is not due to a damaged or broken wire from the coil to the connector; pinched or broken wires can usually be repaired.

Renewal

11 The source coil and pulse generator coil are integral with the alternator stator (see Chapter 9, Section 31).

6 CDI unit – check, removal and installation

Check

1 If the tests shown in the preceding Sections have failed to isolate the cause of an ignition fault, it is possible that the CDI unit itself is faulty. Peugeot provide no test specifications for this unit. In order to determine conclusively that the unit is defective, it should be substituted with a known good one. If the fault is rectified, the original unit is faulty. **Note:** *The CDI unit will be damaged if a non-resistor type spark plug or spark plug cap are fitted. When fitting a new CDI unit, always ensure the spark plug and cap are of the correct specification before starting the engine.*

Removal

2 Remove the kick panel (see Chapter 7) and disconnect the battery negative (-ve) terminal. Disconnect the wiring connectors from the CDI unit. Unscrew the nuts and bolts securing the unit to the frame and remove the unit **(see illustration)**.

Installation

3 Installation is the reverse of removal. Make sure the wiring connector is correctly and securely connected. **Note:** *The ACI 100 ignition system has a combined CDI unit and immobiliser. When a new unit is fitted it must be encoded by a Peugeot dealer using your red master key.*

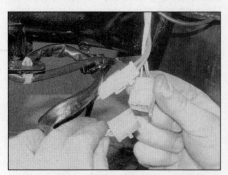

5.2 Disconnect the alternator/pulse generator wiring connector

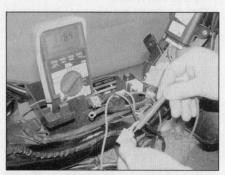

5.7 Measuring the resistance of the pulse generator coil

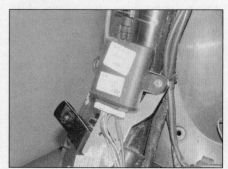

6.2 CDI unit is secured to the frame behind the kick panel

Chapter 6
Frame and suspension

Refer to Chapter 1 for model identification details

Contents

Degrees of difficulty

Easy, suitable for novice with little experience	Fairly easy, suitable for beginner with some experience	Fairly difficult, suitable for competent DIY mechanic	Difficult, suitable for experienced DIY mechanic	Very difficult, suitable for expert DIY or professional

Specifications

Front suspension

Fork oil type	20W fork oil
Fork oil capacity (where applicable)	
Conventional fork	30 cc
Upside-down fork	90 cc
Fork spring free length (upside down fork)	
Compression spring	132 mm
Rebound spring	40 mm

Torque settings

Brake torque arm to suspension leg bolt	56 Nm
Front monolever arm pivot bolt	90 Nm
Front monolever shock absorber lower mounting	25 Nm
Front monolever shock absorber upper mounting	50 Nm
Handlebar stem bolt	40 Nm
Pivot bolt mudguard bracket nut	7 Nm
Rear shock absorber lower mounting	25 Nm
Rear shock absorber upper mounting	50 Nm
Silentblock (engine bracket-to-frame) bolt	60 Nm
Steering head bearing adjuster nut	
Initial setting	40 Nm
Final setting	23 Nm
Steering head bearing locknut	80 Nm

1 General information

All models are fitted with a tubular and pressed steel one-piece frame.

The engine and transmission unit is linked to the frame by a pivoting silentblock assembly at the front and by the rear shock absorber, making the unit an integral part of the rear suspension.

Front suspension on Speedfight models is by a monolever, single-sided leading link with a single, non-adjustable shock. Front suspension on all other models is either by conventional or upside-down telescopic forks.

All models are fitted with a stand, which bolts onto the bottom of the engine.

2 Frame – inspection and repair

1 The frame should not require attention unless accident damage has occurred. In most cases, frame renewal is the only satisfactory remedy for such damage. A few frame specialists have the jigs and other equipment necessary for straightening the frame to the required standard of accuracy, but even then there is no simple way of assessing to what extent the frame may have been over stressed.

2 After a high mileage, the frame should be examined closely for signs of cracking or splitting at the welded joints. Loose engine mount and suspension bolts can cause ovaling or fracturing of the mounting points. Minor damage can often be repaired by specialist welding, depending on the extent and nature of the damage.

3 Remember that a frame which is out of alignment will cause handling problems. If misalignment is suspected as the result of an accident, it will be necessary to strip the machine completely so the frame can be thoroughly checked.

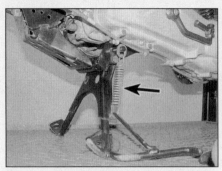

3.2a Stand and stand spring (arrowed) on Speedfight . . .

3.2b . . . and Trekker models

3 Stand –
removal and installation

Removal

1 Support the machine using an auxiliary stand. **Note:** *Do not rest the weight of the machine on the bodywork; remove the belly panels to expose the frame (see Chapter 7). Alternatively, have an assistant support the machine.*
2 Unhook the stand spring, noting how it fits, and remove the spring plate **(see illustrations)**.
3 Unscrew the pivot bolt nut and remove the washer, then withdraw the pivot bolt and remove the stand **(see illustration)**.
4 If required, unscrew the nuts and withdraw the bolts securing the stand bracket to the underside of the engine.
5 Thoroughly clean the stand and remove all road dirt and old grease. Inspect the pivot bolt and the pivot holes in the bracket for wear and renew them if necessary. Inspect the spring; if it is sagged or is cracked a new spring must be fitted. Inspect the rubber stop on the stand and renew it if it is worn or perished.

Installation

6 On installation apply grease to the pivot

bolt and all pivot points and tighten the nuts securely. Check that the spring holds the stand up securely when it is not in use – an accident is almost certain to occur if the stand extends while the machine is in motion.

4 Suspension –
check

1 The suspension components must be maintained in top operating condition to ensure rider safety. Loose, worn or damaged suspension parts decrease the scooter's stability and control.

Front suspension

2 While standing alongside the scooter, apply the front brake and push on the handlebars to compress the suspension several times. See if it moves up-and-down smoothly without binding. If binding is felt, the suspension should be disassembled and inspected (see Section 9).
3 On models with monolever suspension, inspect the shock for fluid leakage and corrosion of the damper rod. If the shock is faulty it should be renewed (see Section 9). Check that the shock mounting bolts are tight.
4 On models with telescopic forks, inspect

the area around the dust seal for signs of grease or oil leakage, then carefully lever off the dust seal using a flat-bladed screwdriver and inspect the area beneath it **(see illustration)**. If corrosion due to the ingress of water is evident, the seals, where fitted, must be renewed (see Section 9).
5 Check the tightness of all suspension nuts and bolts to be sure none have worked loose.

Rear suspension

6 Inspect the shock for fluid leakage and corrosion of the damper rod. If the shock is faulty it should be replaced (see Section 10). Check that the shock mounting bolts are tight.
7 With the aid of an assistant to support the bike, compress the rear suspension several times. It should move up and down freely without binding. If any binding is felt, the worn or faulty component must be identified and renewed. The problem could be due to either the shock absorber or the silentblock assembly.
8 Support the scooter so that the rear wheel is off the ground. Grab the engine/ transmission unit at the rear and attempt to rock it from side to side – there should be no discernible freeplay felt between the engine and frame. If there is movement, inspect the tightness of the rear suspension mountings and the front engine mounting, referring to the torque settings specified at the beginning of this Chapter, then re-check for movement. If freeplay is felt, disconnect the shock absorber lower mounting and displace the shock and check again – any freeplay in the front mounting should be more evident. If there is freeplay, inspect the silentblock assembly for wear (see Section 11).
9 Reconnect the rear shock, then grasp the top of the rear wheel and pull it upwards – there should be no discernible freeplay before the shock absorber begins to compress. Any freeplay indicates a worn shock or shock mountings. The worn components must be renewed (see Section 10).

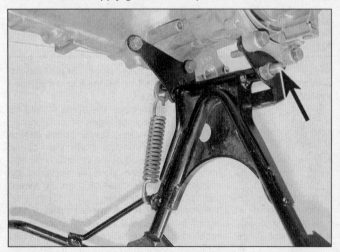

3.3 Unscrew the nut (arrowed) and withdraw the pivot bolt

4.4 Inspect around the dust seals for oil leaks and pitting

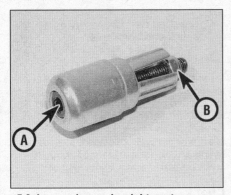

5.3 Loosen bar end weight centre screw (A) to release nut (B)

5.5 Disconnect the brake light switch wiring connectors

5.7 On Speedfight models, detach the turn signal relay from the handlebars

5 Handlebars – removal and installation

Removal

1 Remove the handlebar covers where applicable. On Speedfight and Vivacity models, remove the kick panel (see Chapter 7).

2 If required, the handlebars can be displaced from the steering head for access to the bearings without having to detach any cables, hoses or main wiring looms, or remove the switches, brake levers or master cylinders. If this is the case, ignore the Steps which do not apply.

3 Where fitted, loosen the centre screws for the bar end weights and withdraw the weights from the handlebars. Take care not to undo the screws too far and lose the nuts on the end of the screws **(see illustration)**.

4 Undo the throttle twistgrip housing screws and slide the twistgrip off the end of the handlebar (see Chapter 4).

5 Disconnect the wiring from each brake light switch **(see illustration)**.

6 Undo the handlebar switch housing screws and displace the housing (see Chapter 9).

7 On Speedfight models, detach the turn signal relay from the bracket on the handlebars **(see illustration)**.

8 Unscrew the brake master cylinder assembly clamp bolts and position the assembly clear of the handlebar, making sure no strain is placed on the hydraulic hose (see Chapter 8). Keep the master cylinder reservoir upright to prevent air entering the system. **Note:** *Some models are fitted with hydraulically operated front and rear brakes, on others only the front brake is hydraulically operated.*

9 Remove the left-hand grip; peel the grip off the end of the bar, or if necessary cut it off.

10 On Speedfight 2 Furious and Metal-X Furious models, use a Torx wrench to unscrew the bolts securing the handlebar clamps **(see illustration)**. Support the handlebars and lift the clamps off, then remove the handlebars. On all other models, unscrew the nut on the handlebar stem bolt and remove the nut, washer and shaped spacer, noting how they fit **(see illustration)**.

11 Support the handlebars and withdraw the bolt, then lift the bars off the steering stem. If the handlebar components have been left attached, position the bars so that no strain is placed on any of the cables, hoses or wiring, and protect the bodywork to prevent scratching.

Installation

12 Installation is the reverse of removal, noting the following.

• Refer to the Specifications at the beginning of this Chapter and tighten the handlebar stem bolt to the specified torque setting.

• Use a suitable adhesive between the left-hand grip and the handlebar.

• Don't forget to reconnect the brake light switch wiring connectors.

• Check the operation of the brakes before riding the machine.

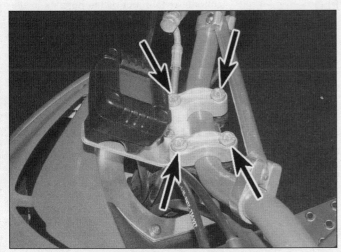

5.10a Handlebar clamps are secured by four bolts

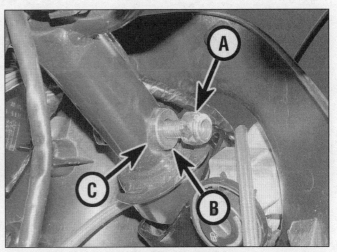

5.10b Remove the nut (A), washer (B) and spacer (C)

6.4 Freeplay in the bearings can be felt as forwards and backwards movement

6.7 Remove the locknut (arrowed) and discard the lockwasher

6.8a Location of the tab washer

6.8b Discard the rubber washer if it is damaged

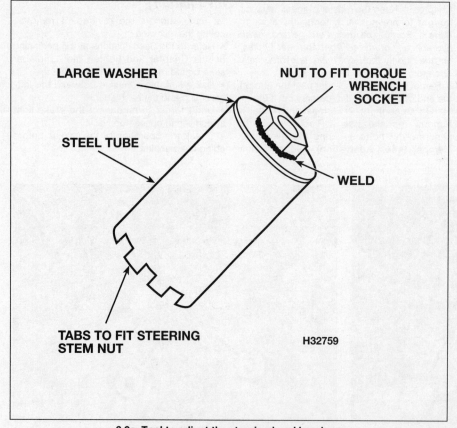

6.9a Tool to adjust the steering head bearings

LARGE WASHER

NUT TO FIT TORQUE WRENCH SOCKET

STEEL TUBE

WELD

TABS TO FIT STEERING STEM NUT

H32759

6 Steering head bearings – check and adjustment

1 Peugeot scooters are equipped with ball steering head bearings which run in races at the top and bottom of the steering head. The races can become dented or rough during normal use and the balls will gradually wear. In extreme cases, worn or loose steering head bearings can cause steering wobble – a condition that is potentially dangerous.

Check

2 Support the machine on its stand. Raise the front wheel off the ground either by having an assistant push down on the rear or by placing a support under the engine. **Note:** *Do not rest the weight of the machine on the bodywork; remove the belly panels to expose the frame (see Chapter 7).*

3 Point the front wheel straight-ahead and slowly turn the handlebars from lock-to-lock. Any dents or roughness in the bearing races will be felt and the bars will not move smoothly and freely.

4 Next, grasp the front suspension and try to move it forwards and backwards **(see illustration)**. Any looseness in the steering head bearings will be felt as front-to-rear movement of the suspension. **Note:** *On models with monolever front suspension, grasp the suspension leg behind the wheel at either end of the monolever arm pivot bolt for this test.*

5 If play is felt in the bearings, adjust them as follows.

Adjustment

6 Displace the handlebars (see Section 5).

7 Some early models are fitted with one locknut above the bearing adjuster nut; most machines have two locknuts above the adjuster nut. If one locknut is fitted, prise the lockwasher tabs out of the notches in the locknut and unscrew the locknut using either a C-spanner or a suitable drift located in one of the notches. Discard the lockwasher as a new one must be fitted on reassembly **(see illustration)**.

8 If two locknuts are fitted, unscrew the upper locknut (see Step 7) then lift off the tab washer, noting how it fits **(see illustration)**. Unscrew the lower locknut. A rubber washer is fitted between the lower locknut and the adjuster nut. Discard it if it crushed or damaged and fit a new one on reassembly **(see illustration)**.

9 To adjust the bearings as specified by Peugeot, a special service tool (Pt. No. 754086) and a torque wrench are required. Alternatively, a similar tool can be made **(see illustration)**. If the tool is available, first loosen the adjuster nut slightly to take pressure off the bearings, then tighten it to the initial torque setting specified at the beginning of

6.9b Bearing adjuster nut

6.9c Adjusting the steering head bearings with the special tool and torque wrench

6.13 Hold the adjuster nut and tighten the locknut with the special tool

this Chapter. Now slacken the nut, and tighten it to the final torque setting specified **(see illustrations)**.

10 If the special tool is not available, using either a C-spanner, a peg spanner or a drift located in one of the notches, loosen the adjuster nut slightly to take pressure off the bearings then tighten the nut until all freeplay is removed. Now tighten the nut a little more to pre-load the bearings. Now loosen the nut and retighten it, setting it so that all freeplay is just removed from the bearings, yet the steering is able to move freely from lock-to-lock.

11 Turn the steering from lock-to-lock five times to settle the bearings, then recheck the adjustment or the torque setting. The object is to set the adjuster nut so that the bearings are under a very light loading, just enough to remove any freeplay.

Caution: Take great care not to apply excessive pressure because this will cause premature failure of the bearings.

12 With the bearings correctly adjusted and where only one locknut is fitted, install a new lockwasher ensuring two of the tabs locate in notches in the adjuster nut. Install the locknut finger-tight, then hold the adjuster nut to prevent it turning and tighten the locknut securely. If the special tool is available, tighten the locknut to the specified torque setting. Bend the remaining lockwasher tabs up to secure the locknut.

13 Where two locknuts are fitted, install the rubber washer and then the lower locknut, tightening it finger-tight. Hold the adjuster nut to prevent it turning, then tighten the lower locknut only enough to align its notches with the

notches in the adjuster nut and install the tab washer **(see illustration 6.8a)**. Install the upper locknut, then hold the adjuster nut to prevent it turning and tighten the upper locknut securely. If the special tool is available, tighten the locknut to the specified torque setting **(see illustration)**.

14 Check the bearing adjustment as described above and re-adjust if necessary, then install the remaining components in the reverse order of removal.

7 Steering stem – removal and installation

Removal

1 Refer to Chapter 8 and remove the front wheel and the brake caliper. On Speedfight models, if required, remove the front mudguard and the wheel hub. On Vivacity models, remove the front mudguard. On Speedfight 2 Furious and Metal-X Furious models, ensure the lower end of the speedometer cable is detached from the front suspension (see Chapter 9).

2 Remove the handlebars (see Section 5). On Speedfight 2 Furious and Metal-X Furious models, remove the bolt securing the instrument cluster bracket and displace the instrument cluster. Unscrew the nut on the steering stem bolt and remove the nut, washer and shaped spacer, noting how they fit. Withdraw the bolt and lift off the handlebar bracket.

3 On Trekker models, remove the mudguard liner from the underside of the steering stem (see Chapter 7).

4 Although not essential, it is advisable to remove adjacent body panels to avoid the possibility of damaging any paintwork (see Chapter 7). **Note:** *The ball bearings in the lower steering head race are not retained by a cage – place a clean rag on the floor beneath the steering head to catch the ball bearings when the steering stem is removed.*

5 Unscrew and remove the bearing adjuster locknut(s) and washer (see Section 6).

6 Support the steering stem, then unscrew the bearing adjuster nut and carefully lower the steering stem out of the steering head **(see illustration)**. Note which way round the adjuster nuts fits – the top inner race is on the underside of the adjuster nut.

7 The ball bearings in the lower race will either fall out of the race or stick to the lower inner race on the steering stem. The top bearing will remain in the top of the steering head.

8 Remove all traces of old grease from the ball bearings and races and inspect them for wear or damage (see Section 8). **Note:** *Do not attempt to remove the outer races from the steering head or the lower bearing inner race from the steering stem unless they are to be renewed.*

Installation

9 Apply a liberal quantity of grease to the bearing inner and outer races and install the top bearing **(see illustration)**.

10 Assemble the lower race ball bearings on the lower inner race on the steering stem; they will be retained by the grease **(see illustration)**. Note that there are 21 balls in the lower race.

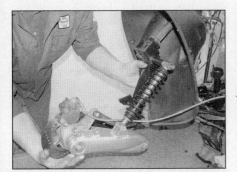

7.6 Lower the steering stem out of the steering head

7.9 Install the top bearing

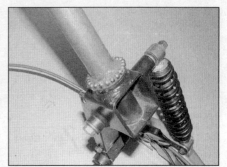

7.10 Hold the lower race ball bearings in place with grease

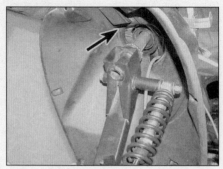

7.11a Lift the steering stem into place . . .

7.11b . . . and install the adjuster nut

8.3a Inspect the races in the top . . .

8.3b . . . and bottom of the steering head

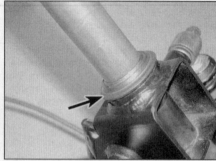
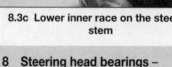

8.3c Lower inner race on the steering stem

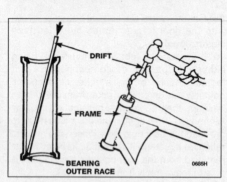

8.4 Drive the bearing outer races out with a brass drift as shown

11 Carefully lift the steering stem up through the steering head, ensuring the lower race ball bearings remain in place, and thread the bearing adjuster nut onto the stem **(see illustrations)**. Ensure the adjuster nut is fitted the right way round.

12 Install the remaining components in the reverse order of removal and adjust the bearings as described in Section 6.

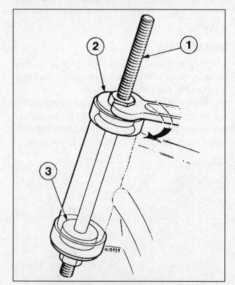

8.6 Using a drawbolt to fit the outer races in the steering head

1 *Long bolt or threaded bar*
2 *Thick washer*
3 *Guide for lower race*

---

8   Steering head bearings – inspection and renewal

Inspection

1 Remove the steering stem (see Section 7).
2 Remove all traces of old grease from the bearings and races and check them for wear or damage.
3 The races should be polished and free from indentations **(see illustrations)**. The outer races are in the steering head, the top inner race is integral with the bearing adjuster nut and the lower inner race is on the steering stem. Inspect the ball bearings for signs of wear, pitting or corrosion, and examine the top bearing retainer cage for signs of cracks or splits. If there are any signs of wear or damage on any of the above components both upper and lower bearing assemblies must be renewed as a set. Only remove the races from the steering head and the stem if they need to be renewed – do not re-use them once they have been removed.

Renewal

4 The outer races are an interference fit in the frame and can be tapped from position with a suitable drift **(see illustration)**. Tap firmly and evenly around each race to ensure that it is driven out squarely. It may prove advantageous to curve the end of the drift slightly to improve access.
5 Alternatively, the races can be pulled out using a slide-hammer with internal expanding extractor.

6 The new outer races can be pressed into the frame using a drawbolt arrangement **(see illustration)**, or by using a large diameter tubular drift which bears only on the outer edge of the race. Ensure that the drawbolt washer or drift (as applicable) bears only on the outer edge of the race and does not contact the working surface. Alternatively, have the races installed by a Peugeot dealer.

> **HAYNES HiNT** *Installation of new bearing outer races is made much easier if the races are left overnight in the freezer. This causes them to contract slightly making them a looser fit.*

7 To remove the lower inner race from the steering stem, first drive a chisel between the base of the race and the bottom yoke. Work the chisel around the race to ensure it lifts squarely. Once there is clearance beneath the race, use two levers placed on opposite sides of the race to work it free, using blocks of wood to improve leverage and protect the yoke. If the race is firmly in place it will be necessary to use a bearing puller. Alternatively, take the steering stem to a Peugeot dealer.
8 Fit the new lower inner race onto the steering stem. A length of tubing with an internal diameter slightly larger than the steering stem will be needed to tap the new bearing into position. Ensure that the drift bears only on the inner edge of the race and does not contact its working surface.
9 Install the steering stem (see Section 8).

9 Front suspension –
disassembly, inspection and reassembly

Monolever suspension (Speedfight models)

Disassembly

1 Remove the front wheel, hub, caliper bracket and axle (see Chapter 8), and the mudguard (see Chapter 7). On Speedfight 2 Furious models, ensure the lower end of the speedometer cable is detached from the front suspension (see Chapter 9).

2 Counterhold the captive nut on the back of the mudguard bracket and undo the bolt securing the lower end of the shock absorber to the monolever arm. Remove the bracket, then support the arm and withdraw the bolt **(see illustration)**.

3 Counterhold the bolt and undo the nut securing the upper end of the shock absorber **(see illustration)**. Remove the nut and washer, then displace the bolt to free the shock. Discard the nut as a new one must be fitted on reassembly. **Note:** *The bolt is supported at either end by a shouldered spacer. If required, remove the left-hand spacer for safe-keeping. The bolt and right-hand spacer can only be removed if the steering stem and suspension leg are lowered out of the steering head (see Section 7).*

4 Counterhold the bolt and undo the nut

9.2 Remove the bracket (A) and withdraw the bolt (B)

securing the caliper bracket torque arm to the suspension leg, then remove the nut, washer and torque arm **(see illustration)**. Discard the nut as a new one must be fitted on reassembly. Withdraw the bolt from the suspension leg.

5 On early models the monolever arm pivot bolt pivots on rubber bushes in the bottom of the suspension leg, on later models the bolt pivots on a pair of bearings. Before separating the arm from the suspension leg, check the condition of the bushes or bearings by moving the arm laterally against the suspension leg. If any play is felt between the arm and the leg, the bushes or bearings must be renewed. Also move the arm up and down. If any roughness is felt or the arm does not move smoothly and freely, the bushes, bearings or pivot bolt must be renewed. If there is no play or roughness in the monolever arm movement there is no

9.3 Remove the nut and washer retaining the upper end of the shock

need to disassemble the suspension further. **Note:** *Peugeot do not list replacement rubber bushes for the front suspension. If it appears that the bushes are worn, remove the monolever arm for further inspection. Component parts from the early and later designs of monolever suspension are not interchangeable.*

6 To remove the monolever arm, counterhold the monolever arm pivot bolt and undo the nut on the right-hand end. Remove the nut, plain washer, special washer, mudguard bracket and special washer **(see illustrations)**. Discard the nut as a new one must be fitted on reassembly. Alternatively, some machines have a separate nut retaining the mudguard bracket; remove the nut, plain washer, special washer and mudguard bracket, then counterhold the pivot bolt and undo the pivot bolt nut.

7 Withdraw the pivot bolt and arm from the

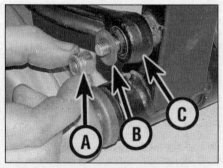

9.4 Remove the nut (A), washer (B) and torque arm (C)

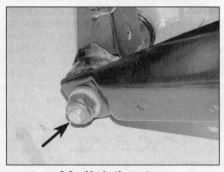

9.6a Undo the nut . . .

9.6b . . . then remove the plain washer . . .

9.6c . . . the special washer . . .

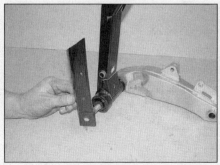

9.6d . . . the mudguard bracket . . .

9.6e . . . and the second special washer

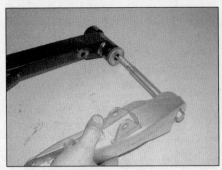

9.7 Withdraw the pivot bolt and arm from the suspension leg

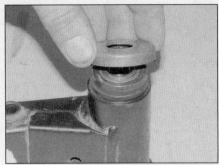

9.8a Remove the left-hand side dust cap and seal . . .

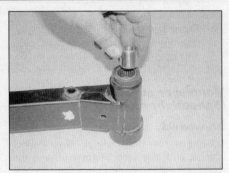

9.8b . . . and the needle bearing sleeve

9.9a Remove the right-hand side seal . . .

9.9b . . . and spacer

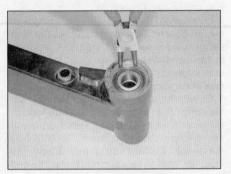

9.11a Remove the circlip . . .

suspension leg (see illustration). The bolt is a press fit in the arm and should not be removed unnecessarily.

8 If bearings are fitted in the end of the suspension leg, remove the dust cap and seal from the left-hand side of the leg and remove the sleeve from inside the needle roller bearing (see illustrations).

9 Carefully lever the seal from the right-hand side of the leg with a screwdriver, taking care not to damage it, and remove the spacer, noting how it fits (see illustrations).

Inspection

10 Clean all components thoroughly, removing all traces of dirt, corrosion and grease. Inspect all components closely, looking for obvious signs of wear such as heavy scoring, or for damage such as cracks or distortion.

11 Check the condition of the caged ball bearing in the right-hand side of the suspension leg. The inner race should turn smoothly without any grating or roughness. If necessary, remove the bearing for further inspection. First remove the circlip retaining the bearing in the leg, then turn the leg over and support it on a block of wood. Use a metal rod (preferably a brass punch) inserted through the middle of the needle roller bearing to tap evenly around the outer race of the ball bearing (see illustrations). The bearing spacer will come out with the bearing. The bearing should be almost silent when spun. If it grates or rattles it should be renewed.

12 Clean the needle roller bearing with a suitable solvent and dry it with compressed air. Inspect the surface of the rollers for wear and pitting. Apply a few drops of clean oil to the rollers and insert the sleeve. The sleeve should turn smoothly; if it does not, or if the rollers show signs of damage, a new bearing should be fitted. Note the position of the bearing before removing it, then drive it out with a metal rod (see Step 11). Note: *The needle roller bearing should only be removed if it is going to be renewed.*

13 Inspect the pivot bolt for wear and remove any corrosion with steel wool. Check the bolt for straightness with a straight-edge. If the bolt is worn or bent, renew it.

14 Inspect the condition of the bearing seals and renew them if they show signs of wear or deterioration.

15 Inspect the bush in the caliper bracket torque arm (see illustration). If it is a loose fit or shows signs of wear, renew it.

16 Inspect the shock absorber for obvious physical damage and the shock spring for looseness, cracks or signs of fatigue.

17 Inspect the damper rod for signs of bending, pitting and oil leakage and check the mountings at the top and bottom of the shock for wear or damage (see illustration).

9.11b . . . then tap out the bearing

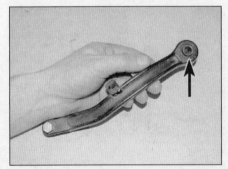

9.15 Inspect the bush (arrowed) in the torque arm

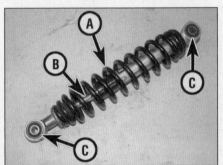

9.17 Inspect the shock spring (A), damper rod (B) and mountings (C)

Individual components are not available for the shock. If any parts are worn or damaged, a new shock must be fitted.

Reassembly

18 Ensure the housings for the pivot bolt bearings are thoroughly clean. Install the caged ball bearing with the marked or sealed side facing outwards. Using an old bearing, a bearing driver or a socket large enough to contact the outer race of the bearing, drive it in only as far as is necessary to install the retaining circlip, then install the circlip **(see illustration)**.

19 Turn the suspension leg over and install the bearing spacer, then install the new needle roller bearing. The needle bearing should be pressed or drawn into place rather than driven in. In the absence of a press, a similar drawbolt arrangement can be used as is shown for fitting the steering head bearing outer races **(see illustration 8.6)**.

20 Lubricate the needle roller bearing with molybdenum disulphide grease, then install the bearing sleeve. Smear the seal inside the dust cap with grease and install the cap.

21 Turn the suspension leg over. Smear the spacer and seal with grease then install the spacer and press the seal into place.

22 Smear the pivot bolt with grease and install it from the left-hand side, ensuring the seals remain in position. Install the special washer, mudguard bracket, special washer, plain washer and new nut in that order **(see illustrations 9.6e, d, c, b and a)**. Tighten the nut sufficiently to allow final positioning of the mudguard bracket when the mudguard is fitted. Alternatively, on machines fitted with a separate nut retaining the mudguard bracket, first install the pivot bolt nut and tighten it to the specified torque setting. Then install the mudguard bracket, special washer, plain washer and mudguard bracket nut and tighten the nut sufficiently to allow final

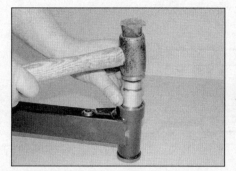

9.18 Fitting a new caged ball bearing

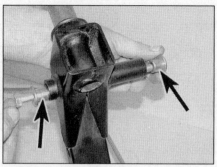

9.25 Ensure the spacers (arrowed) are correctly located in the suspension leg

positioning of the mudguard bracket when the mudguard is fitted.

23 Install the bolt for the caliper bracket torque arm in the suspension leg from the right-hand side, then install the arm, washer and new nut **(see illustration 9.4)**. Tighten the nut sufficiently to allow final alignment of the torque arm when the caliper bracket is installed.

24 Install the lower end of the shock absorber in the bracket on the monolever arm, then install the bolt and mudguard bracket. Tighten the bolt finger-tight to allow final positioning of the mudguard bracket when the mudguard is fitted. **Note:** *This bolt must be thread locked before final tightening.*

25 Ensure the spacers on the upper shock mounting bolt are correctly positioned in the suspension leg **(see illustration)**. Support the monolever arm and fit the shock onto the bolt and install the washer and new nut. Counterhold the bolt and tighten the nut to the torque setting specified at the beginning of this Chapter.

26 Install the mudguard (see Chapter 7).

27 Support the monolever arm and undo the bolt on the lower end of the shock. Apply a suitable non-permanent thread locking

compound to the bolt. Install the bolt, then counterhold the captive nut on the back of the mudguard bracket and tighten the bolt to the specified torque setting **(see illustrations)**.

28 Counterhold the monolever arm pivot bolt and tighten the nut to the specified torque setting. On machines fitted with a separate nut retaining the mudguard bracket, tighten the bracket nut to the specified torque setting.

29 Install the axle and caliper bracket (see Chapter 8). Counterhold the bolt and tighten the nut securing the caliper bracket torque arm to the suspension leg to the specified torque setting.

30 Install the hub and front wheel (see Chapter 8). On Speedfight 2 Furious models, install the lower end of the speedometer cable (see Chapter 9).

Conventional forks (Trekker models)

Disassembly

Note: *Always dismantle the fork legs separately to avoid interchanging parts.*

31 Remove the steering stem (see Section 7).

32 Place a suitable oil drain tray below the fork, then unscrew the bolt in the bottom of the fork slider and pull the slider off the tube.

9.27a Thread lock the lower shock mounting bolt . . .

9.27b . . . and tighten it to the specified torque

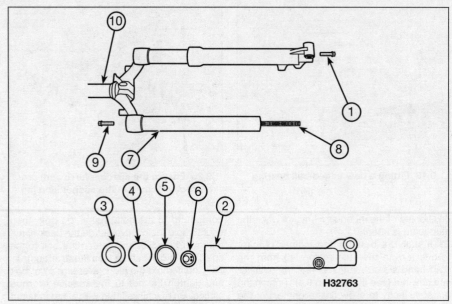

9.32 Conventional fork – Trekker models

1 Bottom bolt	5 Oil seal	8 Spring
2 Fork slider	6 Compression limiting	9 Top bolt
3 Dust seal	cone	10 Steering stem
4 Circlip	7 Fork tube	

Pull the dust seal off the slider and drain the oil from the slider **(see illustration)**.

33 Remove the circlip from inside the top of the slider, then carefully prise out the oil seal, taking care not to gouge the rim of the slider when doing this. Discard the seal as a new one must be fitted on reassembly.

34 Remove the compression limiting cone from inside the bottom of the slider, noting which way round it fits.

35 To remove the spring, unscrew the bolt in the top of the fork tube and draw the spring out of the tube. Hold the spring to prevent it from turning with the bolt.

Inspection

36 Clean all parts in a suitable solvent and dry them with compressed air. Inspect the fork tubes for score marks, pitting or flaking of the chrome finish and excessive or abnormal wear. Check the straightness of the tubes with a straight-edge.

37 Inspect the springs for cracks, sagging and other damage. No service data is available for the springs, but ensure they are both the same length.

38 Individual components are not available for the forks, apart from the dust seal, circlip and oil seal. If any parts are worn or damaged, the whole fork will have to be renewed.

39 The dust seals should be a sliding fit on the fork legs. Discard the dust seals if they are worn or perished and fit new ones (it is good practice to renew the dust seals when the forks are disassembled).

Reassembly

40 Install the compression limiting cone.

41 Lubricate the new oil seal with fork oil

then press it squarely into the slider using a suitable piece of tubing or a socket until the circlip groove is visible above the seal.

 Place a suitably sized washer on top of the oil seal to protect it when pressing it into place.

42 Once the seal is installed, fit the circlip, making sure it is correctly located in its groove.

43 Check that both plugs are in the ends of the spring, then insert the spring into the slider. Install the bolt into the bottom of the slider and thread it into the plug in the base of the spring. Hold the spring to prevent it from turning and tighten the bolt securely.

44 Carefully pour the correct quantity of the specified fork oil into the slider.

45 Fit the dust seal and apply some fork oil to the lips of the seal, then insert the top of the spring into the bottom of the fork tube. Ensure the fork tube fits squarely through the oil seal and into the slider, and install the slider onto the tube until the spring contacts the top of the tube. Hold the slider in position, then install the bolt in the top of the fork tube and thread it into the plug in the top of the spring. Tighten the bolt securely.

46 Install the steering stem (see Section 7).

Upside-down forks (Trekker models)

Seal renewal

47 Remove the front wheel and brake caliper (see Chapter 8). On Metal-X Furious models, ensure the lower end of the speedometer cable is detached from the front suspension (see Chapter 9).

48 Unscrew the bolt from the base of the fork slider which retains the axle/brake caliper bracket and draw the bracket off the slider **(see illustration)**. Lever the dust seal off the bottom of the fork tube and remove it.

49 Carefully prise the oil seal out of the bottom of the fork tube, taking care not to gouge the rim of the tube or the surface of the slider.

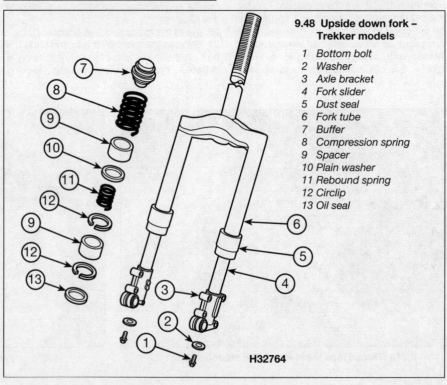

9.48 Upside down fork – Trekker models

1 Bottom bolt
2 Washer
3 Axle bracket
4 Fork slider
5 Dust seal
6 Fork tube
7 Buffer
8 Compression spring
9 Spacer
10 Plain washer
11 Rebound spring
12 Circlip
13 Oil seal

50 Clean the bottom of the slider and the inside of the axle/brake caliper bracket and remove any traces of corrosion.

51 Smear the new oil seal with fork oil, then fit it over the slider and press it into position on the bottom of the tube.

52 Smear the inside of the new dust seal with fork oil and install the seal.

53 Install the axle/brake caliper bracket and tighten the retaining bolt securely. Use the axle inserted through the bracket to prevent the fork slider rotating when tightening the bolt.

54 Install the brake caliper and front wheel (see Chapter 8).

Disassembly

Note: *The forks on these models are difficult to disassemble. Also, some models have had undocumented changes to the internal components of the forks and they may differ to those components described. A certain amount of reader input and common sense will have to be applied if the forks are to be disassembled.*

Note: *Always dismantle the fork legs separately to avoid interchanging parts.*

55 Remove the steering stem (see Section 7).

56 Remove the dust and oil seals (see Steps 48 and 49).

57 Remove the lower circlip from inside the bottom of the fork leg, then draw out the lower bush and remove the upper circlip. Discard the circlips as new ones must be fitted on reassembly.

58 Pull the slider out of the fork leg together with the rebound spring, washer and upper bush. Drain the fork oil out of the slider.

59 Withdraw the compression spring and buffer from the leg.

Inspection

60 Clean all parts in a suitable solvent and dry them with compressed air. Inspect the fork sliders for score marks, pitting or flaking of the chrome finish and excessive or abnormal wear. Check the straightness of the sliders with a straight-edge. Peugeot do not list the sliders as separate items. If a slider is worn or damaged a new fork assembly will have to be fitted.

61 Inspect the springs for cracks, sagging and other damage. Measure the spring free length and compare the result to the specifications at the beginning of this Chapter. If a spring is defective, renew all the springs as a set.

62 Examine the working surfaces of each bush; if worn or scuffed, renew the bushes as a set.

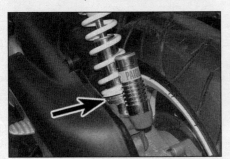

10.5 Location of the rear shock spring preload adjuster (arrowed)

Reassembly

63 Install the various components in the reverse order of removal. Pour the correct quantity of the specified fork oil into each slider before installing the sliders.

64 Install the new upper circlip using a suitable piece of tubing to ensure it is squarely positioned inside the fork tube, then install the lower bush a new lower circlip using the same method. Take care not to scratch the slider. Make sure the circlips are correctly located in their grooves.

Upside-down forks (Vivacity 50 cc models)

65 The forks on these models are outwardly similar to the Trekker forks. However, Peugeot only list replacement oil seals for the Vivacity. The replacement procedure for the seals is the same as for the Trekker. If the fork action is suspect, consult a Peugeot dealer. If the fork is damaged a new fork assembly will have to be fitted. To remove the fork, first remove the steering stem (see Section 7).

Upside-down forks (Vivacity 100 cc models)

66 The forks on these models are outwardly similar to the Trekker forks. However, fork action is controlled by an hydraulic cartridge in the left-hand tube and a spring in the right-hand tube, and the forks are maintenance-free. If the fork action is suspect, consult a Peugeot dealer. If the fork is damaged a new fork assembly will have to be fitted. To remove the fork, first remove the steering stem (see Section 7).

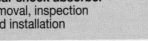

10 Rear shock absorber – removal, inspection and installation

Removal

1 Support the machine on its stand and position a support under the rear wheel so that the engine does not drop when the shock absorber is removed, but also making sure that the weight of the machine is off the rear suspension so that the shock is not compressed.

2 The shock absorber is secured to the frame at the top and the transmission casing at the bottom. To access the nut securing it at the top, remove the body panels as necessary

11.2 Undo the nut (arrowed) and withdraw the bolt

according to model (see Chapter 7). Remove the air filter housing (see Chapter 4).

3 Undo and remove the nut and bolt securing the top of the shock absorber to the frame.

4 Undo the nut and bolt securing the bottom of the shock absorber to the transmission casing. Support the shock and remove the bolt, then manoeuvre the shock away from the machine.

Inspection

5 Inspect the shock absorber for obvious physical damage and the shock spring for looseness, cracks or signs of fatigue. Later Speedfight 2 and TKR models are fitted with a remote reservoir shock with adjustable spring preload **(see illustration)**; use a C-spanner to ensure the preload adjuster turns freely and locks in position under spring pressure.

6 Inspect the damper rod for signs of bending, pitting and oil leakage and check the mountings at the top and bottom of the shock for wear or damage **(see illustration 9.17)**. Individual components are not available for the shock. If any parts are worn or damaged, a new shock must be fitted.

Installation

7 Installation is the reverse of removal. Tighten the shock absorber mounting bolts to the torque settings specified at the beginning of this Chapter.

11 Silentblock assembly – removal, inspection and installation

Removal

1 Remove the engine/transmission unit (see Chapter 2A or 2B).

2 Counterhold the engine bracket-to-frame bolt and undo the nut, then withdraw the bolt and remove the engine bracket, noting how the silentblock fits to the bracket **(see illustration)**.

Inspection

3 Thoroughly clean all components, removing all traces of dirt, corrosion and grease.

4 Inspect the silentblock closely, looking for obvious signs of wear such as compression and cracks, or distortion due to accident damage. It should be necessary to compress the silentblock in order to remove and install the engine bracket-to-frame bolt. If the bracket is not a tight fit, renew the silentblock.

5 Check the bolts for wear and check the holes in the engine bracket for wear. If the bolts are not a precise fit in the bracket the components must be renewed.

6 Check the condition of the engine mounting bushes (see Chapter 2A or 2B).

Installation

7 Installation is the reverse of removal. Smear some grease on the engine bracket bolt and tighten the nut and bolt to the torque setting specified at the beginning of this Chapter.

Notes

Chapter 7
Bodywork

Refer to Chapter 1 for model identification details

Contents

Degrees of difficulty

Easy, suitable for novice with little experience	**Fairly easy,** suitable for beginner with some experience	**Fairly difficult,** suitable for competent DIY mechanic	**Difficult,** suitable for experienced DIY mechanic	**Very difficult,** suitable for expert DIY or professional

1 General information

Almost all the functional components of Peugeot scooters are enclosed by body panels, making removal of relevant panels a necessary part of most servicing and maintenance procedures. Panel removal is straightforward, and as well as facilitating access to mechanical components, it avoids the risk of accidental damage to the panels.

The panels are retained by screws and inter-locking tabs; be sure to follow the advice given at the beginning of Section 6 before removing the panels.

2 Rear view mirrors – removal and installation

Removal

1 The stem of the rear view mirror locates in the front half of the handlebar switch housing and is retained by a nut.

2 To remove the mirror on early models, pull back the lower end of the boot on the stem to expose the top of the fixing **(see illustration)**. Counterhold the fixing and undo the nut, then withdraw the mirror from the switch housing. On later models with 'carbon look' mirrors, remove the plug from the top of the bracket, then counterhold the fixing and undo the nut **(see illustration)**.

Installation

3 Installation is the reverse of removal. Position the mirror as required then tighten the nut.

4 On early models, to adjust the angle of the mirror head, pull back the upper end of the boot on the stem to expose the adjuster screws **(see illustration)**. Loosen the screws and set the mirror to the required position, then tighten the screws and refit the boot.

3 Passenger footrests – removal and installation

Note: Folding passenger footrests are fitted to Speedfight and Trekker models. The floor panel on the Vivacity extends back to provide passenger footrests.

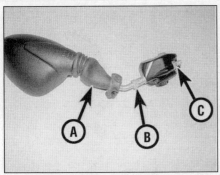

2.2a Mirror boot (A), top fixing (B) and retaining nut (C)

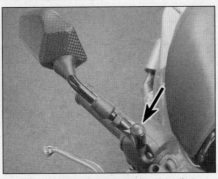

2.2b Prise out the plug (arrowed) to access the fixing

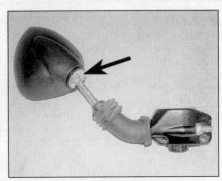

2.4 Rear view mirror adjuster screws

3.1 On Speedfight models, undo the screws (arrowed) and remove the cover

3.2 Undo the nut to remove the footrest

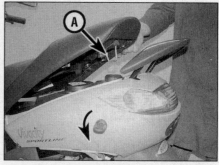

4.1 Turn the lock to release the seat catch (A)

Removal

1 On Speedfight models, undo the two screws that retain the footrest cover and remove the cover **(see illustration)**.

2 On all models, counterhold the footrest pivot bolt and undo the nut on the underside of the footrest, then remove the nut and plain washer **(see illustration)**.

3 Withdraw the bolt and spring washer from the footrest bracket and slide the footrest out of the bracket. Note the bush inside the footrest pivot hole.

Installation

4 Installation is the reverse of removal. Apply a smear of grease to the pivot bolt and ensure the spring washer is fitted on the bolt before it is installed. Tighten the nut enough to allow the footrest to pivot without binding in the bracket.

---

4   Seat and storage compartment – removal and installation

Seat

1 To remove the seat, insert the ignition key into the seat lock and turn it anti-clockwise. This will release the catch on the rear underside of the seat base **(see illustration)**. Swing the seat upright.

2 The seat is retained by the hinge at the front of the seat base **(see illustration)**. Support the seat and undo the hinge bolts, then lift the seat away.

3 The seat latch mechanism is actuated either by a rod or cable from the seat lock **(see illustrations)**. To remove the seat lock, first remove the storage compartment (see Steps 7 to 11). Unclip the rod from the lock or

unclip the cable from the back of the panel and the lock **(see illustrations)**, then remove the body panel (see Section 6).

4 The lock is retained in a recess in the panel by a spring clip. Pull off the spring clip, note how the lock locates in the panel recess, then remove the lock **(see illustration)**.

5 Check the operation of the latch mechanism and lubricate it with a smear of grease.

6 Installation is the reverse of removal.

⚠️ *Warning: Ensure the actuating rod or cable is properly connected to the lock before closing the seat, otherwise you will have no way of releasing the latch.*

Storage compartment

7 Unlock the seat and swing it upright. An engine access panel is fitted in the bottom of the compartment. To open the panel, unclip

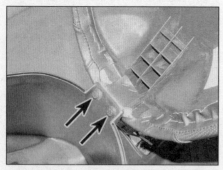

4.2 Undo the hinge bolts to remove the seat

4.3a Latch mechanism is actuated either by rod . . .

4.3b . . . or by cable

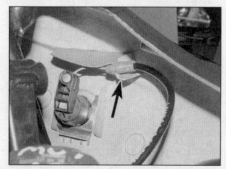

4.3c Unclip the cable from the stop on the panel . . .

4.3d . . . then from the back of the lock

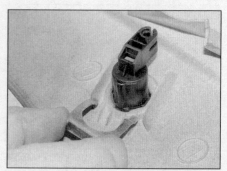

4.4 Pull off the clip to remove the lock

4.7 Engine access panel in the bottom of the storage compartment

4.9 Remove the tool tray fitted to Speedfight models

4.10 Remove the collars from the fuel and oil tank filler necks

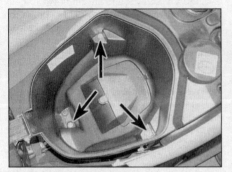

4.11a Storage compartment is retained by flange nuts (arrowed)

4.11b Lift the assembly off the machine

4.11c Rear panel screws also retain storage compartment on Trekker

the top edge and either fold it back or swivel it around on its hinge **(see illustration)**. The panel offers limited access to the engine; for better access remove the storage compartment as follows.

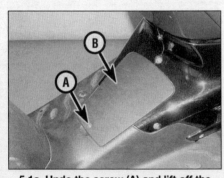

5.1a Undo the screw (A) and lift off the panel (B) . . .

8 The storage compartment can be removed with the seat attached.
9 On Speedfight models, remove the tool tray clipped inside the rear cowling **(see illustration)**.
10 Sealing collars are fitted around the fuel and oil tank filler necks. Where fitted, disconnect the drain hose from the collar on the fuel tank filler neck, then unscrew the fuel and oil tank caps and remove the collars **(see illustration)**. Refit the tank caps.
11 The storage compartment is retained by three or four flange nuts, as applicable **(see illustration)**. Undo the nuts, then lift the compartment and seat assembly off the machine **(see illustration)**. **Note:** *On Trekker models the storage compartment is retained by two of the rear cowling screws in addition to the nuts **(see illustration)**.*
12 Installation is the reverse of removal.

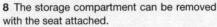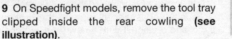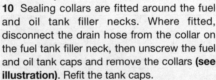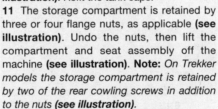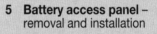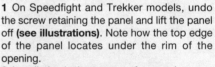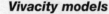

5 Battery access panel – removal and installation

Speedfight and Trekker models

1 On Speedfight and Trekker models, undo the screw retaining the panel and lift the panel off **(see illustrations)**. Note how the top edge of the panel locates under the rim of the opening.
2 Installation is the reverse of removal.

Vivacity models

3 On Vivacity models, undo the lower fixing screw, then raise the seat to access the two fixing screws on the top edge of the panel **(see illustration)**.
4 Undo the top screws and lift the panel off the machine **(see illustration)**.

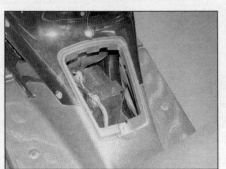

5.1b . . . to access the battery

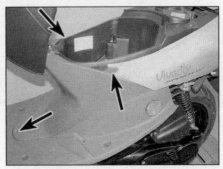

5.3 On Vivacity models, undo the three screws (arrowed) . . .

5.4 . . . and lift off the battery panel

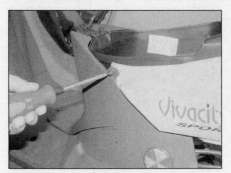

5.5 Battery panel screws also retain front of seat cowling

5 Installation is the reverse of removal. Note that the two top screws also retain the front edge of the seat cowling **(see illustration)**.

6 Body panels – removal and installation

General information

Before removing any body panel, study it closely, noting the position of the fasteners and associated fittings. In some cases the aid of an assistant will be required when removing panels, to avoid the risk of straining tabs or damaging paintwork.

Once the evident fasteners have been removed, try to remove the panel as described but DO NOT FORCE IT – if it will not release, check that all fasteners have been removed and try again. Where a panel engages another by means of tabs, be careful not to break the tab or its mating slot. Remember that a few moments of patience at this stage will save you a lot of money in replacing broken body panels!

Note any fasteners and associated fittings removed with the panel to be sure of returning everything to its correct place on installation.

Before installing a body panel, check that all fasteners and fittings are in good condition and renew any that are damaged. Also check that all mounting brackets are straight and repair or renew them if necessary before attempting to install the panel. Where assistance was required to remove a panel, make sure your assistant is on hand to install it.

Tighten the fasteners securely, but be careful not to overtighten any of them or the panel may break (not always immediately) due to uneven stress. Take particular care when tightening self-tapping screws into plastic lugs on the backs of panels – if the lugs break the panel will have to be renewed.

> **HAYNES HINT** *Note that a small amount of lubricant (liquid soap or similar) applied to rubber mounting grommets will assist the lugs to engage without the need for undue pressure.*

In the case of damage to the body panels, it is usually necessary to remove the broken panel and replace it with a new (or used) one.

There are however some shops that specialise in 'plastic welding', so it may be worthwhile seeking the advice of one of these specialists before consigning an expensive component to the bin. Additionally proprietary repair kits can be obtained for small repairs.

Speedfight models

Handlebar covers

1 The top cover is retained by five screws on the underside of the handlebars. Access to the front middle screw is restricted and may require removal of the front panel (see Step 6) **(see illustrations)**.

2 Undo the screws and lift the cover to gain access to the speedometer cable connector and instrument cluster wiring connectors and disconnect them, then remove the cover from the machine. (see Chapter 9).

3 The instrument cluster is retained in the cover by four screws; undo the screws and remove the cluster **(see illustrations)**.

4 The lower cover is retained by four bolts. Undo the bolts to detach the cover from the handlebars and pull the throttle cable grommet out of the slot in the lower edge of the cover **(see illustrations)**. To remove the cover from the machine, first remove the handlebars (see Chapter 6). Note the routing of the cables, hoses and wiring looms before removing the cover **(see illustration)**.

5 Installation is the reverse of removal. Ensure that all the connectors are secure and check the operation of the instruments and switches, including the brake light switches.

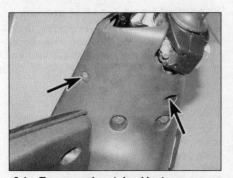

6.1a Top cover is retained by two screws on each side . . .

6.1b . . . and one at the front

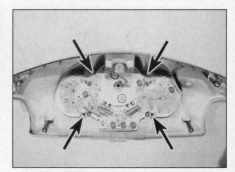

6.3a Undo the four screws (arrowed) . . .

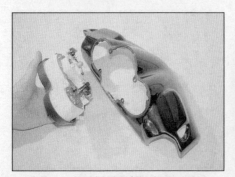

6.3b . . . and remove the instrument cluster

6.4a Undo the lower cover fixing bolts . . .

6.4b . . . and detach the throttle cable

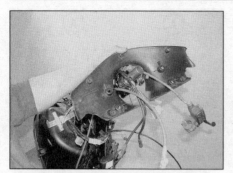

6.4c All cables, hoses and wiring pass through the centre of the cover

Front panel (liquid-cooled models)

6 On the Speedfight 1, the front panel is retained by one screw on the top edge of the panel. On the Speedfight 2, the panel is retained by three screws **(see illustration)**. Undo the screw(s) and lift off the panel **(see illustration)**.

7 Installation is the reverse of removal.

Headlight panel

Note: *Although visually similar, the arrangement of the front body panels differs between the liquid and air-cooled models to allow access to the coolant reservoir and radiator. Air-cooled Speedfight 1 variants have a one-piece front/headlight panel with no grille or separate front panel. The front body panels were redesigned for the Speedfight 2 models. If required, the headlight panel can be removed with the front panel attached to it. On air-cooled Speedfight 2 variants, the grille was blanked off.*

8 Undo the four screws in the kick panel **(see illustration)**.

9 Undo the two screws on the lower front edge of the panel **(see illustration)**.

10 Pull the panel forward to disengage the fixing tabs from the kick panel and the front side panels, and disconnect the headlight wiring connector **(see illustrations)**.

11 The headlight unit is retained in the panel by four screws; undo the screws and remove the unit **(see illustration)**.

12 The grille is retained by two of the headlight unit screws and a third screw in the centre top of the grille **(see illustration)**. Remove the screws and unclip the tabs on the grille to remove it **(see illustration)**.

6.6a On Speedfight 2 models, undo the three screws (arrowed) . . .

13 Installation is the reverse of removal. Ensure the headlight unit and grille are properly located in the panel and the fixings are tightened securely. Ensure the U-clips are in place **(see illustration 6.12b)**. Ensure the

6.8 Headlight panel is retained by four screws in the kick panel . . .

6.10a Pull the panel forward to disengage the tabs (arrowed) . . .

6.11 Four screws retain the headlight unit

6.12a Grille is retained by central screw . . .

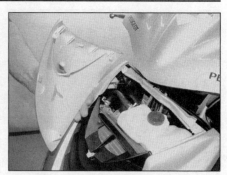

6.6b . . . and lift off the front panel

tabs on the sides and lower edge of the panel are correctly located before tightening the fixing screws. Connect the headlight wiring connector and check the operation of the headlight.

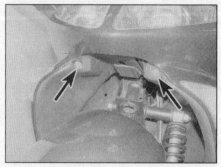

6.9 . . . and two screws on the front lower edge

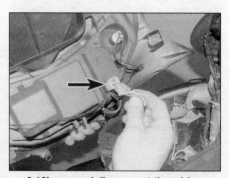

6.10b . . . and disconnect the wiring connector

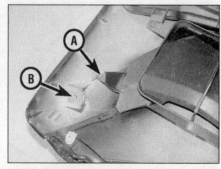

6.12b . . . and tabs at either side (A). Note the U-clip on the panel fixing (B)

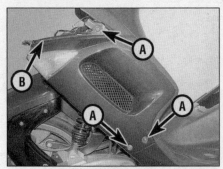

6.15 Panel is retained by screws (A) and tab (B)

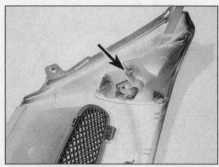

6.16a Undo the screw to remove the turn signal

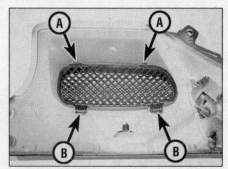

6.16b Grille is retained by two tabs (A) and two clips (B)

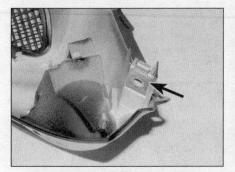

6.17a Ensure the U-clip is in place . . .

6.17b . . . and reconnect the turn signal wiring

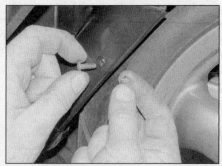

6.18 Mudguard is retained by two nuts and bolts on right-hand side . . .

Front side panels

14 Remove the headlight panel and disconnect the wiring connectors for the front turn signals.

15 The panel is retained by three screws **(see illustration)**. Undo the screws and unclip the tab from the mudflap, then lift the panel off.

16 The turn signal is retained in the panel by one screw **(see illustration)**. The grille is retained by two tabs and two clips **(see illustration)**.

17 Installation is the reverse of removal. Ensure the U-clip for the headlight panel fixing is in place and connect the turn signal wiring before installing the retaining screws **(see illustrations)**. Check the operation of the turn signals.

Front mudguard

18 Counterhold the nuts and undo the bolts

securing the mudguard to the bracket at the rear right-hand side of the mudguard **(see illustration)**.

19 Undo the screws securing the mudguard to the bracket at the rear left-hand side of mudguard **(see illustration)**.

20 Undo the screws securing the mudguard bracket to the monolever arm and remove the mudguard and bracket **(see illustration 6.19)**.

21 If required, undo the screws securing the bracket to the mudguard.

22 Installation is the reverse of removal. Ensure the U-clips are in place and tighten all fixings securely. **Note:** *The rear right-hand side mudguard bracket is retained by the front suspension pivot bolt; the rear left-hand side mudguard bracket is retained by the shock absorber lower mounting bolt (see Chapter 6).*

Kick panel

23 Remove the headlight panel, then undo

the two screws securing the kick panel to the frame **(see illustration)**.

24 Undo the two flange bolts securing the floor panel and lower edge of the kick panel to the frame and lift off the kick panel **(see illustration)**.

25 Installation is the reverse of removal. Ensure no cables, hoses or wiring are trapped between the panel and the frame before tightening the fixings.

Belly panels

26 Remove the passenger footrest cover (see Section 3).

27 Undo the screws joining the two panels on their lower edge **(see illustration)**.

28 Undo the two screws securing the top front edge of the panel to the front side panel **(see illustration 6.15)**.

29 Undo the screw securing the front edge of the panel to the mudflap **(see illustration)**.

6.19 . . . and four screws on the left-hand side

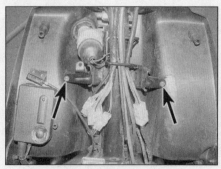

6.23 Kick panel is retained by two screws . . .

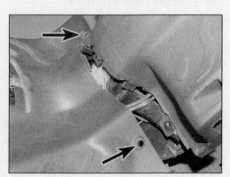

6.24 . . . and two flange bolts

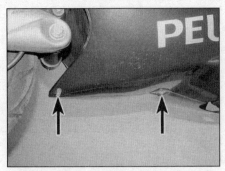

6.27 Belly panels are joined on the lower edge

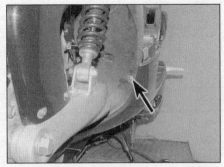

6.29 Screw secures belly panel to mudflap

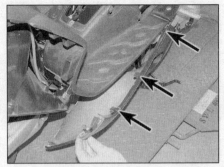

6.30 Tabs locate in side of floor panel

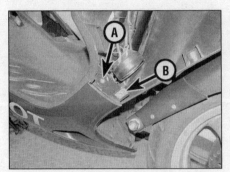

6.31 Ensure U-clips are in place on frame (A) and belly panel (B)

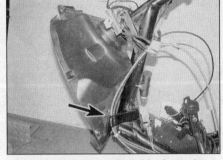

6.32 Mudflap is supported by frame lugs on both sides

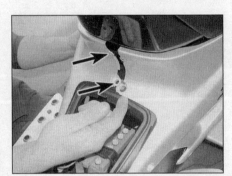

6.34 Side panels are joined by two screws

30 Tabs along the top edge of the belly panel fit into slots along the side of the floor panel. Lift the panel off carefully to avoid damaging the tabs **(see illustration)**.

31 Installation is the reverse of removal. Ensure the U-clips are in place on the frame bracket and fixing point on the belly panel **(see illustration)**.

Mudflap

32 The mudflap is secured by the assembly of front body panels and belly panels. Once the headlight panel, front side panels, kick panel and belly panels have been removed, remove the front suspension (see Chapter 6). If still attached, note the route of the speedometer cable and front brake hose through the mudflap, then lift the mudflap off the lugs on the frame and remove it **(see illustration)**. *Note: The mudflap is split at the front to facilitate fitting the speedometer cable and front brake hose.*

33 Installation is the reverse of removal. Ensure the speedometer cable and brake hose are correctly routed before installing the mudflap on the frame lugs.

Side panels

34 Remove the battery access panel (see Section 5) and undo the screws joining the two side panels above the battery compartment **(see illustration)**.

35 Undo the two screws securing the side panel to the floor panel and the two screws securing the side panel to the rear cowling, then remove the panel **(see illustration)**.

36 Installation is the reverse of removal. Ensure the U-clips are in place on the floor panel and rear cowling fixing points.

Floor panel

37 Remove the belly panels and the side panels.

38 Undo the four flange bolts securing the floor panel to the frame and lift off the panel **(see illustration)**.

39 The floor panel trim, where fitted, is secured to the floor panel by three screws; undo the screws to remove the trim.

40 Installation is the reverse of removal. Ensure no cables, hoses or wiring are trapped between the panel and the frame before tightening the flange bolts.

Rear cowling

41 Lift out the tool tray **(see illustration 4.9)**. The seat lock is located in the left-hand side of the cowling; before removing the cowling, the lock must be disconnected (see Section 4).

42 Undo the screws securing the cowling to the side panels **(see illustration 6.35)** and to the rear mudguard **(see illustration)**.

43 Undo the screws securing the cowling to

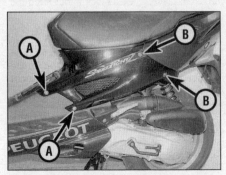

6.35 Screws secure the side panel to the floor (A) and rear cowling (B)

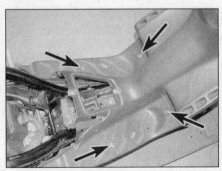

6.38 Four flange bolts secure floor panel

6.42 Screw secures cowling to the rear mudguard

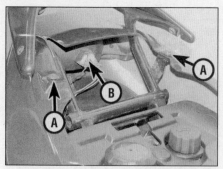

6.43 Screws (A) secure cowling to frame. Note wiring connectors (B)

6.44 Ease the cowling off carefully

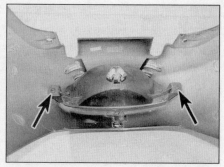

6.45 Undo screws to remove light unit

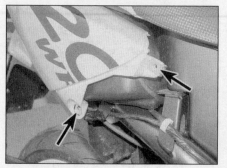

6.46 U-clips on side panel fixings

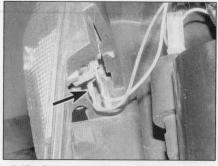

6.47a Disconnect the wiring for the turn signals . . .

6.47b . . . and the number plate light

the frame and disconnect the rear light unit wiring connectors **(see illustration)**.

44 Carefully ease the sides of the cowling away from the frame and draw the cowling rearwards off the machine **(see illustration)**.

45 The rear light unit is retained in the cowling by two screws **(see illustration)**. **Note:** *Although the rear cowling on Speedfight 1 models is a three-piece assembly, the joints are fragile and the*

cowling should only be disassembled if a component part is damaged and in need of repair or renewal. The cowling on Speedfight 2 models it is a two-piece assembly but Peugeot only list the complete cowling as a replacement part.

46 Installation is the reverse of removal. Ensure the U-clips are in place on the fixing points for the side panels **(see illustration)**. Connect the wiring for the rear light unit and check the operation of the tail light and brake light.

Rear mudguard

47 Remove the rear cowling and disconnect the wiring connectors for the rear turn signals and, where fitted, the number plate light **(see illustrations)**.

48 If a Boa lock is fitted, undo the two screws retaining the Boa lock panel and remove the panel **(see illustrations)**. The Boa lock can remain in place. If a Boa lock is not fitted the panel can remain in place.

49 The rear mudguard is retained by four screws and a lug on the underside of the frame tube in front of the oil tank **(see illustrations)**. Undo the screws and unclip the mudguard from the lug, then lift the mudguard off the machine.

50 The turn signals are retained in the mudguard by one screw each **(see illustration 6.16a)**. The number plate light unit is retained by three nuts and bolts **(see illustration)**.

51 Installation is the reverse of removal. Ensure the U-clips are in place on the fixing points for the retaining screws and locate the

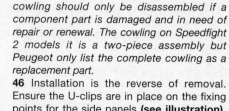

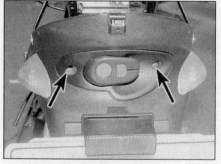

6.48a Undo the two screws . . .

6.48b . . . and lift off the Boa lock panel

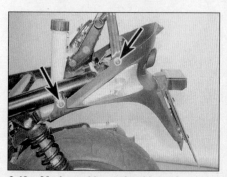

6.49a Mudguard is retained by two screws on each side . . .

6.49b . . . and a lug on the frame

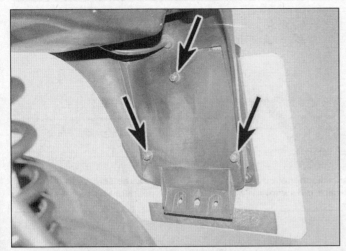

6.50 Three bolts secure the number plate light unit

6.52 Spoiler is retained by three screws

mudguard in the frame lug before installing the screws. Connect the wiring for the turn signals and, where fitted, the number plate light. Check the operation of the turn signals and, where fitted, the number plate light.

Rear spoiler

52 The spoiler is retained by three screws **(see illustration)**. Undo the screws to detach the spoiler.

Trekker, TKR and Metal-X Furious models

Handlebar covers

53 The rear cover is retained by five screws. Undo the screws and lift the cover away **(see illustrations)**.

54 To remove the front cover, first remove the instrument cluster. Undo the three screws securing the cluster to the front cover, then lift the cover to gain access to the speedometer cable and wiring connectors and detach them **(see illustrations)**.

55 Disconnect the wiring connectors for the front turn signals, then remove the two screws securing the front cover to the handlebars and remove the cover **(see illustration 6.54a)**.

56 Installation is the reverse of removal. Ensure that all the connectors are secure and check the operation of the instruments and turn signals.

Headlight panel

57 Undo the four screws in the kick panel, then lift the headlight panel away from the machine and disconnect the headlight wiring connectors **(see illustrations)**.

58 The headlight unit is retained in the panel by three screws; undo the screws and remove the unit **(see illustration)**.

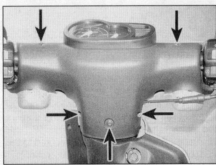

6.53a Undo the five screws . . .

6.53b . . . and lift off the panel

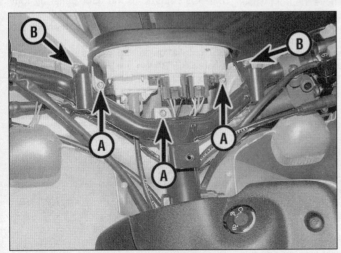

6.54a Screws (A) secure instrument cluster to front cover, screws (B) secure front cover to the handlebars

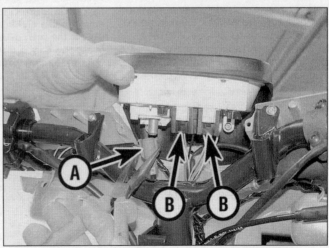

6.54b Detach the speedometer cable (A) and the wiring connectors (B)

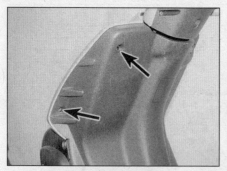

6.57a Headlight panel is retained by two screws on each side

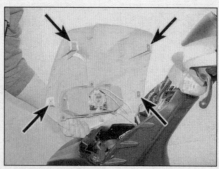

6.57b Lift panel off and disconnect the wiring. Note the U-clips (arrowed)

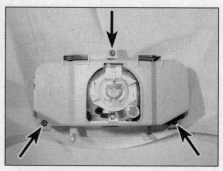

6.58 Undo the three screws to remove headlight unit

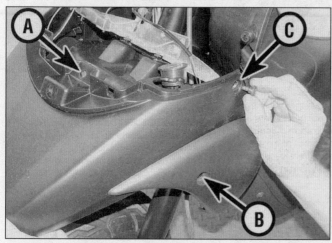

6.60 Mudguard is secured by screws to the mudflap (A), belly panel (B) and frame bracket (C)

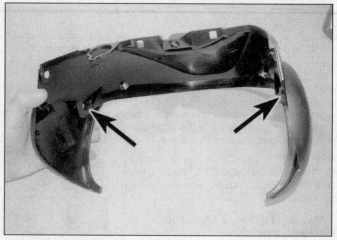

6.61 Side trims are secured by one nut on each side

59 Installation is the reverse of removal. Ensure the headlight unit is properly located in the panel and the fixings are tightened securely. Ensure the U-clips are in place on the back of the panel (see illustration 6.57b). Connect the headlight wiring connectors and check the operation of the headlight.

Front mudguard

Note: To remove and install the front mudguard on WRC 206 and Metal-X Furious models, follow the procedure in Steps 101 to 103.

60 Remove the headlight panel and lift the turn signal relay out of its mounting on the mudguard. The mudguard is secured to the mudflap by one screw, to the belly panel by two screws and to the frame bracket by two screws (see illustration). Undo the screws and remove the mudguard.

61 The mudguard side trims are secured to the mudguard by one nut each (see illustration).

62 A mudguard liner is bolted to the underside of the steering stem (see illustration). To remove the liner, first remove the front wheel (see Chapter 8). Grommets on the speedometer cable and front brake hose clip into slots in the liner; detach them from the liner, noting how they fit, then undo the two retaining bolts and remove the liner (see illustration).

63 Installation is the reverse of removal.

Ensure the grommets on the speedometer cable and brake hose are properly clipped into the mudguard liner. Ensure the U-clips are in place on the fixing points for the retaining screws.

Belly panel

64 Remove the front mudguard. The belly panel is secured to the floor panel by four screws along each side. Support the belly panel and remove the screws, then lift the panel away (see illustration).

65 Installation is the reverse of removal. Ensure the U-clips are in place on the fixing points for the retaining screws.

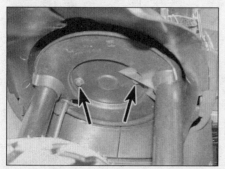

6.62a Mudguard liner is retained by two bolts

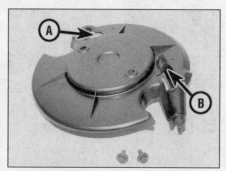

6.62b Mudguard liner has slots for speedometer cable (A) and brake hose (B)

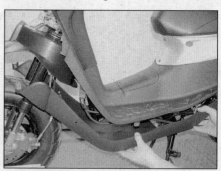

6.64 Belly panel is a one-piece moulding

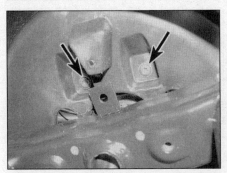

6.66a Mudflap is secured by two screws at the front . . .

6.66b . . . and two screws at the back

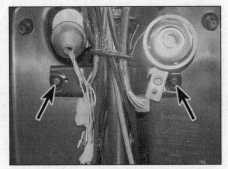

6.69 Two screws secure the kick panel to the frame

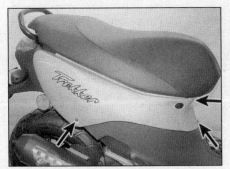

6.73 Side panel is retained by three screws

6.74 Lower the panel to release the tab (arrowed)

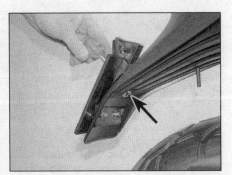

6.82 Mudguard and liner are held together by screw and clip (arrowed)

Mudflap

66 The mudflap is secured to the frame by four screws **(see illustrations)**.

67 Remove the steering stem (see Chapter 6), then unscrew the retaining screws. If still attached, note the route of the speedometer cable and front brake hose through the mudflap, then detach them and lift the mudflap off the machine. **Note:** *The mudflap is split at the back to facilitate fitting the speedometer cable and front brake hose.*

68 Installation is the reverse of removal. Ensure the speedometer cable and brake hose are correctly routed before installing the mudflap retaining screws.

Kick panel

69 Remove the headlight panel, then undo the two screws securing the kick panel to the frame **(see illustration)**.

70 Tabs on the lower edge of the kick panel locate in slots in the top edge of the floor panel. Lift the kick panel off carefully to avoid damaging the tabs.

71 Installation is the reverse of removal. Ensure the tabs on the kick panel are properly engaged in the slots before installing the retaining screws.

Side panels

72 The seat lock is located in the left-hand side panel; before removing the left-hand panel, the lock must be disconnected (see Section 4).

73 Each panel is retained by three screws **(see illustration)**. Undo the screw joining the two side panels below the front of the seat first. Support the panel and undo the retaining screw

on the lower rear edge, then undo the retaining screw at the front and remove the panels.

74 When removing the right-hand panel only, undo the screws and lower the panel to disengage the tab on the upper rear edge from underneath the seat, then lift the panel off **(see illustration)**.

75 Installation is the reverse of removal. Ensure the U-clips are in place on the floor panel fixing points.

Floor panel

76 Remove the belly panel, kick panel and the side panels.

77 Undo the four flange bolts securing the floor panel to the frame and lift off the panel.

78 Floor panel trim, where fitted, is secured to the floor panel by three screws; undo the screws to remove the trim.

79 Installation is the reverse of removal. Ensure no cables, hoses or wiring are trapped

between the panel and the frame before tightening the flange bolts.

Rear cowling/mudguard

80 Remove the storage compartment (see Section 4) and the side panels.

81 If a Boa lock is fitted, undo the two screws retaining the Boa lock panel and remove the panel **(see illustration 6.48)**. If no Boa lock is fitted, the panel can remain in place.

82 Undo the screw securing the mudguard to the mudguard liner **(see illustration)**.

83 Undo the two screws securing the sides of the cowling to the frame. **Note:** *These screws also secure the mudguard liner.*

84 Pull the cowling back and disconnect the wiring for the rear light unit, turn signals and, where fitted, the number plate light, then remove the cowling **(see illustration)**.

85 The rear light unit is retained in the cowling by two screws **(see illustration)**.

6.84 Lift the cowling off and disconnect the wiring connectors

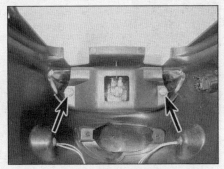

6.85a Light unit is retained by two screws

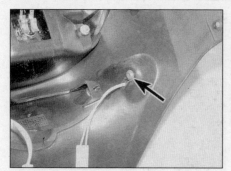

6.85b Turn signal is retained by nut and bolt

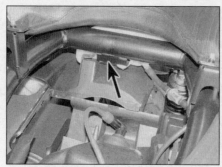

6.86 Front edge of the mudguard liner clips into lug on frame

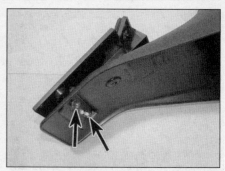

6.87 Number plate bracket is secured by nuts and bolts

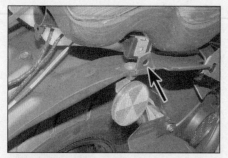

6.88 Align lug on mudguard liner with U-clip before installing cowling screw

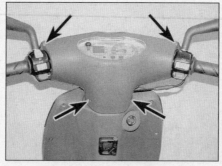

6.90a Undo the four screws . . .

6.90b . . . and lift off the panel

The turn signals are retained by a nut and bolt (see illustration).

86 The mudguard liner is retained by a lug on the underside of the frame tube forward of the oil tank (see illustration). Unclip the liner and remove it from the machine.

87 The rear number plate bracket is secured to the mudguard by two nuts and bolts (see illustration).

88 Installation is the reverse of removal. Ensure the U-clips are in place on the fixing points for the retaining screws and locate the mudguard liner in the frame lug before installing the screws. Connect the wiring for the rear light unit, turn signals and, where

fitted, the number plate light. Ensure the screws securing the sides of the cowling pass through the lugs on the mudguard liner before engaging in the U-clips on the frame (see illustration). Check the operation of the tail light, brake light, turn signals and, where fitted, the number plate light.

Rear spoiler

89 The spoiler is retained by three screws (see illustration 6.52). Undo the screws to detach the spoiler.

Vivacity models

Handlebar covers

90 The front cover is retained by four screws;

undo the screws and lift the panel away (see illustrations). Note the cut-out in the front panel for the throttle cable.

91 To remove the rear cover, first disconnect the speedometer cable and wiring connectors (see illustration 6.54b). Undo the four screws securing the cover to the handlebars and remove the cover (see illustration).

92 The instrument cluster is retained in the rear cover by four screws; undo the screws and remove the cluster (see illustration 6.91).

93 On models with an electrically operated speedometer, first pull back the boot on the instrument cluster wiring connector and disconnect the connector (see illustration).

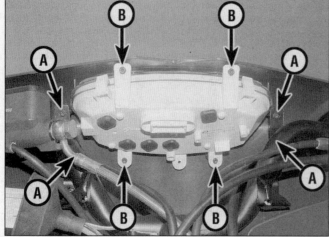

6.91 Screws (A) secure the rear cover to the handlebars, screws (B) retain the cluster in the cover

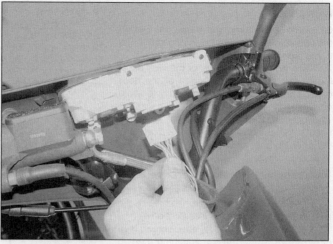

6.93 Multi-pin connector on Vivacity Sportline 2 models

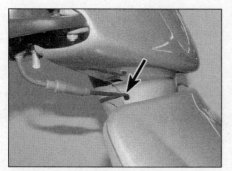

6.94 Route throttle cable through cut-out in front cover

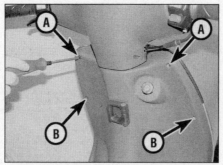

6.95a Screws (A) secure the front panel, screws (B) secure the headlight panel

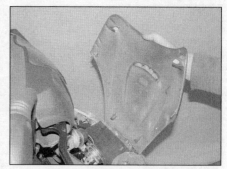

6.95b Lift off the front panel

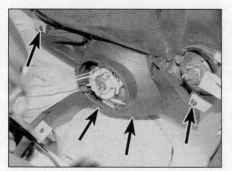

6.98 Headlight/turn signal assembly is retained by four screws

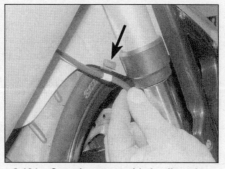

6.101a Speedometer cable is clipped to the mudguard

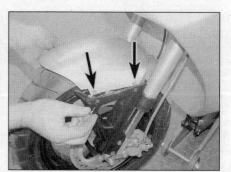

6.101b Mudguard is secured by two screws on each side

Undo the four screws securing the rear cover to the handlebars and remove the cover, then undo the four screws and remove the cluster from the cover.

94 Installation is the reverse of removal. Ensure that the instrument cluster wiring connections are secure and check the operation of the instruments. Ensure the throttle cable is correctly routed through the cut-out in the front cover **(see illustration)**.

Front panel

95 The front panel is retained by two screws **(see illustration)**. Undo the screws and pull the panel forward, then unclip the lower edge from the headlight panel and lift it off **(see illustration)**.

96 Installation is the reverse of removal.

Headlight panel

97 To displace the headlight panel to gain access to the headlight unit, first remove the front panel and the belly panels (see Steps 106 to 109).

98 Cover the front mudguard to protect the paintwork, then undo the two headlight panel fixing screws and pull the panel forward **(see illustration 6.95a)**. The combined headlight and turn signal assembly is retained in the panel by four screws **(see illustration)**.

99 To remove the headlight panel, first remove the steering stem (see Chapter 6) and the front panel. Undo the two headlight panel fixing screws **(see illustration 6.95a)**, then lift the panel away from the machine and disconnect the headlight and turn signal wiring connectors.

100 Installation is the reverse of removal. Ensure the headlight and turn signal assembly is properly located in the panel and the fixings are tightened securely. Connect the headlight and turn signal wiring connectors and check the operation of the headlight and turn signals.

Front mudguard

101 Release the speedometer cable from the clip on the front mudguard, then undo the four screws securing the mudguard to the mudguard brackets and remove the mudguard **(see illustrations)**.

102 Undo the mudguard bracket mounting bolts and remove the brackets from the front forks **(see illustration)**.

103 Installation is the reverse of removal. Check the condition of the plastic U-clips on the mudguard and renew them if they are damaged **(see illustration)**.

104 On some Vivacity variants, the front mudguard is mounted on a bracket on the underside of the steering stem. To remove the mudguard, first remove the front wheel (see Chapter 6). Undo the two screws securing the mudguard to the bracket and carefully lower the mudguard off the machine.

105 Installation is the reverse of removal. Ensure the U-clips are in place on the mudguard bracket and tighten the screws securely.

Belly panels

106 Undo the screws joining the two panels on their lower edge **(see illustration)**.

107 Undo the screw securing the front edge of the panel to the headlight panel **(see illustration)**.

108 Undo the screw securing the rear of the panel to the mounting bracket **(see illustration)**.

6.102 Each mudguard bracket is retained by two bolts

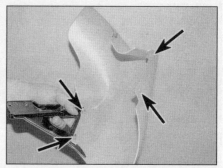

6.103 Check the condition of the U-clips before installing the mudguard

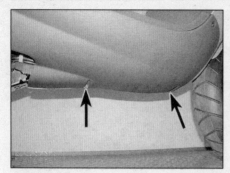

6.106 Belly panels are joined on the lower edge

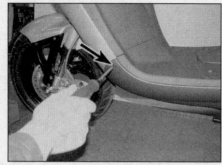

6.107 Belly panel is retained by one screw at the front . . .

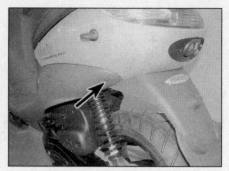

6.108 . . . and one at the back

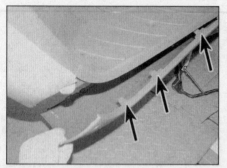

6.109a Unclip the panel tabs from the floor panel . . .

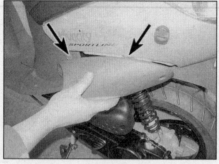

6.109b . . . and the seat cowling

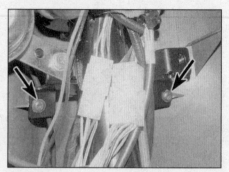

6.112 Two screws secure the kick panel to the frame

109 The belly panel is clipped to the lower edge of the floor panel and the lower edge of the seat cowling; unclip it carefully to avoid damaging the tabs and lift it off **(see illustrations)**.

110 Installation is the reverse of removal. Ensure the panel is securely clipped in position before installing the retaining screws.

Kick panel

111 Remove the front panel and the fixing screws for the headlight panel and bag hook **(see illustration 6.95a)**.

112 Undo the two screws securing the kick panel to the frame **(see illustration)**.

113 Tabs on the lower edge of the kick panel locate in slots in the top edge of the floor panel. Lift the kick panel off carefully to avoid damaging the tabs.

114 Installation is the reverse of removal.

Ensure the tabs on the kick panel are properly engaged in the slots before installing the retaining screws.

Floor panel

115 Remove the battery access panel (see Section 5) and the belly panels.

116 Undo the screws securing the seat cowling to the floor panel **(see illustration)**.

117 Undo the four flange bolts securing the floor panel to the frame and lift off the panel **(see illustration)**.

118 Installation is the reverse of removal. Ensure no cables, hoses or wiring are trapped between the panel and the frame before tightening the flange bolts.

Seat cowling

119 The seat lock is located in the left-hand

side of the cowling; before removing the cowling, the lock must be disconnected (see Section 4).

120 If a Boa lock is fitted, undo the two screws retaining the Boa lock panel and remove the panel **(see illustration 6.48)**. If no Boa lock is fitted, the panel can remain in place.

121 Remove the battery access panel (see Section 5) and the belly panels.

122 Undo the screws securing the cowling to the floor panel **(see illustration 6.116)**.

123 Undo the screws securing the cowling to the frame **(see illustration)**. **Note:** *These screws also secure the mudguard.*

124 Pull the cowling back and disconnect the wiring for the rear light and turn signal assembly, then remove the cowling **(see illustration)**.

6.116 Undo one screw each side . . .

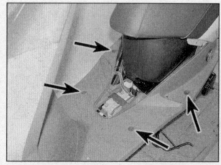

6.117 . . . and four flange bolts

6.123 Undo one screw each side

6.124 Lift the cowling off

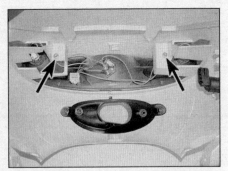

6.125 Undo screws to remove light unit

125 The rear light and turn signal assembly is retained in the cowling by two screws **(see illustration)**.

126 Installation is the reverse of removal. Connect the wiring for the rear light and turn signal assembly. Ensure the screws securing the cowling to the frame engage in the U-clips on the mudguard. Check the operation of the tail light, brake light and turn signals.

Rear mudguard

127 Remove the rear cowling and disconnect the wiring connector, where fitted, for the number plate light.

128 Undo the screws securing the mudguard to the frame, then unclip the guard from the lug on the underside of the frame tube in front of the oil tank and remove it.

129 Installation is the reverse of removal.

Ensure the tab on the mudguard is located in the frame lug before installing the fixing screws. Connect the wiring, where fitted, for the number plate light and check the operation of the light.

Rear spoiler

130 The spoiler is retained by three screws **(see illustration 6.52)**. Undo the screws to detach the spoiler.

Chapter 8
Brakes, wheels and tyres

Refer to Chapter 1 for model identification details

Contents

Degrees of difficulty

Easy, suitable for novice with little experience	Fairly easy, suitable for beginner with some experience	Fairly difficult, suitable for competent DIY mechanic 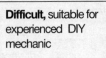	Difficult, suitable for experienced DIY mechanic	Very difficult, suitable for expert DIY or professional

Specifications

Disc brake
Fluid type	DOT 4
Pad minimum thickness	1.5 mm
Disc thickness	
Standard	3.5 mm
Service limit	3.0 mm

Drum brake
Lining thickness – standard	4 mm
Internal diameter – standard	110 mm

Wheels
Axial (side-to-side) wheel runout – front and rear wheel	0.8 mm maximum

Tyres
Tyre pressures and sizes	see Chapter 1

Torque settings
All models
Front brake caliper mounting bolts	35 Nm

Speedfight
Front and rear wheel bolts	40 Nm
Front brake disc mounting bolts	35 Nm
Front hub nut	70 Nm
Rear brake caliper mounting bolts	32 Nm
Rear brake disc mounting bolts	32 Nm
Rear hub nut	120 Nm
Rear wheel nut (drum brake)	120 Nm

Trekker and Vivacity
Front axle nut	70 Nm
Front brake disc mounting bolts	32 Nm
Rear wheel nut	120 Nm

2.2a Brake pad retaining pins (arrowed)

2.2b Withdraw the pins . . .

2.2c . . . and lift out the pads

2.3 Measure the amount of friction
material on each pad

1 General information

The front brake on all models is a single, hydraulically operated disc. The front brake master cylinder is integral with the brake lever and fluid reservoir on the right handlebar.

The rear brake is either an hydraulically operated disc or a cable operated single leading shoe drum. The rear disc brake master cylinder and fluid reservoir assembly is mounted on the left handlebar.

All models covered in this manual are fitted with cast alloy wheels designed for tubeless tyres only.

Caution: Disc brake components rarely require disassembly. Do not disassemble components unless absolutely necessary. If an hydraulic brake hose is loosened, the

entire system must be disassembled, drained, cleaned and then properly filled and bled upon reassembly. Do not use solvents on internal brake components. Solvents will cause the seals to swell and distort. Use only clean brake fluid, a dedicated brake cleaner or denatured alcohol for cleaning. Use care when working with brake fluid as it can injure your eyes and it will damage painted surfaces and plastic parts.

2 Front brake pads – renewal

⚠ *Warning: The dust created by the brake system may contain asbestos, which is harmful to your health. Never blow it out with compressed air and don't inhale any of it. An approved*

filtering mask should be worn when working on the brakes.

1 Unscrew the brake caliper mounting bolts and slide the caliper off the disc (see Section 3). **Note:** *Do not operate the brake lever while the caliper is off the disc.*

2 The pads are retained in the caliper by two spring wire pins **(see illustration)**. Withdraw the pins, noting how they fit, then lift the pads out of the caliper **(see illustrations)**.

3 Inspect the surface of each pad for contamination and check that the friction material has not worn to or beyond the minimum thickness specified at the beginning of this Chapter **(see illustration)**. If either pad is worn down to, or beyond, the service limit, is fouled with oil or grease, or heavily scored or damaged, both pads must be renewed. **Note:** *It is not possible to degrease the friction material; if the pads are contaminated in any way they must be renewed.*

4 If the pads are in good condition, clean them carefully using a fine wire brush which is completely free of oil and grease to remove all traces of road dirt and corrosion. Spray the caliper with a dedicated brake cleaner to remove any dust and remove any traces of corrosion which might cause sticking of the caliper/pad operation.

5 Check the condition of the brake disc (see Section 4).

6 Remove all traces of corrosion from the pad pins. Inspect the pins for damage and loss of spring tension and renew them if necessary.

7 If new pads are being installed, slowly push the pistons as far back into the caliper as possible using hand pressure or a piece of wood for leverage. This will displace brake fluid back into the hydraulic reservoir, so it may be necessary to remove the reservoir cap, plate and diaphragm and siphon out some fluid (depending on how much fluid was in there in the first place and how far the pistons have to be pushed in). If the pistons are difficult to push back, attach a length of clear hose to the bleed valve and place the open end in a suitable container, then open the valve and try again. Take great care not to draw any air into the system and don't forget to tighten the valve once the pistons have been sufficiently displaced. If in doubt, bleed the brakes afterwards (see Section 8). *Caution: Never lever the caliper against the brake disc to push the pistons back into the caliper as damage to the disc will result.*

8 Smear the backs of the pads with copper-based grease, making sure that none gets on the front or sides of the pads.

9 Installation is the reverse of removal. Fit the pads into the caliper so that the friction material faces the disc, then install the pad pins and check that they lock in the recesses at the back of the caliper **(see illustrations)**.

10 Install the caliper onto the disc ensuring the pads fit over each side of the disc, then tighten the caliper bolts to the specified torque. Operate the brake lever several times to bring the pads into contact with the disc.

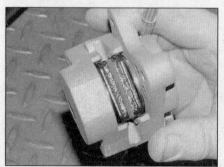

2.9a Ensure the pads are correctly
installed . . .

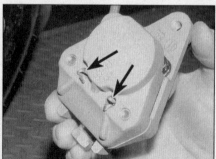

2.9b . . . and ensure the pins lock in the
back of the caliper

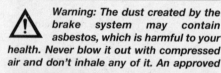

11 Check the level of fluid in the hydraulic reservoir and top-up if necessary (see *Daily (pre-ride) checks*).
12 Check the operation of the brake before riding the machine.

3 Front brake caliper – removal, inspection and installation

Note: *Caliper rebuild kits are not available for the models covered. If the caliper is leaking fluid from the piston seal area it must be renewed.*

⚠️ **Warning: If a caliper indicates the need for renewal (usually due to leaking fluid or sticky operation), all old brake fluid should be flushed from the system at the same time. Also, the dust created by the brake system may contain asbestos, which is harmful to your health. Never blow it out with compressed air and don't inhale any of it. An approved filtering mask should be worn when working on the brakes. Do not, under any circumstances, use petroleum-based solvents to clean brake parts. Use a dedicated brake cleaner or denatured alcohol only, as described. To prevent damage from spilled brake fluid, always cover paintwork when working on the braking system.**

Note: *On Speedfight models, the front wheel must be removed before the caliper can be removed (see Section 14).*

Removal

1 Unscrew the brake caliper mounting bolts and slide the caliper off the disc **(see illustrations)**. **Note:** *Do not operate the brake lever while the caliper is off the disc.*
2 If the caliper is just being displaced, the brake pads can be left in place. Support the caliper with a cable tie to ensure no strain is placed on the hydraulic hose.
3 If the caliper is being cleaned and inspected, remove the brake pads (see Section 2). **Note:** *It is not necessary to disconnect the brake hose to clean and inspect the caliper. Do not disconnect the brake hose from the caliper unless the caliper is being removed from the machine.*
4 To remove the caliper from the machine, first note the alignment of the banjo fitting on the caliper, then unscrew the banjo bolt and separate the hose from the caliper **(see illustration)**. Plug the hose end or wrap a plastic bag tightly around it to minimise fluid loss and prevent dirt entering the system. Discard the sealing washers as new ones must be used on installation.

Inspection

5 Clean the exterior of the caliper with denatured alcohol or brake system cleaner. Inspect the caliper for signs of damage, especially around the mounting lugs and the bleed screw and renew it if necessary. If

3.1a Undo the mounting bolts . . .

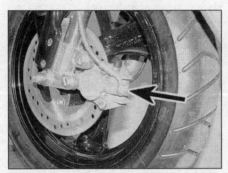

3.4 Unscrew the bolt to detach the hose

hydraulic fluid is leaking from around the edge of the piston, the internal piston seal has failed **(see illustration)**. Peugeot do not list caliper rebuild kits for the models covered and the caliper will have to be renewed – overhaul is not possible.

Installation

6 If the brake pads have been removed, install the pads (see Section 2).
7 Install the caliper onto the disc ensuring the pads fit over each side of the disc, then tighten the caliper bolts to the specified torque **(see illustration 3.1a)**. Operate the brake lever several times to bring the pads into contact with the disc.
8 If the caliper was removed from the machine, or a new caliper is being fitted, connect the brake hose to the caliper, using new sealing washers on each side of the banjo fitting. Align the banjo fitting as noted

4.2 Measuring the thickness of a disc with a micrometer

3.1b . . . and remove the caliper

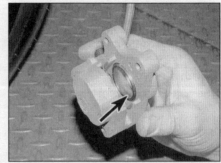

3.5 Fluid leaks indicate a failed seal

on removal. Tighten the banjo bolt securely and top-up the hydraulic reservoir with DOT 4 brake fluid (see *Daily (pre-ride) checks*). Bleed the hydraulic system (see Section 8).
9 Check for fluid leaks and check the operation of the brake before riding the machine.

4 Front brake disc – inspection, removal and installation

Note: *Always renew the brake pads if fitting a new disc.*

Inspection

1 Visually inspect the surface of the disc for score marks and other damage. Light scratches are normal after use and won't affect brake operation, but deep grooves and heavy score marks will reduce braking efficiency and accelerate pad wear. If a disc is badly scored it must be machined or renewed.
2 The disc must not be machined or allowed to wear down to a thickness less than the service limit as listed in this Chapter's Specifications. Check the thickness of the disc with a micrometer and renew it if necessary **(see illustration)**.
3 To check disc warpage, position the machine upright so that the wheel is raised off the ground. Attach a dial gauge to the suspension with the tip of the gauge touching the surface of the disc about 10 mm from the outer edge. Rotate the wheel and watch the

4.5 Unscrew the bolts (arrowed) to remove the disc

gauge needle; a small amount of movement is acceptable. If excessive movement is indicated, first check the wheel bearings for play (see Section 16). If the bearings are good, the disc is warped and should be renewed.

Removal

4 Remove the front wheel (see Section 14). On Speedfight models, also remove the hub assembly.

Caution: Do not lay the wheel down and allow it to rest on the disc – the disc could become warped.

5 If you are not renewing the disc, mark the relationship of the disc to the wheel so that it can be installed in the same position. Unscrew the disc retaining bolts, loosening them a little at a time to avoid distorting the disc, then remove the disc **(see illustration)**.

Installation

6 Before installing the disc, make sure there is no dirt or corrosion where the disc seats on the hub. If the disc does not sit flat when it is bolted down, it will appear to be warped when checked or when the front brake is used.

7 Align the previously applied register marks, if you are reinstalling the original disc, then install the bolts and tighten them evenly and a little at a time to the torque setting specified at the beginning of this Chapter. Clean the brake disc

using acetone or brake system cleaner. If a new brake disc has been installed, remove any protective coating from its working surfaces.

8 Install the hub assembly on Speedfight models, and the front wheel (see Section 14).

9 Operate the brake lever several times to bring the pads into contact with the disc. Check the operation of the brake before riding the machine.

5 Front brake master cylinder
– removal and installation

Note: *Master cylinder rebuild kits are not available for the models covered. If the master cylinder is leaking fluid, or if the lever does not produce a firm feel when the brake is applied, and bleeding the brakes does not help (see Section 8), and the hydraulic hoses are all in good condition, then the master cylinder must be renewed.*

Removal

1 Remove the handlebar covers for access (see Chapter 7).

2 If the master cylinder is just being displaced, ensure the fluid reservoir cover is secure. Unscrew the master cylinder clamp bolts and remove the back of the clamp **(see illustration)** . Position the assembly clear of the handlebar, making sure no strain is placed on the brake hose and the brake light switch wiring. Keep the fluid reservoir upright to prevent air entering the hydraulic system.

3 If the master cylinder is being removed, disconnect the brake light switch wiring connector and, if required unscrew the brake light switch (see Chapter 9).

4 Unscrew the brake hose banjo bolt and detach the banjo fitting, noting its alignment with the master cylinder **(see illustration)**. Once disconnected, clamp the hose and secure it in an upright position to minimise fluid loss. Wrap a clean plastic bag tightly

around the end to prevent dirt entering the system. Discard the sealing washers as new ones must be fitted on reassembly.

6 Undo the master cylinder clamp bolts and remove the back of the clamp, then lift the master cylinder and reservoir away from the handlebar **(see illustration 5.2)**.

7 Undo the reservoir cover retaining screws and lift off the cover, the diaphragm plate and the rubber diaphragm. Drain the brake fluid from the reservoir into a suitable container. Wipe any remaining fluid out of the reservoir with a clean rag.

8 If required, remove the brake lever (see Section 11).

Installation

9 Attach the master cylinder to the handlebar and fit the clamp, then tighten the bolts securely **(see illustration 5.2)**.

10 Connect the brake hose to the master cylinder, using new sealing washers on each side of the banjo union, and aligning the union as noted on removal **(see illustration 5.4)**. Tighten the banjo bolt securely.

11 If removed, install the brake lever and the brake light switch, and connect the wiring connector.

12 Fill the fluid reservoir with new DOT 4 brake fluid as described in *Daily (pre-ride) checks*, then bleed the air from the system (see Section 8).

13 Ensure the reservoir diaphragm is correctly seated and that the cover screws are tightened securely.

14 Check the operation of the brake before riding the machine.

6 Rear disc brake –
inspection, removal and installation

1 The procedures for removal, inspection and installation of the rear disc brake pads, caliper, disc and master cylinder are the same

5.2 Unscrew the clamp bolts

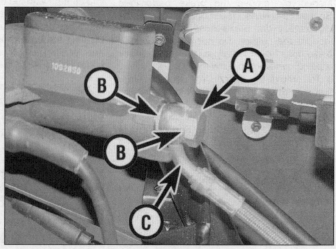

5.4 Brake hose banjo bolt (A), sealing washers (B) and banjo fitting (C)

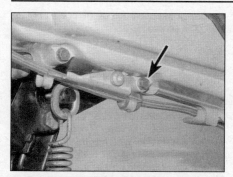

6.2 Undo the screw and remove the bracket

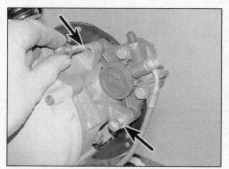

6.3 Brake caliper is secured by two bolts

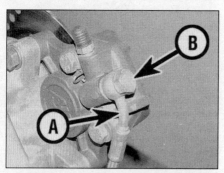

7.5 Note the alignment of the fitting (A) before undoing the bolt (B)

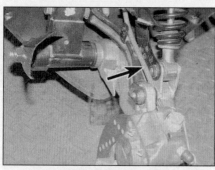

7.6 Ensure the brake hose is routed correctly

as for the front brake. **Note:** *The rear wheel must be removed before the caliper can be removed (see Section 15).*

2 Note the routing of the rear brake hose before displacing the caliper, then undo the screw securing the hose bracket to the underside of the drive belt cover and remove the bracket **(see illustration)**.

3 The caliper is secured to the transmission casing by two bolts **(see illustration)**.

4 If the caliper is just being displaced, secure it to the machine with a cable tie to avoid straining the hose. **Note:** *Do not operate the brake lever while the caliper is off the disc.*

5 After working on any component in the brake system, always check the operation of the brake before riding the machine.

7 Brake hose(s) and unions – inspection and renewal

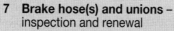

Inspection

1 Brake hose condition should be checked regularly and the hose(s) renewed at the specified interval (see Chapter 1).

2 Remove the body panels as necessary (see Chapter 7).

3 Twist and flex the hose while looking for cracks, bulges and seeping fluid. Check extra carefully around the areas where the hose connects with the banjo fittings, as these are common areas for hose failure.

4 Inspect the banjo fittings; if they are rusted, cracked or damaged, fit a new hose.

Renewal

5 The brake hose(s) have banjo fittings on each end. Cover the surrounding area with plenty of rags and unscrew the banjo bolt at each end of the hose, noting the alignment of the fitting with the master cylinder or brake caliper **(see illustration)**. Free the hose from any clips or guides and remove it, noting its routing. Discard the sealing washers. **Note:** *Do not operate the brake lever while a brake hose is disconnected.*

6 Position the new hose, making sure it is not twisted or otherwise strained, and ensure that it is correctly routed through any clips or

guides and is clear of all moving components **(see illustration)**.

7 Check that the fittings align correctly, then install the banjo bolts, using new sealing washers on both sides of the fittings **(see illustration 5.4)**. Tighten the banjo bolts securely.

8 Flush the old brake fluid from the system, refill with new DOT 4 brake fluid and bleed the air from the system (see Section 8).

9 Check the operation of the brakes before riding the scooter.

8 Brake hydraulic system – bleeding and fluid change

Bleeding

Caution: Support the machine in a upright position and turn the handlebars so that the hydraulic reservoir is level while carrying-out these procedures.

1 Bleeding the brakes is simply the process of removing air from the brake fluid reservoir, master cylinder, the hose and the brake caliper. Bleeding is necessary whenever a brake system connection is loosened, or when a component is replaced or renewed. Leaks in the system may also allow air to enter, but leaking brake fluid will reveal their presence and warn you of the need for repair.

2 To bleed the brake, you will need some new DOT 4 brake fluid, a small container partially filled with clean brake fluid (from a freshly opened container), a length of clear vinyl or

plastic hose, some rags and a spanner to fit the brake caliper bleed valve.

3 Remove the handlebar covers for access to the fluid reservoir (see Chapter 7) and cover any painted components to prevent damage in the event that brake fluid is spilled.

4 Remove the reservoir cover, diaphragm plate and diaphragm and slowly pump the brake lever a few times, until no air bubbles can be seen floating up from the holes in the bottom of the reservoir. This bleeds air from the master cylinder end of the line. Temporarily refit the reservoir cover.

5 Pull the dust cap off the caliper bleed valve **(see illustration)**. Attach one end of the clear vinyl or plastic hose to the bleed valve and submerge the other end in the brake fluid in the container **(see illustration)**. **Note:** *To avoid damaging the bleed valve during the procedure, loosen it and then tighten it temporarily with a ring spanner before*

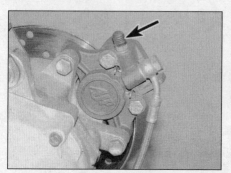

8.5a Pull the dust cap off the bleed valve (arrowed) . . .

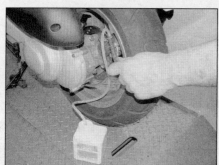

8.5b . . . and attach the hose

attaching the hose. With the hose attached, the valve can then be opened and closed with an open-ended spanner.

6 Check the fluid level in the reservoir. Do not allow the fluid level to drop below the half-way mark on the inspection window during the procedure **(see illustration)**.

7 Carefully pump the brake lever three or four times and hold it in while opening the caliper bleed valve. When the valve is opened, brake fluid will flow out of the caliper into the clear hose and the lever will move toward the handlebar.

8 Tighten the bleed valve, then release the brake lever gradually. Repeat the process until no air bubbles are visible in the brake fluid leaving the caliper and the lever is firm when applied. On completion, disconnect the hose, then tighten the bleed valve and fit the dust cap.

9 Top-up the reservoir, install the diaphragm, diaphragm plate and cover, and wipe up any spilled brake fluid. Check the entire system for fluid leaks.

 HAYNES HiNT *If it is not possible to produce a firm feel to the lever the fluid my be aerated. Let the brake fluid in the system stabilise for a few hours and then repeat the procedure when the tiny bubbles in the system have settled out.*

Fluid change

10 Changing the brake fluid is a similar process to bleeding the brakes and requires the same materials plus a suitable syringe for emptying the hydraulic reservoir and back-filling the system with fluid.

11 Remove the reservoir cover, diaphragm plate and diaphragm and siphon the old fluid out of the reservoir. Temporarily refit the reservoir cover but do not tighten the fixing screws.

12 Remove the brake caliper and slowly push the pistons as far back into the caliper as possible using hand pressure or a piece of wood for leverage, then siphon any residual

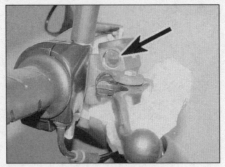
8.6 Check the fluid level

fluid from the reservoir. Refit the brake caliper. Leave the cover off the reservoir.

13 Fill the syringe with approximately 40 ml of new brake fluid and connect a short length of hose to the syringe. Bleed any air from the syringe and hose, then connect the hose to the caliper bleed valve. **Note:** *To avoid damaging the bleed valve during the procedure, loosen it and then tighten it temporarily with a ring spanner before attaching the hose. With the hose attached, the valve can then be opened and closed with an open-ended spanner.*

14 Open the bleed valve and carefully inject fluid into the system until the level in the reservoir is up to the half-way mark on the inspection window. Tighten the bleed valve, disconnect the hose and refit the dust cap.

15 Operate the brake lever carefully several times to bring the pads into contact with the disc, then check the fluid level in the reservoir and top-up if necessary (see *Daily (pre-ride) checks*).

 HAYNES HiNT *Old brake fluid is invariably much darker in colour than new fluid, making it easy to see when all old fluid has been expelled from the system.*

16 Install the diaphragm, diaphragm plate and cover, and wipe up any spilled brake fluid. Check the system for fluid leaks.

17 Check the operation of the brakes before riding the scooter.

9 Rear drum brake – inspection and shoe renewal

> ⚠ **Warning: The dust created by the brake system may contain asbestos, which is harmful to your health. Never blow it out with compressed air and don't inhale any of it. An approved filtering mask should be worn when working on the brakes.**

Inspection

1 Remove the wheel (see Section 15).

2 Check the condition of the friction material on the brake shoes **(see illustration)**. No minimum thickness specification is given, but if the wear indicator aligns with the index mark when the brake is applied, the shoes should be renewed.

3 Inspect the friction material for contamination. If it is fouled with oil or grease, or heavily scored or damaged, both shoes must be renewed as a set. Note that it is not possible to degrease the friction material; if the shoes are contaminated in any way they must be renewed.

4 If the shoes are in good condition, clean them carefully using a fine wire brush which is completely free of oil and grease to remove all traces of dust and corrosion.

5 Check the condition of the brake shoe springs; they should hold the shoes tightly in place against the operating cam and pivot post **(see illustration 9.2)**. Remove the shoes (see Steps 10 to 12) and renew the springs if they appear weak or are obviously deformed or damaged.

6 Clean the brake drum surface using acetone or brake system cleaner. Examine the surface for scoring and excessive wear **(see illustration)**. While light scratches are to be expected, heavy score marks will impair braking and there is no satisfactory way of

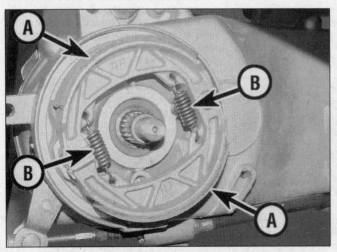
9.2 Check the friction material (A) and springs (B)

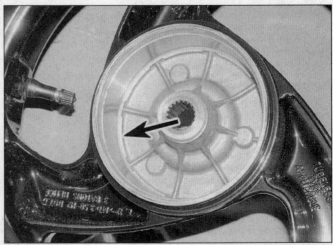
9.6 Check the surface of the brake drum (arrowed)

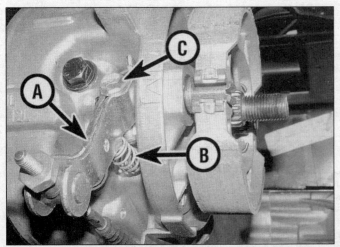

9.8 Brake arm (A), spring (B) and pinch bolt (C)

10.2 Release the cable from the brake arm

removing them; in this event the wheel should be renewed, although you could consult a specialist engineer who might be able to skim the surface.

7 Measure the internal diameter of the brake drum with a vernier caliper and compare the result with the standard specification at the beginning of this Chapter. Take several measurements to ensure the drum has not worn out-of-round. If the drum has worn, or is out-of-round, consult a Peugeot dealer or specialist engineer.

8 To check and lubricate the brake cam, first remove the brake shoes (see Steps 10 to 12). Note the position of the brake arm and spring, then loosen the brake arm pinch bolt and pull the cam out of the casing **(see illustration)**. Clean all traces of old grease off the cam and shaft. If the bearing surfaces of the cam or shaft are worn the cam should be renewed.

9 Lubricate the shaft with a smear of copper grease; position the brake arm and spring and install the cam in the casing, then tighten the pinch bolt securely. Lubricate the cam and the pivot post with a smear of copper grease and install the brake shoes.

Shoe renewal

10 Remove the wheel (see Section 15).

11 If the shoes are not going to be renewed they must be installed in their original positions; mark them to aid reassembly. Note how the springs are fitted.

12 Grasp the outer edge of each shoe and fold them inwards towards each other to release the spring tension and remove the shoes. Remove the springs from the shoes.

13 To install the shoes, first lubricate the cam and the pivot post with a smear of copper grease and hook the springs into the shoes. Position the shoes in a V on the cam and pivot post, then fold them down into position. Operate the brake arm to check that the cam and shoes work correctly.

14 Install the wheel and test the operation of the brake before riding the scooter.

10 Rear drum brake cable – renewal

1 Remove the body panels as necessary (see Chapter 7).

2 Fully unscrew the adjuster nut on the lower end of the cable, then pull the cable out of the brake arm **(see illustration)**.

3 Free the cable from any clips or guides.

4 Pull the outer cable out of the handlebar lever bracket and free the inner cable nipple from its socket in the underside of the lever **(see illustrations)**.

5 Withdraw the cable from the machine, noting its routing.

> **HAYNES HINT** *When fitting a new cable, tape the lower end of the new cable to the upper end of the old cable before removing it from the machine. Slowly pull the lower end of the old cable out, guiding the new cable down into position. Using this method will ensure the cable is routed correctly.*

6 Installation is the reverse of removal. Make sure the cable is correctly routed and clipped into place. Lubricate the cable nipple at the handlebar end with grease before fitting it into the lever and adjust the cable freeplay (see Chapter 1, Section 5).

7 Check the operation of the brake before riding the scooter.

11 Brake levers – removal and installation

1 Unscrew the lever pivot bolt locknut, then withdraw the pivot bolt and remove the lever **(see illustration)**. Where applicable, detach

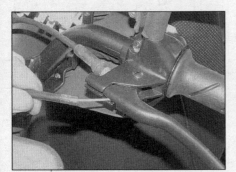

10.4a Pull the cable out of the bracket . . .

10.4b . . . and release the nipple from the lever

11.1 Brake lever pivot bolt locknut

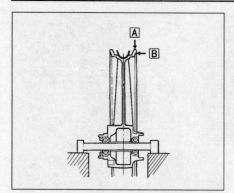

12.2 Check the wheel for radial (out-of-round) runout (A) and axial (side-to-side) runout (B)

the brake cable from the underside of the lever as you remove it.

2 Installation is the reverse of removal. Apply grease to the pivot bolt shank and the contact areas between the lever and its bracket, and to the brake cable nipple (where applicable).

12 Wheels –
inspection and repair

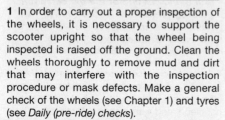

1 In order to carry out a proper inspection of the wheels, it is necessary to support the scooter upright so that the wheel being inspected is raised off the ground. Clean the wheels thoroughly to remove mud and dirt that may interfere with the inspection procedure or mask defects. Make a general check of the wheels (see Chapter 1) and tyres (see *Daily (pre-ride) checks*).

2 Attach a dial gauge to the suspension (front) or the transmission casing (rear) with the tip of the gauge touching the side of the rim **(see illustration)**. Spin the wheel slowly and check the axial (side-to-side) runout of the rim, then compare the result with the specifications at the beginning of this Chapter.

3 In order to accurately check radial (out-of-round) runout with the dial gauge, the wheel should be removed from the machine, and the tyre from the wheel. With the axle clamped in a vice or jig and the dial gauge positioned on the top of the rim, the wheel can be rotated to check the runout.

4 An easier, though slightly less accurate, method is to attach a stiff wire pointer to the front suspension or transmission casing with the end of the pointer a fraction of an inch from the edge of the wheel rim where the wheel and tyre join. If the wheel is true, the distance from the pointer to the rim will be constant as the wheel is rotated. **Note:** *If wheel runout is excessive, check the wheel bearings very carefully before renewing the wheel (see Section 16).*

5 The wheels should also be visually inspected for cracks, flat spots on the rim and other damage. Look very closely for dents in

the area where the tyre bead contacts the rim. Dents in this area may prevent complete sealing of the tyre against the rim, which leads to deflation of the tyre over a period of time. If damage is evident, or if runout is excessive, the wheel will have to be renewed. Never attempt to repair a damaged cast alloy wheel.

13 Wheels –
alignment check

1 Misalignment of the wheels can cause strange and potentially serious handling problems and will most likely be due to bent frame or suspension components as the result of an accident. If the frame or suspension are at fault, repair by a frame specialist or replacement with new parts are the only options.

2 To check wheel alignment you will need an assistant, a length of string or a perfectly straight piece of wood and a ruler. A plumb bob or spirit level for checking that the wheels are vertical will also be required. Support the scooter in an upright position on its stand.

3 If a string is used, have your assistant hold one end of it about halfway between the floor and the rear axle, with the string touching the back edge of the rear tyre sidewall.

4 Run the other end of the string forward and pull it tight so that it is roughly parallel to the floor. Slowly bring the string into contact with the front sidewall of the rear tyre, then turn the front wheel until it is parallel with the string. Measure the distance (offset) from the front tyre sidewall to the string **(see illustration)**. **Note:** *Where the same size tyre is fitted front and rear, there should be no offset.*

5 Repeat the procedure on the other side of the machine. The distance from the front tyre sidewall to the string should be equal on both sides.

6 As previously mentioned, a perfectly straight length of wood or metal bar may be substituted for the string **(see illustration)**.

7 If the distance between the string and tyre is greater on one side, or if the rear wheel appears to be out of alignment, have your machine checked by a Peugeot dealer.

8 If the front-to-back alignment is correct, the wheels still may be out of alignment vertically.

9 Using a plumb bob or spirit level, check the rear wheel to make sure it is vertical. To do

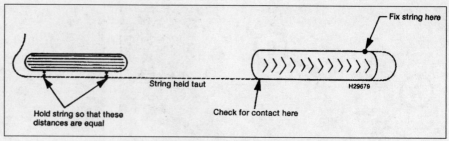

13.4 Wheel alignment check using string

this, hold the string of the plumb bob against the tyre upper sidewall and allow the weight to settle just off the floor. If the string touches both the upper and lower tyre sidewalls and is perfectly straight, the wheel is vertical. If it is not, adjust the stand by inserting spacers under its feet until it is.

10 Once the rear wheel is vertical, check the front wheel in the same manner. If both wheels are not perfectly vertical, the frame and/or major suspension components are bent.

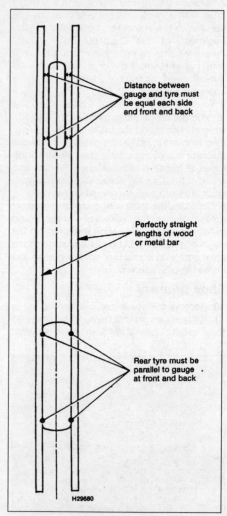

13.6 Wheel alignment check using a straight edge

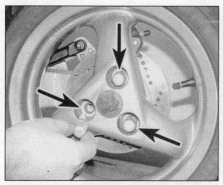

14.2 Front wheel is retained by three bolts

14.4 Speedometer cable retaining screw

14.5 Loosen the hub nut (arrowed)

14 Front wheel and hub assembly – removal and installation

Speedfight models – wheel

1 Support the machine in an upright position with the front wheel off the ground.
2 Undo the three bolts securing the wheel to the hub assembly and lift the wheel off the hub (see illustration).
3 To install the wheel, position it on the hub and align the bolt holes. Install the bolts and tighten them to the torque setting specified at the beginning of this Chapter.

Speedfight models – hub assembly

Removal

4 Remove the wheel (see above). On Speedfight 2 Furious models, remove the screw securing the lower end of the speedometer cable to the caliper bracket and disconnect the cable (see illustration).
5 Have an assistant apply the front brake, then loosen the hub nut (see illustration). Undo the brake caliper mounting bolts and slide the caliper off the disc (see Section 3). **Note**: *Do not operate the brake lever while the caliper is off the disc.*

6 Unscrew the hub nut and remove the nut and washer (see illustration).
7 Draw the hub assembly off the axle. Note how the speedometer drive tabs on the back of the hub locate in the speedometer gearbox in the brake caliper bracket (see illustration). Remove the plain washer fitted on the axle inside the speedometer gearbox (see illustration).
8 If required, unscrew the knurled ring that secures the speedometer cable to the speedometer gearbox, then undo the bolt securing the torque arm to the caliper bracket and disconnect the arm from the bracket (see illustration). Slide the bracket off the axle and draw the axle out of the monolever arm (see illustration).

14.6 Remove the nut and washer

14.7a Note how the speedometer drive tabs (arrowed) . . .

14.7b . . . locate on the speedometer gearbox tabs (arrowed)

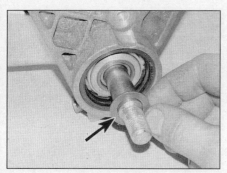

14.7c Remove the plain washer (arrowed)

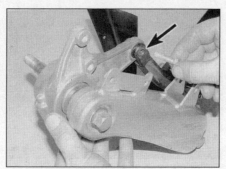

14.8a Undo the torque arm bolt (arrowed) . . .

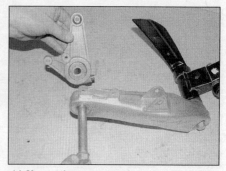

14.8b . . . then remove the caliper bracket and axle

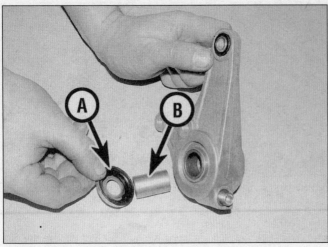

14.11a Check the condition of the dust cap (A) and sleeve (B) . . .

14.11b . . . speedometer gearbox seal (arrowed) . . .

9 Check the condition of the bearings in the hub (see Section 16).
10 Clean the axle and remove any corrosion using steel wool. Check the axle for straightness by rolling it on a flat surface such as a piece of plate glass. If available, place the axle in V-blocks and check it using a dial gauge. If the axle is bent, renew it.
11 Remove the dust cap from the caliper bracket and withdraw the sleeve (see illustration). Check the condition of the seal inside the cap and inspect the sleeve for wear. Check the condition of the seal inside the speedometer gearbox (see illustration). Press the sleeve out of the torque arm fixing point and check the condition of the sleeve

and the seals (see illustration). Renew any components that are worn or damaged. If new seals are being fitted, the old seals can be levered out of the caliper bracket with a flat-bladed screwdriver and a piece of wood. Take care not to damage the seal housings. Grease the new seals to aid installation and press them into place with a flat piece of wood.

Installation

12 Installation is the reverse of removal, noting the following:
• Lubricate the axle, bearings, sleeves and speedometer drive with grease.
• Ensure the dust cap is installed on the caliper bracket before sliding the bracket onto the axle.

• Ensure the plain washer is installed inside the speedometer gearbox before sliding the hub onto the axle.
• Apply non-permanent thread locking compound to the torque arm bolt.
• Tighten the hub nut to the torque setting specified at the beginning of this Chapter.

Trekker and Vivacity models – wheel

Removal

13 Support the machine in an upright position with the front wheel off the ground.
14 Unscrew the brake caliper mounting bolts and slide the caliper off the disc (see Section 3).
Note: *Do not operate the brake lever while the caliper is off the disc.*
15 Unscrew the knurled ring that secures the speedometer cable to the speedometer gearbox and disconnect the cable (see illustration).
Note: *On certain models the speedometer is electronically activated and the speedometer cable and drive housing are a one-piece unit. Do not attempt disconnected them.*
16 Counterhold the axle and undo the axle nut, then remove the nut and washer (see illustration). Note how the speedometer gearbox locates against the right-hand fork slider, then support the wheel and withdraw the axle from the wheel and front suspension (see illustration). Remove the speedometer

14.11c . . . and torque arm fixing sleeve (arrowed)

14.15 Disconnect the speedometer cable

14.16a Remove the axle nut and washer

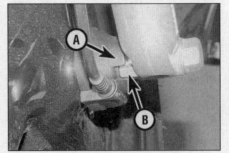

14.16b Note how the speedometer gearbox (A) locates against the fork slider (B)

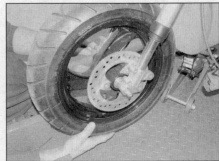

14.16c Support the wheel and withdraw the axle . . .

14.16d . . . then remove the speedometer gearbox (arrowed)

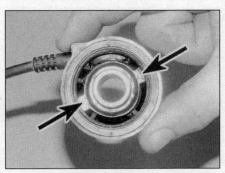

14.19a Tabs inside the speedometer gearbox (arrowed) . . .

14.19b . . . locate against tabs on the wheel hub (arrowed)

gearbox from the right-hand side of the wheel, noting how it fits, and remove the wheel **(see illustration)**.
Caution: Don't lay the wheel down and allow it to rest on the disc – the disc could become warped. Set the wheel on wood blocks so the disc doesn't support the weight of the wheel.
17 Clean the axle and remove any corrosion using steel wool. Check the axle for straightness by rolling it on a flat surface such as a piece of plate glass. If available, place the axle in V-blocks and check it using a dial gauge. If the axle is bent, renew it.
18 Check the condition of the wheel bearings (see Section 16).

Installation

19 Manoeuvre the wheel into position, making sure the brake disc is on the correct side. On models with a cable activated

speedometer, apply some grease to the inside of the speedometer gearbox. Install the speedometer gearbox, ensuring it locates correctly on the wheel hub **(see illustrations)**.
20 Lubricate the axle with a smear of grease, then lift the wheel into place between the forks. Check that the stepped section on the outside of the speedometer gearbox is located correctly against the corresponding section on the inside of the fork. Slide the axle in carefully from the right-hand side, ensuring the fork legs and wheel remain in alignment.
21 Install the washer and axle nut and tighten the nut to the torque setting specified at the beginning of this Chapter.
22 Install the brake caliper, making sure the pads fit on each side of the disc (see Section 3). Tighten the caliper bolts to the specified torque.
23 Connect the speedometer cable and tighten the knurled ring.
24 Move the scooter off its stand, apply the

front brake and pump the front forks a few times to settle all components in position.
25 Check the operation of the front brake before riding the scooter.

15 Rear wheel and hub assembly – removal and installation

Speedfight models – wheel

Note: *It is not possible to remove the rear wheel on its own with the exhaust system in place. If the exhaust system has been removed, undo the three wheel bolts and lift the wheel off the hub. To remove the wheel without disturbing the exhaust system, the wheel and hub assembly have to be removed together as follows.*

Removal

1 Position the scooter on its stand and support it so that the rear wheel is off the ground.
2 Lever the centre cap off with a small flat-bladed screwdriver **(see illustration)**.
3 Have an assistant apply the rear brake, then loosen the hub nut **(see illustration)**.
4 Undo the three bolts securing the wheel to the hub assembly and displace the wheel **(see illustration)**.
5 Undo the brake caliper mounting bolts (see Section 6) and slide the caliper off the disc **(see illustration)**. **Note:** *Do not operate the brake lever while the caliper is off the disc.*
6 Temporarily fit the wheel back onto the hub and secure it with one bolt, then unscrew the hub nut and remove the nut and washer **(see illustration)**. Slide the wheel and hub

15.2 Remove the cap . . .

15.3 . . . then loosen the hub nut

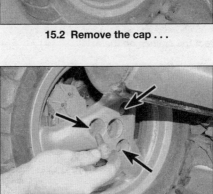

15.4 Remove the three wheel bolts

15.5 Slide the brake caliper off the disc

15.6a Remove the hub nut and washer

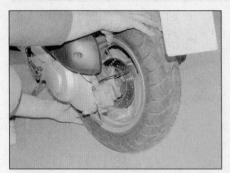

15.6b Slide the wheel off the axle . . .

15.6c . . . and withdraw it from the machine

assembly off the axle, then tilt the wheel and withdraw it from the machine on the left-hand side **(see illustrations)**.

7 Undo the remaining wheel bolt and separate the hub assembly from the wheel. Inspect the components for wear and damage (see Step 11).

Installation

8 Installation is the reverse of removal. When fitting the hub onto the wheel prior to installing the wheel, only tighten the wheel bolt finger-tight. When the hub, wheel and brake caliper are all in place, tighten the caliper mounting bolts, the wheel bolts and the hub nut in that order to the specified torque settings.

Speedfight models – hub assembly

Removal

9 If the wheel has already been removed from the hub assembly, have an assistant apply the rear brake, then loosen the hub nut. Undo the brake caliper mounting bolts and slide the caliper off the disc (see Section 6). **Note**: *Do not operate the brake lever while the caliper is off the disc.*

10 Unscrew the hub nut and remove the nut and washer, then draw the hub assembly off the axle **(see illustration)**.

11 Inspect the splines on the axle and on the inside of the hub for wear and damage **(see**

illustrations). Fit the hub onto the axle and check for backlash in the splines. If the splines are worn, both components should be renewed. To renew the axle, the transmission relay box must first be disassembled (see Chapter 2C).

Installation

12 Installation is the reverse of removal (see Step 8).

Trekker and Vivacity models – wheel

Caution: It is not possible to remove the rear wheel on Trekker models with the exhaust system in place. Do not remove the exhaust system mounting bolts and attempt to lever the wheel behind the silencer with the exhaust manifold still connected. Damage to the manifold studs and cylinder will result.

Removal

13 Position the scooter on its stand and support it so that the rear wheel is off the ground.

14 On Trekker models, remove the exhaust system (see Chapter 4).

15 Lever the centre cap off with a small flat-bladed screwdriver **(see illustration)**.

16 Have an assistant apply the rear brake, then unscrew the wheel nut and remove the nut and washer **(see illustration)**.

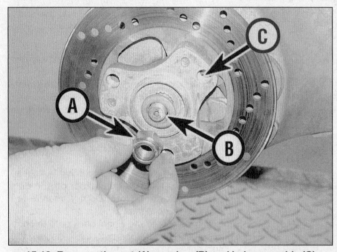

15.10 Remove the nut (A), washer (B) and hub assembly (C)

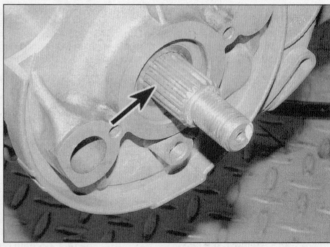

15.11a Inspect the splines on the axle . . .

15.11b . . . and inside the hub (arrowed)

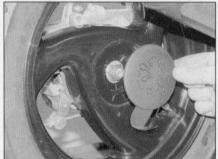

15.15 Remove the cap . . .

15.16 . . . and remove the hub nut and washer

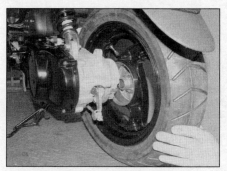

15.17a Slide the wheel off the axle . . .

15.17b . . . and withdraw it from the machine

15.18 Inspect the splines for wear and damage

17 Slide the wheel off the axle and manoeuvre it out of the back of the machine **(see illustrations)**.

18 Inspect the splines on the axle and on the inside of the hub for wear and damage **(see illustration)**. If the splines are worn, both components should be renewed. To renew the axle, the transmission relay box must first be disassembled (see Chapter 2C).

Installation

19 Installation is the reverse of removal. Slide the wheel onto the axle carefully to avoid disturbing the alignment of the brake shoes. Tighten the wheel nut to the specified torque setting.

16 Wheel bearings –
check and renewal

1 The front wheel bearings are housed in the separate hub assembly on Speedfight models and in the wheel hub on Trekker and Vivacity models. There are no rear wheel bearings as such, the rear axle/output shaft bearings are housed in the transmission relay box (see Chapter 2C).

Front wheel bearings

Speedfight models

2 Remove the wheel and the hub assembly (see Section 14).

3 Inspect the bearings – check that the inner race turns smoothly without any rough spots, and that the outer race is a tight fit in the hub. If a bearing grates or rattles, it is worn and must be renewed. **Note:** *Always renew the wheel bearings in pairs, never individually.*

4 To remove the bearings, stand the hub assembly on a suitable spacer to allow the bearings to be driven out.

Caution: Do not support the hub on the brake disc when driving out the bearings.

5 Use a metal rod (preferably a brass drift punch) inserted through the centre of the bearing on the one side of the hub, to tap evenly around the outer race of the bearing on the other side **(see illustrations)**. The bearing spacer will come out with the bearing.

6 Turn the hub over and drive out the remaining bearing using the same procedure.

7 Thoroughly clean the hub with a suitable solvent and inspect the bearing seats for scoring and wear. If the seats are damaged, consult a Peugeot dealer before reassembling the wheel.

8 Install a new bearing into its seat in one side of the hub, with the marked or sealed side facing outwards. Using the old bearing, a bearing driver or a socket large enough to contact the outer race of the bearing only (it must not contact the inner race or balls), drive it in squarely until it's completely seated **(see illustration)**.

9 Turn the hub over, install the bearing spacer and drive the other new bearing into place.

10 Install the hub assembly and the wheel (see Section 14).

Trekker and Vivacity models

Caution: Don't lay the wheel down and allow it to rest on the brake disc – it could become warped. Set the wheel on wood blocks so the wheel rim supports the weight of the wheel.

11 Remove the wheel (see Section 14). Remove the spacer and dust cap from the right-hand side of the wheel hub.

12 Inspect the bearings – check that the inner race turns smoothly without any rough spots, and that the outer race is a tight fit in the hub. If a bearing grates or rattles, it is worn and must be renewed. **Note:** *Always renew the wheel bearings in pairs, never individually.*

13 To remove the bearings, set the wheel on blocks. Use a metal rod (preferably a brass drift punch) inserted through the centre of the bearing on the one side of the wheel hub, to tap evenly around the outer race of the bearing on the other side. The bearing spacer will come out with the bearing.

14 Turn the wheel over and drive out the remaining bearing using the same procedure.

15 Thoroughly clean the hub with a suitable solvent and inspect the bearing seats for scoring and wear. If the seats are damaged, consult a Peugeot dealer before reassembling the wheel.

16 Install a new bearing into its seat in one side of the wheel hub, with the marked or sealed side facing outwards. Using the old

16.5a Driving a bearing out of the hub

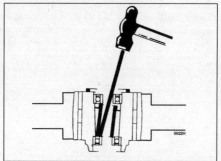

16.5b Locate the rod as shown when driving out a bearing

16.8 Installing a new bearing `

bearing, a bearing driver or a socket large enough to contact the outer race of the bearing only (it must not contact the inner race or balls), drive it in squarely until it's completely seated.

17 Turn the wheel over, install the bearing spacer and drive the other new bearing into place.

18 Install the dust cap and spacer into the right-hand side of the hub and install the wheel (see Section 14).

Rear wheel bearings

19 There are no bearings fitted in the rear wheel or the rear hub. Refer to Chapter 2C for renewal of the rear axle/output shaft bearings in the transmission relay box.

17 Tyres –
general information and fitting

General information

1 The wheels fitted to all models are designed to take tubeless tyres only. Tyre sizes are given in the *Service specifications* in Chapter 1.

2 Refer to *Daily (pre-ride) checks* at the beginning of this manual for tyre maintenance.

Fitting new tyres

3 When selecting new tyres, refer to the tyre information given in the owners handbook. Ensure that front and rear tyre types are compatible, the correct size and correct speed rating. If necessary seek advice from a Peugeot dealer or tyre fitting specialist **(see illustration)**.

4 It is recommended that tyres are fitted by a tyre specialist rather than attempted in the home workshop. This is particularly relevant in the case of tubeless tyres because the force required to break the seal between the wheel rim and tyre bead is substantial, and is usually beyond the capabilities of an individual working with normal tyre levers. Additionally, the specialist will be able to balance the wheels after tyre fitting.

5 Note that although punctured tubeless tyres can in some cases be repaired, Peugeot do not recommend the use of repaired tyres. Do not fit an inner tube inside a tubeless tyre.

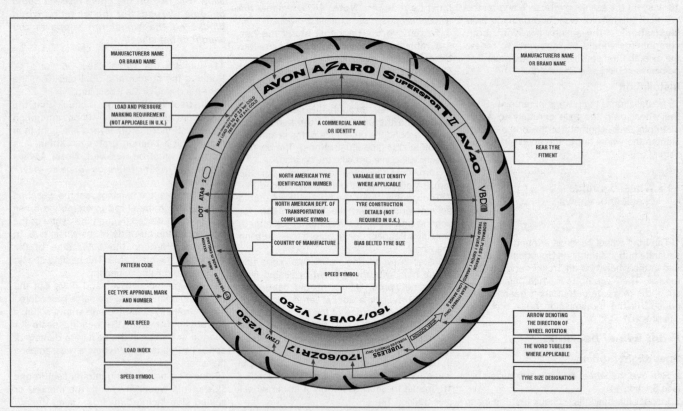

17.3 Common tyre sidewall markings

Chapter 9
Electrical system

Refer to Chapter 1 for model identification details

Contents

Degrees of difficulty

Easy, suitable for novice with little experience	Fairly easy, suitable for beginner with some experience	Fairly difficult, suitable for competent DIY mechanic	Difficult, suitable for experienced DIY mechanic	Very difficult, suitable for expert DIY or professional

Specifications

Battery
Capacity . . . . 12 V, 4 Ah (5 Ah on MF gel batteries)
Voltage
   Fully charged @ 20°C . . . . 14.0 to 15.0 V
   Discharged @ 20°C . . . . 10.7 V
Recharge rate (all models) . . . . 0.5 Amps for 5 to 10 hrs

Alternator
Voltage output (unregulated) . . . . 18 to 22 V (AC) at ½ to ¾ throttle
Lighting coil resistance @ 20°C . . . . 0.48 to 0.72 ohms
Charging coil resistance @ 20°C . . . . 0.64 to 0.96 ohms

Regulator/rectifier
Regulated voltage output
   Battery charging . . . . 14 to 15 V (DC) at ½ to ¾ throttle
   Lighting circuit . . . . 12.6 to 13.6 V (AC) at ½ to ¾ throttle

Fuse
Main . . . . 5 Amps

Lighting resistor
Resistance . . . . 4.7 to 7 ohms

Fuel level sender
Resistance with tank full . . . . 0 to 12 ohms
Resistance with tank empty . . . . 90 to 120 ohms

Oil level sensor
Resistance with tank full . . . .   Infinite resistance
Resistance with tank empty . . . .   0.1 to 0.5 ohms

Starter relay
Primary resistance . . . .   65.8 ohms
Secondary resistance . . . .   0.1 to 0.5 ohms

Bulbs
Headlight (main/dipped) . . . .   35/35 W
Sidelight (where fitted) . . . .   5 W
Tail/brake light . . . .   21/5 W
Licence plate light (where fitted) . . . .   5 W
Turn signal lights . . . .   10 W
Instrument and warning lights . . . .   1.2 W

Torque settings
Alternator stator bolts . . . .   10 Nm
Alternator rotor nut . . . .   40 Nm

1 General information

All models have a 12-volt electrical system charged by a three-phase alternator with a separate regulator/rectifier.

The regulator maintains the charging system output within the specified range to prevent overcharging, and the rectifier converts the AC (alternating current) output of the alternator to DC (direct current) to power the lights and other components and to charge the battery. The alternator rotor is mounted on the right-hand end of the crankshaft.

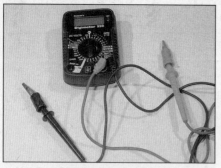

2.5 A multimeter is capable of reading ohms, amps and volts

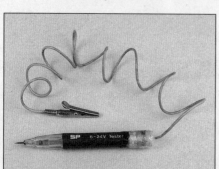

2.6a A test light . . .

All models are fitted with an electric starter motor. The starting system includes the motor, the battery, the relay and the various wires and switches.

Note: *Keep in mind that electrical parts, once purchased, cannot be returned. To avoid unnecessary expense, make very sure the faulty component has been positively identified before buying a replacement part.*

2 Electrical system – fault finding

⚠ *Warning: To prevent the risk of short circuits, the ignition (main) switch must always be OFF and the battery negative (-ve) terminal should be disconnected before any of the scooter's other electrical components are disturbed. Don't forget to reconnect the terminal securely once work is finished or if battery power is needed for circuit testing.*

Tracing faults

1 A typical electrical circuit consists of an electrical component, the switches, relays, etc related to that component and the wiring and connectors that hook the component to both the battery and the frame. To aid in locating a problem in any electrical circuit, refer to the

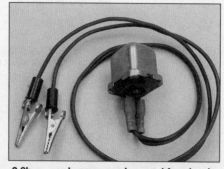

2.6b . . . or buzzer can be used for simple voltage checks

Wiring Diagrams at the end of this Chapter.
2 Before tackling any troublesome electrical circuit, first study the wiring diagram thoroughly to get a complete picture of what makes up that individual circuit. Trouble spots, for instance, can often be narrowed down by noting if other components related to that circuit are operating properly or not. If several components or circuits fail at one time, chances are the fault lies in the fuse or earth connection.
3 Electrical problems often stem from simple causes, such as loose or corroded connections or a blown fuse. Prior to any electrical fault finding, always visually check the condition of the fuse, wires and connections in the problem circuit. Intermittent failures can be especially frustrating, since you can't always duplicate the failure when it's convenient to test. In such situations, a good practice is to clean all connections in the affected circuit, whether or not they appear to be good. All of the connections and wires should also be wiggled to check for looseness which can cause intermittent failure.
4 If testing instruments are going to be utilised, use the wiring diagram to plan where you will make the necessary connections in order to accurately pinpoint the trouble spot.

Using test equipment

5 The basic tools needed for electrical fault finding include a battery and bulb test circuit, a continuity tester, a test light, and a jumper wire. A multimeter capable of reading volts, ohms and amps is also very useful as an alternative to the above, and is necessary for performing more extensive tests and checks **(see illustration)**.
6 Voltage checks should be performed if a circuit is not functioning properly. Connect one lead of a test light or voltmeter to either the negative battery terminal or a known good earth **(see illustrations)**. Connect the other lead to a connector in the circuit being tested, preferably nearest to the battery or fuse. If the

bulb lights, voltage is reaching that point, which means the part of the circuit between that connector and the battery is problem-free. Continue checking the remainder of the circuit in the same manner. When you reach a point where no voltage is present, the problem lies between there and the last good test point. Most of the time the problem is due to a loose connection. Keep in mind that some circuits only receive voltage when the ignition is ON.

7 An earth check should be done to see if a component is earthed properly. Disconnect the battery and connect one lead of a self-powered test light (continuity tester) to a known good earth **(see illustrations)**. Connect the other lead to the wire or earth connection being tested. If the bulb lights, the earth is good. If the bulb does not light, the earth is not good.

8 A continuity check is performed to see if a circuit, section of circuit or individual component is capable of passing electricity through it. Disconnect the battery and connect one lead of a self-powered test light (continuity tester) to one end of the circuit being tested and the other lead to the other end of the circuit. If the bulb lights, there is continuity, which means the circuit is passing electricity through it properly. Switches can be checked in the same way.

 Remember that all electrical circuits are designed to conduct electricity from the battery, through the wires, switches, relays, etc. to the electrical component (light bulb, motor, etc.). From there it is directed to the frame (earth) where it is passed back to the battery. Electrical problems are basically an interruption in the flow of electricity from the battery or back to it.

3 Battery –
removal, installation and checks

⚠️ **Warning: Be extremely careful when handling or working around the battery. Do not allow electrolyte to come in contact with your skin or painted or plastic surfaces of the scooter. Rinse off any spills immediately with plenty of water. Check with the local authorities about disposing of an old battery. Many communities will have collection centres which will see that batteries are disposed of safely.**

Removal and installation

1 On all models the battery holder is located on the frame in front of the engine unit. Remove the battery access panel (see Chapter 7).
2 Undo the negative (-ve) terminal screw first

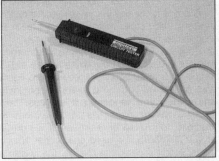
2.7a Continuity can be checked with a battery powered tester . . .

and disconnect the lead from the battery, then unscrew the positive (+ve) terminal screw and disconnect the lead.
3 Undo the screw securing the battery strap or displace the strap and lift the battery from its holder **(see illustrations)**.
4 Before installation, clean the battery terminals, terminal screws, nuts and lead ends with a wire brush, knife or steel wool to ensure a good electrical connection.
5 Install the battery, then reconnect the leads, connecting the positive (+ve) lead first, and secure the battery strap.

 Battery corrosion can be kept to a minimum by applying a layer of petroleum jelly to the terminals after the cables have been connected.

6 Fit the battery access panel.

Inspection and maintenance – conventional battery

7 The battery fitted to most models is of the conventional lead/acid type, requiring regular checks of the electrolyte level (see Chapter 1) in addition to those detailed below.
8 Check the battery terminals and leads for tightness and corrosion. If corrosion is evident, undo the terminal screws and disconnect the leads from the battery, disconnecting the negative (-ve) terminal first. Wash the terminals and lead ends in a solution of baking soda and hot water and dry them thoroughly. If necessary, further clean

3.3a Battery strap is retained by a screw (arrowed) . . .

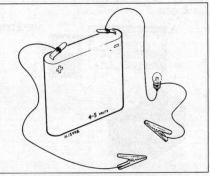
2.7b . . . or a battery and bulb circuit

the terminals and lead ends with a wire brush, knife or steel wool. Reconnect the leads, connecting the negative (-ve) terminal last, and apply a thin coat of petroleum jelly to the connections to slow further corrosion.
9 The battery case should be kept clean to prevent current leakage, which can discharge the battery over a period of time (especially when it sits unused). Wash the outside of the case with a solution of baking soda and water. Rinse the battery thoroughly, then dry it.
10 Look for cracks in the case and renew the battery if any are found. If acid has been spilled on the battery holder or surrounding bodywork, neutralise it with a baking soda and water solution, dry it thoroughly, then touch up any damaged paint.
11 If the machine is not used for long periods of time, disconnect the leads from the battery terminals, negative (-ve) terminal first. Refer to Section 4 and charge the battery once every month to six weeks.
12 The condition of the battery can be assessed by measuring the voltage present at the battery terminals with a multimeter. Connect the meter positive (+ve) probe to the battery positive (+ve) terminal, and the negative (-ve) probe to the battery negative (-ve) terminal. Compare the reading with the specifications given at the beginning of this Chapter. If the voltage falls below 12 volts the battery must be removed, disconnecting the negative (-ve) terminal first, and recharged as described below in Section 4. **Note:** *Before taking the measurement, wait at least 30 minutes after any charging has taken place (including running the engine).*

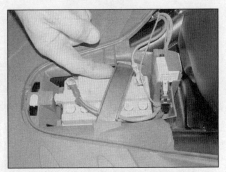
3.3b . . . or in a slot in the holder

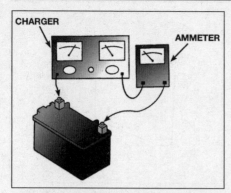

4.3 If the charger has no built-in ammeter, connect one in series as shown. DO NOT connect the ammeter between the battery terminals or it will be ruined

13 If battery condition is suspect, connect the multimeter to the battery terminals as before (see Step 12), turn the ignition ON and press the starter button. If the meter reading drops below 8 volts a new battery is required.

Inspection and maintenance – maintenance-free battery

14 Later models are fitted with a maintenance-free battery, either a lead-acid type or gel type. Inspect the terminals and case as for a conventional battery (see Steps 8 to 10). If the machine is not used for long periods of time, disconnect the leads from the battery terminals and charge the battery periodically (see Section 4).

15 Battery condition can be assessed as for a conventional battery (see Steps 12 and 13).

4 Battery – charging

Caution: Be extremely careful when handling or working around the battery. The electrolyte is very caustic and an explosive gas (hydrogen) is given off when the battery is charging.

1 Ensure the charger is suitable for charging a 12V battery.

2 Remove the battery (see Section 3). Connect the charger to the battery **BEFORE** switching the charger ON. Make sure that the

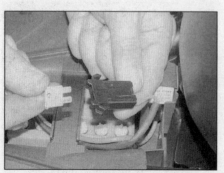

5.1 Remove the fuse to check it

positive (+ve) lead on the charger is connected to the positive (+ve) terminal on the battery, and the negative (-ve) lead is connected to the negative (-ve) terminal.

3 Peugeot recommend that a discharged battery is charged at a maximum rate of 0.5 amps for 5 to 10 hours. Exceeding this figure can cause the battery to overheat, buckling the plates and rendering it useless. Few owners will have access to an expensive current controlled charger, so if a normal domestic charger is used check that after a possible initial peak, the charge rate falls to a safe level **(see illustration)**. If the battery becomes hot during charging **STOP**. Further charging will cause damage. **Note:** *In emergencies the battery can be charged at a higher rate of around 5.0 amps for a period of 30 minutes. However, this is not recommended and the low amp charge is by far the safer method of charging the battery.*

4 When charging a maintenance-free battery, make sure that you use a regulated battery charger. If using a constant voltage charger, ensure that the voltage does not exceed 15.2V otherwise the battery could be ruined.

5 If the recharged battery discharges rapidly if left disconnected it is likely that an internal short caused by physical damage or sulphation has occurred. A new battery will be required. A sound item will tend to lose its charge at about 1% per day.

6 Install the battery (see Section 3).

5 Fuse – check and replacement

1 The electrical system is protected by a fuse which is located in a holder next to the battery. Pull the fuse out of its holder to check it visually **(see illustration)**.

2 A blown fuse is easily identified by a break in the element **(see illustration)**. The fuse is clearly marked with its rating and must only be replaced by a fuse of the correct rating (see Specifications at the beginning of this Chapter). It is advisable to carry a spare fuse on the scooter at all times.

⚠ *Warning: Never put in a fuse of a higher rating or bridge the terminals with any other*

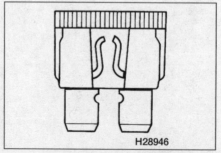

5.2 A blown fuse can be identified by a break in the element

substitute, however temporary it may be. Serious damage may be done to the circuit, or a fire may start.

3 If the fuse blows, be sure to check the wiring circuit very carefully for evidence of a short-circuit. Look for bare wires and chafed, melted or burned insulation. If the fuse is renewed before the cause is located, the new fuse will blow immediately.

4 Occasionally the fuse will blow or cause an open-circuit for no obvious reason. Corrosion of the fuse ends and fuseholder terminals may occur and cause poor fuse contact. If this happens, remove the corrosion with a wire brush or steel wool, then spray the fuse end and fuseholder terminals with electrical contact cleaner.

6 Lighting system – check

1 The alternator provides power for operation of the headlight, rear light, brake light, turn signal lights and instrument cluster lights. The engine must be running for any of these to work. If none of the lights work, always check the alternator lighting coil before proceeding (see Section 30). Also, check the condition of the lighting resistor (see Step 23).

Headlight

2 If the headlight fails to work, first check the bulb and the terminals in the bulbholder or the bulb wiring connector (see Section 7). Next check for voltage on the supply side of the bulbholder or wiring connector with a test light or multimeter. Refer to *Wiring Diagrams* at the end of this Chapter, then connect the negative (-ve) probe of the multimeter to earth (ground) and the positive (+ve) probe to first the high beam connector terminal (yellow/blue wire) and then the low beam connector terminal (white wire) with the engine running and light switch ON. Don't forget to select either high or low beam at the handlebar switch while conducting this test. Turn the engine OFF.

3 If no voltage is indicated at either terminal, check the wiring between the bulbholder or wiring connector and the light switch, then check the switch (see Section 22).

4 If voltage is indicated, check for continuity between the green wire terminal and earth (ground). If there is no continuity, check the earth (ground) circuit for a broken or poor connection.

5 On Speedfight 2 models, check the terminals in the headlight unit wiring connector **(see illustration)**.

Sidelight (where fitted)

6 If the sidelight fails to work, first check the bulb and the terminals in the bulbholder (see Section 7). Next check for voltage on the supply side of the bulbholder (brown wire) with the engine running and light switch in the 'sidelights' position. Turn the engine OFF.

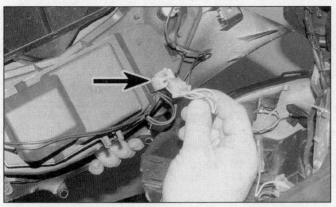

6.5 Check the headlight wiring connector terminals

6.23 Lighting resistor is located behind the headlight panel

7 If no voltage is indicated, check the wiring between the bulbholder and the light switch, then check the switch (see Section 22).

8 On Speedfight 2 models, check the terminals in the headlight unit wiring connector **(see illustration 6.5)**.

Tail light

9 If the tail light fails to work, first check the bulb and the terminals in the bulbholder (see Section 9). Next check for voltage on the supply side of the bulbholder wiring connector (brown wire) with the engine running and light switch ON. Turn the engine OFF.

10 If no voltage is indicated, check the rear light wiring circuit (see *Wiring Diagrams* at the end of this Chapter).

11 If voltage is indicated, check for continuity between the green wire terminal and earth (ground). If there is no continuity, check the earth (ground) circuit for a broken or poor connection.

Brake light

12 If the brake light fails to work, first check the bulb and the terminals in the bulbholder (see Section 9). Next check for voltage on the supply side of the bulbholder wiring connector (yellow/green wire) with the engine running and the brake lever pulled in. Turn the engine OFF.

13 If no voltage is indicated, check the brake light switches (see Section 11), then the brake light wiring circuit (see *Wiring Diagrams* at the end of this Chapter).

14 If voltage is present, check the earth (ground) circuit for a broken or poor connection (see Step 11). Note that a resistor is fitted in the earth wire to the brake light to prevent the current backfeed as the starter button is released from blowing the brake light bulb. If the resistor has failed, there will be no continuity in the earth circuit.

Licence plate light (where fitted)

15 If the light fails to work, first check the bulb and the terminals in the bulbholder (see Section 12). Next check for voltage on the supply side of the bulbholder wiring connector (brown wire) with the engine

running and light switch ON. Turn the engine OFF.

16 If no voltage is indicated, check the number plate light wiring circuit (see *Wiring Diagrams* at the end of this Chapter).

17 If voltage is indicated, check for continuity between the green wire terminal and earth (ground). If there is no continuity, check the earth (ground) circuit for a broken or poor connection.

Turn signal lights

18 If one light fails to work, check the bulb, the bulb terminals in the bulb socket and the wiring connectors (see Section 14). If none of the turn signals work, check the turn signal circuit (see Section 13).

Instrument cluster lights

Note: *On Speedfight 2 Furious and Metal-X Furious models, the warning lights are illuminated by LEDs. If a light fails to work, and the fault cannot be traced to a wiring or component failure, the instrument cluster will have to be replaced with a new one.*

19 If one light fails to work, check the bulb and the bulb terminals (see Section 18). If none of the lights work, refer to *Wiring Diagrams* at the end of this Chapter, then check for voltage at the brown wire terminal on the supply side of the instrument cluster wiring connector, with the engine running and light switch ON. Turn the engine OFF.

20 If no voltage is indicated, check the wiring between the connector, the light switch and the ignition switch, then check the switches themselves (see Section 22).

21 If voltage is indicated, disconnect the multi-pin wiring connector and check for continuity between the brown wire terminal on the instrument cluster and the corresponding terminals in the bulbholders; no continuity indicates a break in the circuit.

22 If continuity is present, check for continuity between the green wire terminal in the wiring connector and earth (ground). If there is no continuity, check the earth (ground) circuit for a broken or poor connection.

Lighting system resistor

23 The lighting system incorporates a resistor to absorb current from the alternator when the lights are turned off (see *Wiring Diagrams* at the end of this Chapter). Remove the headlight panel (see Chapter 7) and disconnect the resistor wiring connectors **(see illustration)**.

24 To check the resistor, measure the resistance between the terminals on the resistor side of the connectors with a multimeter set to the ohms x 1 scale. If the result is not as specified at the beginning of this Chapter, renew the resistor.

---

7 Headlight bulb and sidelight bulb – renewal

Note: *If the headlight bulb is of the quartz-halogen type, do not touch the bulb glass as skin acids will shorten the bulb's service life. If the bulb is accidentally touched, it should be wiped carefully when cold with a rag soaked in methylated spirit and dried before fitting.*

⚠️ **Warning: Allow the bulb time to cool before removing it if the headlight has just been on.**

Headlight

1 Displace the headlight panel (see Chapter 7). On Speedfight models, unclip the back of the headlight unit and remove it **(see illustrations)**.

7.1a Unclip the back of the headlight panel . . .

7.1b . . . and remove it

7.1c Lift the flap on Vivacity models

7.2a Remove the wiring connector . . .

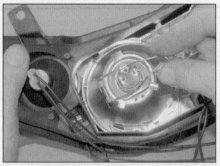

7.2b . . . then release the clip . . .

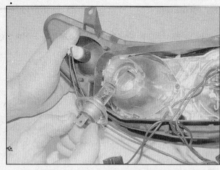

7.2c . . . and remove the bulb

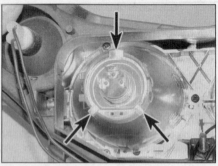

7.2d Ensure the tabs are properly located

On Vivacity models, lift the flap to access the back of the headlight unit **(see illustration)**.

2 On Speedfight 2 models, disconnect the wiring connector from the back of the headlight bulb **(see illustration)**. Release the

bulb retaining clip, noting how it fits, then remove the bulb **(see illustrations)**. Check that the contacts inside the bulbholder are clean and free from corrosion, then fit the new bulb, bearing in mind the information in the

Note above. Make sure the tabs on the bulb fit correctly in the slots in the bulb housing **(see illustration)**. Secure the bulb in position with the retaining clip. Check that the contacts inside the wiring connector are clean and free from corrosion, then install the connector.

3 On all other models, twist the bulbholder anti-clockwise and draw it out of the headlight unit, then push the bulb in and twist it anti-clockwise to release it from the holder **(see illustrations)**. Check that the contacts inside the bulbholder are clean and free from corrosion, then fit the new bulb, bearing in mind the information in the **Note** above. Make sure the pins on the bulb fit correctly in the slots in the bulbholder. Install the holder in the headlight unit and twist it clockwise to lock it in position. Check that the bulbholder wiring connections are tight, clean and free from corrosion

4 Check the operation of the headlight, then install the headlight panel (see Chapter 7).

7.3a Twist the bulbholder to remove it . . .

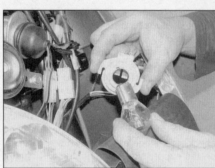

7.3b . . . then push and twist the bulb

HAYNES HiNT

Always use a paper towel or dry cloth when handling new bulbs to prevent injury if the bulb should break and to increase bulb life.

Sidelight

5 Displace the headlight panel (see Chapter 7). On Speedfight models, unclip the back of the headlight unit and remove it **(see illustration 7.1a)**.

6 Pull the bulbholder out of its socket in the headlight unit, then carefully pull the bulb out of the holder **(see illustrations)**. Check the

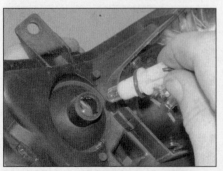

7.6a Pull the bulbholder out of its socket . . .

7.6b . . . and pull the bulb out of the holder

9.1a Rear light lens screws (arrowed) on Speedfight . . .

9.1b . . . Trekker . . .

9.1c . . . and Vivacity

condition of the seal on the bulbholder and renew it if necessary.

7 Check that the contacts inside the bulbholder are clean and free from corrosion, then carefully press the new bulb into the bulbholder, then install the bulbholder in the headlight unit.

8 Check the operation of the sidelight, then install the headlight panel (see Chapter 7).

8 Headlight unit – removal and installation

Removal

1 Remove the headlight panel (see Chapter 7).
2 The headlight unit is secured to the panel by screws. Undo the screws and lift the headlight unit out of the panel (see Chapter 7). **Note:** *On Vivacity models, the front turn signals are clipped to the headlight unit. Separate the turn signals from the headlight if required.*

Installation

3 Installation is the reverse of removal. Take care not to overtighten the fixing screws. Make sure all the wiring is correctly connected and secured. Check the operation of the lights, then install the headlight panel (see Chapter 7). Check the headlight aim (see Chapter 1).

9 Tail/brake light bulb – renewal

1 Remove the screws securing the tail light lens and remove the lens, noting how it fits **(see illustrations)**. **Note:** *On Speedfight 2 models, the screw on the centre lower edge of the lens retains the rear cowling, not the light lens.*
2 Push the bulb into the socket and twist it anti-clockwise to remove it **(see illustration)**.
3 Check the socket terminals for corrosion and clean them if necessary **(see illustration)**. Line up the pins of the new bulb with the slots in the socket, then push the bulb in and turn it

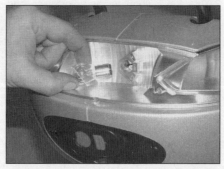

9.2 Push the bulb and twist to remove it

clockwise until it locks into place. **Note:** *The pins on the bulb are offset so it can only be installed one way. It is a good idea to use a paper towel or dry cloth when handling the new bulb to prevent injury if the bulb should break and to increase bulb life.*
4 Check the operation of the rear/brake light, then install the lens and tighten the screws securely.

10 Tail light unit – removal and installation

1 On Speedfight and Trekker models, remove the rear cowling; on Vivacity models remove the seat cowling (see Chapter 7). On all models the tail light unit is retained by two screws; undo the screws and lift the unit out of the body panel (see Chapter 7).

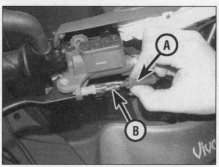

11.2a Pull back the boot (A) and disconnect the wires (B)

9.3 Ensure the socket terminals (arrowed) are clean

2 Installation is the reverse of removal. Check the operation of the tail light and the brake light.

11 Brake light switches – check and renewal

Check

1 Before checking the electrical circuit, check the bulb (see Section 9).
2 Remove the handlebar cover (see Chapter 7). Pull back the boot on the switch and disconnect the wiring connectors **(see illustration)**. Using a continuity tester, connect a probe to each terminal on the switch. With the brake lever at rest, there should be no continuity. Pull the brake lever in – there should now be continuity **(see illustration)**. If not, fit a new switch.

11.2b Testing the continuity of the brake light switch

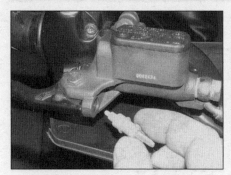

11.5 Switch screws into brake lever bracket

12.1 Displace the licence plate . . .

12.2 . . . then remove the bulbholder . . .

3 If continuity is shown with the lever pulled in, the switch is functioning correctly and the fault lies elsewhere in the circuit. Using a multimeter or test light connected to a good earth, check for voltage at the black wire terminal on the switch with the engine running. Turn the engine OFF. If there's no voltage present, check the wire between the switch and the ignition switch (see the *Wiring Diagrams* at the end of this Chapter).

4 If both continuity and voltage are obtained the switch and its power supply are proved good. Go on to check the wiring between both switches and the switch and the brake light bulb (see the *Wiring Diagrams* at the end of this Chapter).

Renewal

5 The switches are mounted in the brake lever brackets. Remove the front handlebar cover (see Chapter 7), then disconnect the wiring connectors from the switch **(see illustration 11.2a)**. Using pliers on the knurled section of the switch, unscrew it from the lever bracket **(see illustration)**.

6 Installation is the reverse of removal. Don't forget to pull the boot over the wiring connectors before refitting the handlebar cover.

12 Licence plate light bulb – renewal

1 Undo the screws securing the licence plate to the rear mudguard and displace the licence plate **(see illustration)**.

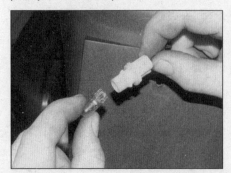

12.3 . . . and pull out the bulb

2 Turn the bulbholder anti-clockwise and withdraw it from the back of the light unit **(see illustration)**.

3 Carefully pull the bulb out of the holder **(see illustration)**. Check the condition of the seal on the bulbholder and renew it if necessary.

4 Check that the contacts inside the bulbholder are clean and free from corrosion. Carefully press the new bulb into the bulbholder, then check the operation of the light.

5 Install the bulbholder in the light unit, then install the licence plate.

13 Turn signal circuit – check

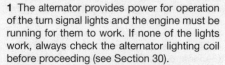

1 The alternator provides power for operation of the turn signal lights and the engine must be running for them to work. If none of the lights work, always check the alternator lighting coil before proceeding (see Section 30).

2 Most turn signal problems are the result of a failed bulb or corroded socket. This is especially true when the turn signals function properly in one direction, but not in the other. Check the bulbs and the sockets (see Section 14). Also check the operation of the turn signal switch (see Section 22) and the turn signal warning light (see Section 18).

3 If the bulbs and sockets are good, test the signal relay. On Speedfight models remove the top handlebar cover, on Trekker models remove the headlight panel and on Vivacity models remove the front panel to access the

13.4a Relay location on Trekker . . .

relay (see Chapter 7). **Note:** *The signal relay on later Vivacity Sportline models (with the electronic speedometer) is integral with the instrument cluster (see Step 7).*

4 Disconnect the wiring connector and check for voltage at the black wire terminal in the connector with the engine running, using a multimeter or test light connected to a good earth (ground) **(see illustrations)**. Turn the engine OFF. If there is no voltage, check the wiring between the connector and the ignition switch (see *Wiring Diagrams* at the end of this Chapter).

5 If there is voltage, reconnect the wiring connector to the relay and use the test light to check the output from the purple wire terminal with the engine running. The light should flash; if it does not, fit a new relay.

6 If the light flashes, check the wiring between the relay, the turn signal switch and the turn signal lights.

7 On Vivacity Sportline models, remove the rear handlebar cover and disconnect the instrument cluster multi-pin connector (see Chapter 7). Check for voltage at the black wire terminal in the connector (see Step 4). If there is voltage, reconnect the connector and use the test light to check the output from the purple wire terminal in the connector (see Step 5). The light should flash; if it does not, the relay has failed. It is not possible to renew the cluster relay, but a new relay can be wired into the turn signal circuit (consult a Peugeot dealer or electrical specialist).

8 If the light flashes, check the wiring between the connector, the turn signal switch and the turn signal lights.

13.4b . . . and on Speedfight. Disconnect the wiring connector

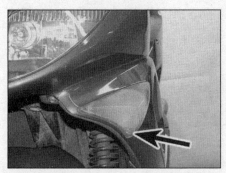

14.1a Retaining screw on front turn signal lens

14.1b Retaining screw on rear turn signal lens

14.5a Retaining screw is in the back of the turn signal unit

14.5b Note the clip on the inner edge of the lens

14.9a Undo the screw . . .

14.9b . . . and lift off the lens

14 Turn signal bulbs – renewal

Speedfight models

1 Undo the screw securing the turn signal lens and lift off the lens **(see illustrations)**. Where fitted, unclip the bulb cover, then push the bulb into the socket and turn it anti-clockwise to remove it.

2 Check that the contacts inside the socket are clean and free from corrosion. Line up the pins on the bulb body with the slots in the socket, then push the bulb in and turn it clockwise until it locks into place.

3 Where fitted, fit the bulb cover. Install the lens and tighten the fixing screw securely.

4 Check the operation of the turn signal light.

Trekker models

5 Undo the screw securing the turn signal lens and lift off the lens noting how it fits **(see illustrations)**. Where fitted, unclip the bulb cover, then push the bulb into the socket and turn it anti-clockwise to remove it.

6 Check that the contacts inside the socket are clean and free from corrosion. Line up the pins on the bulb body with the slots in the socket, then push the bulb in and turn it clockwise until it locks into place.

7 Where fitted, fit the bulb cover. Install the lens and tighten the fixing screw securely.

8 Check the operation of the turn signal light.

Vivacity models

9 To access the front turn signal bulbs, first remove the front panel (see Chapter 7). Undo the screw securing the turn signal lens and lift off the lens **(see illustrations)**.

10 To access the rear turn signal bulbs, undo the screws securing the rear light lens and remove the lens, then unclip the turn signal lens **(see illustrations)**.

11 Unclip the bulb cover, then push the bulb into the socket and turn it anti-clockwise to remove it **(see illustrations)**.

14.10a Remove the rear light lens . . .

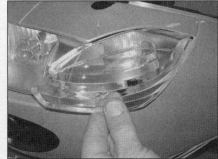

14.10b . . . then unclip the lens

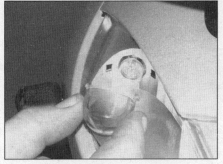

14.11a Unclip the bulb cover . . .

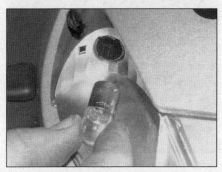

14.11b . . . and remove the bulb

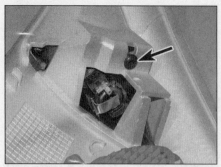

15.2 Screw retains turn signal assembly in panel

12 Check that the contacts inside the socket are clean and free from corrosion. Line up the pins on the bulb body with the slots in the socket, then push the bulb in and turn it clockwise until it locks into place.

13 Refit the lens and any other components disturbed.

15 Turn signal assembly – removal and installation

Speedfight models

1 The turn signals are retained in the front side panels and the rear mudguard body panel by a screw on the rear of each signal assembly. Remove the panels as required (see Chapter 7).

2 Undo the screw securing the signal lens

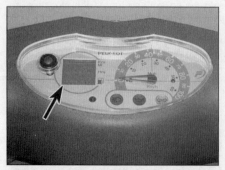

16.2a Digital display (arrowed) on Vivacity Sportline 2

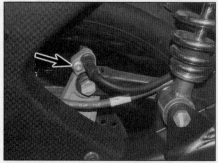

16.4a Screw (arrowed) securing the speed sensor to the front suspension – Speedfight 2 Furious shown

15.5 Retaining bolt for turn signal is inside rear cowling

and lift off the lens (see Section 14), then undo the screw securing the signal assembly in the panel and withdraw the assembly **(see illustration)**.

3 Installation is the reverse of removal.

Trekker models

4 The front turn signals are integral with the front handlebar cover (see Chapter 7).

5 To remove the rear turn signals, first remove the rear cowling (see Chapter 7). Undo the bolt securing the signal assembly and remove the assembly, noting the routing of the wiring **(see illustration)**. Note the captive nut in the signal body.

6 Installation is the reverse of removal.

Vivacity models

7 To remove the front turn signals, first remove the front panel (see Chapter 7).

16.2b All-electronic instrument cluster as fitted to Speedfight 2 Furious and Metal-X Furious models

16.4b Instrument cluster is secured by two bolts

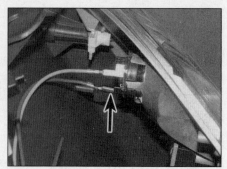

15.7 Wiring connectors for front turn signal

Disconnect the turn signal wiring and unclip the signal assembly from the headlight unit **(see illustration)**.

8 Installation is the reverse of removal.

9 The rear turn signals are integral with the rear light unit (see Section 10).

16 Instrument cluster – check, removal and installation

Check

1 Special instruments are required to check the operation of the speedometer. If it is believed to be faulty, first check the operation of the speedometer cable (see Section 17), then take the scooter to a Peugeot dealer for assessment. **Note:** *On Speedfight 2 Furious and Metal-X Furious models, the speedometer is actuated by a permanent magnet glued to the front wheel rim. If the speedometer fails to work, first check that the magnet is held securely to the rim.*

2 On models with an electronically operated speedometer, digital odometer, clock and fuel level display, the instruments are powered by the machine's battery **(see illustrations)**. Check for voltage at the supply terminal (black) on the instrument cluster wiring connector (see *Wiring Diagrams* at the end of this Chapter) if the display fails, then consult a Peugeot dealer for further assessment.

3 Refer to Section 19 to check the fuel gauge and Section 20 to check the oil level warning circuit. Refer to Chapter 3 to check the temperature gauge (where fitted). Individual components are not available, so if an instrument is faulty, the entire cluster must be renewed.

Removal

4 On Speedfight 2 Furious and Metal-X Furious models, undo the screw and detach the speed sensor on the lower end of the speedometer cable from the front suspension **(see illustration)**. Remove the bolts securing the instrument cluster and lift it off **(see illustration)**. Note that the cable cannot be detached from the instrument cluster – draw it out of the bodywork noting its routing.

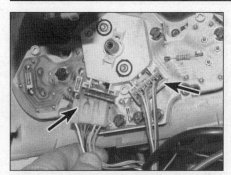

16.5a Speedfight instrument cluster wiring connectors

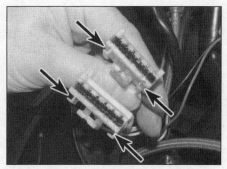

16.5b Note the arrangement of the tabs (arrowed)

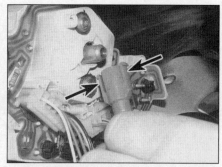

16.5c Press the clips (arrowed) together to release the speedometer cable

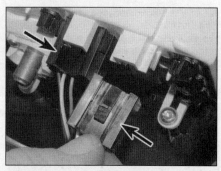

16.6 Instrument cluster wiring connectors on Trekker models

5 On all other models, remove the handlebar cover (see Chapter 7). On Speedfight models, unclip the two wiring connectors on the back of the instrument cluster and disconnect the connectors, noting the two different arrrangments of the tabs on the connector bodies **(see illustrations)**. Press the clips together on the speedometer cable connector and disconnect the cable **(see illustration)**. Undo the screws and detach the cluster from the top cover (see Chapter 7).

6 On Trekker models, detach the instrument cluster from the front handlebar cover (see Chapter 7), then disconnect the speedometer cable and wiring connectors **(see illustration)**.

7 On Vivacity models, disconnect the speedometer cable and wiring connectors, then detach the rear cover from the machine and remove the instrument cluster from the cover (see Chapter 7).

8 On models with electronic instruments, pull back the boot on the instrument cluster wiring connector and disconnect the connector, then detach the rear cover from the machine and remove the instrument cluster from the cover (see Chapter 7).

Installation

9 Installation is the reverse of removal. Make sure that the speedometer cable and wiring connectors are correctly routed and secured.

17 Speedometer cable – check and renewal

Note: *Certain models are fitted with an electronically activated speedometer. The speedometer drive cannot be checked on these models.*

Check

1 To check the operation of the speedometer cable, support the machine on its stand with the front wheel off the ground.

2 Remove the handlebar cover (see Chapter 7), then disconnect the cable from the instrument cluster (see Section 16).

3 Turn the rear wheel in the normal direction of rotation and observe that the squared

upper end of the inner cable rotates **(see illustration)**. If the cable does not rotate, the cable or the speedometer gearbox is damaged or broken.

4 Unscrew the knurled ring and disconnect the lower end of the cable from the speedometer gearbox to check the inner cable **(see illustration)**. Remove the front wheel on Trekker and Vivacity models, and the front wheel, hub assembly and caliper bracket on Speedfight models, to check the speedometer gearbox (see Chapter 8).

Renewal

5 To remove the cable from the machine, first remove the front panel or headlight panel. Disconnect the cable from the instrument cluster and the speedometer gearbox (see Steps 2 and 4), then withdraw it from the machine, noting its routing.

6 On Vivacity models, disconnect the cable from the instrument cluster, then remove the front wheel and detach the speedometer gearbox from the wheel. Unclip the cable from the front mudguard, then withdraw the cable and gearbox assembly from the machine, noting its routing.

7 Installation is the reverse of removal. On Speedfight models, ensure the cable is correctly routed along the monolever arm. On Trekker models, ensure the cable is correctly routed through the mudguard liner on the underside of the steering stem.

8 Check that the cable doesn't restrict steering movement or interfere with any other components.

17.3 Inner cable should rotate with front wheel

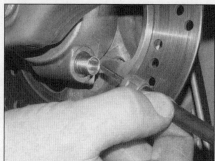

17.4 Disconnect the lower end of the cable

18 Instrument cluster bulbs – renewal

Note: *On Speedfight 2 Furious and Metal-X Furious models, the warning lights are illuminated by LEDs. If a light fails to work, and the fault cannot be traced to a wiring or component failure, the instrument cluster will have to be replaced with a new one.*

1 On Speedfight and Trekker models, remove the instrument cluster; on Vivacity models, remove the handlebar front cover and disconnect the multi-pin wiring connector (see Section 16).

2 On Speedfight and Trekker models, twist the bulbholder anti-clockwise and draw it out of the instrument casing, then pull the bulb

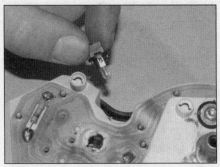

18.2a Bulbholder locks in the back of the cluster

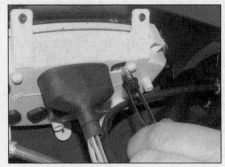

18.2b Remove the bulbholder . . .

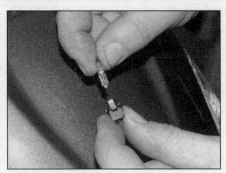

18.2c . . . then pull out the bulb

out of the bulbholder **(see illustration)**. On Vivacity models, grip the bulbholder with tweezers and pull it out, then pull the bulb out of the bulbholder **(see illustrations)**.

3 Check with the Specifications to ensure you fit a new bulb of the correct wattage.

4 Check that the contacts inside the bulbholder are clean and free from corrosion and spray with electrical contact cleaner before a new bulb is installed.

5 Carefully push the new bulb into the holder, then install the holder into the casing.

6 Installation of the instrument cluster is the reverse of removal.

19 Fuel gauge and level sender – check and renewal

⚠ *Warning: Petrol (gasoline) is extremely flammable, so take extra precautions when you work on any part of the fuel system. Don't smoke or allow open flames or bare light bulbs near the work area, and don't work in a garage where a natural gas-type appliance is present. If you spill any fuel on your skin, rinse it off immediately with soap and water. When you perform any kind of work on the fuel system, wear safety glasses and have a fire extinguisher suitable for a class B type fire (flammable liquids) on hand.*

Fuel gauge

Check

1 Remove the storage compartment to access the top of the fuel tank (see Chapter 7). Disconnect the wiring connector from the top of the fuel level sender **(see illustrations)**.

2 Connect a jumper wire between the terminals on the wiring loom side of the connector. With the ignition switched ON, the fuel gauge should read FULL. If it doesn't, check the wiring between the connector and the gauge, and check for voltage at the supply terminal (black) on the instrument cluster wiring connector (see *Wiring Diagrams* at the end of this Chapter). If the wiring is good, then the gauge is confirmed faulty.

Renewal

3 The fuel gauge is integral with the instrument cluster, for which no individual parts are available. If the fuel gauge is faulty, the entire cluster must be renewed (see Section 16).

Fuel level sender

Check

4 Disconnect the wiring connector from the fuel level sender (see Step 1), then unscrew the sender from the tank and remove the sender unit **(see illustrations)**. **Note:** *On some models the sender is retained by a locking ring (see illustrations).*

19.1a Fuel level sender wiring connector plugs into the sender . . .

19.1b . . . or into a wiring connector

19.4a Unscrew the sender . . .

19.4b . . . . and withdraw it from the tank

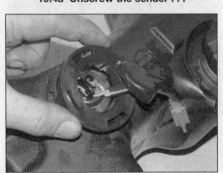

19.4c Unscrew the retaining ring . . .

19.4d . . . and withdraw the sender

Warning: Block the opening in the tank to prevent the escape of petrol fumes and accidental fuel spillage.

5 Test the operation of the sender with a multimeter set to the ohms x 100 scale. Connect the meter probes to the terminals on the top of the sender and measure the resistance with the sender float UP (tank full) and DOWN (tank empty) **(see illustration)**. If the readings obtained differ greatly from those given in the Specifications at the beginning of this Chapter, the sender is faulty and must be renewed.

6 Check the operation of the sender; the arm should move freely without binding. Also check that the float is held securely on the arm and that it is not damaged. This will usually be apparent by the presence of fuel inside the float. If any of the component parts are faulty or damaged, fit a new sender.

7 If the sender is good, check the wiring between the sender and the gauge (see *Wiring Diagrams* at the end of this Chapter).

Renewal

8 Remove the sender as described in Step 4.
9 Check the condition of the sender O-ring and fit a new one if it is deformed or perished. Insert the sender carefully into the tank, then turn it clockwise to lock it in position.

20 Oil level sensor – check and renewal

Check

1 The oil level warning light in the instrument cluster should come on temporarily when the ignition is first turned on as a check of the warning circuit. If the light fails to come on, first check the bulb (see Section 18), then check the wiring between the instrument cluster wiring connector and the starter relay (see *Wiring Diagrams* at the end of this Chapter).

2 If the warning light in the instrument cluster fails to come on when the oil is low, first check the bulb (see Section 18). If the bulb is good, remove the storage compartment to access the oil level sensor in the top of the oil tank (see Chapter 7).

21.1a Displace the boot . . .

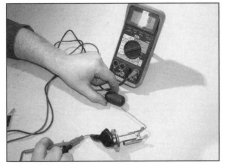

19.5 Measuring resistance in the fuel level sender

20.5 Measuring resistance in the oil level sensor

3 Disconnect the wiring connector from the top of the sensor **(see illustration)**. With the ignition switched on, check for voltage at the black wire terminal in the connector. If there is no voltage, check the wiring between the connector and the ignition switch (see *Wiring Diagrams* at the end of this Chapter).

4 To test the sensor, remove it from the oil tank as described below.

5 Using a multimeter set to the ohms x 1 scale, connect the meter probes to the terminals on the top of the sensor and measure the resistance with the sensor float UP (tank full) and DOWN (tank empty) **(see illustration)**. If the readings obtained differ from those given in the Specifications at the beginning of this Chapter, the sensor is faulty and must be renewed.

6 If the sensor is good, check the wiring between the sensor and the instrument cluster (see *Wiring Diagrams* at the end of this Chapter).

21.1b . . . and disconnect the ignition switch

20.3 Oil level sensor wiring connector

20.8 Withdraw the sensor from the tank

Renewal

7 Remove the storage compartment (see Chapter 7).
8 Disconnect the sensor wiring connector and withdraw the sensor from the tank **(see illustration)**.
9 Installation is a reverse of the removal procedure. Check the operation of the warning light on completion.

21 Ignition (main) switch – check, removal and installation

Warning: To prevent the risk of short circuits, disconnect the battery negative (-ve) lead before making any ignition (main) switch checks.

Check

1 Remove any body panels as required for access (see Chapter 7). Disconnect the battery negative (-ve) lead, then pull back the boot on the wiring connector and disconnect the connector **(see illustrations)**.

2 Using an multimeter or a continuity tester, check the continuity of the connector terminal pairs (see the *Wiring Diagrams* at the end of this Chapter). Continuity should exist between the connected terminals when the switch is in the indicated position.

3 If the switch fails any of the tests it must be renewed. **Note:** *For machines fitted with an ignition immobiliser, from July 2002 it was possible to transfer the transponder from the old ignition key to a new one if a new switch was*

21.4 Unclip the transponder aerial

21.5 Ignition switch is secured by a shear bolt (arrowed)

22.3a Trace the wiring to the connectors . . .

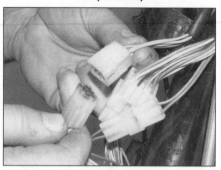

22.3b . . . and disconnect them to test the switches

using a multimeter or test light and battery. Always disconnect the battery negative (-ve) lead, which will prevent the possibility of a short circuit, before making the checks.

3 Remove the handlebar covers and front or headlight panel as necessary to trace the wiring from the switch in question back to its connector (see Chapter 7). Disconnect the relevant wiring connector **(see illustrations)**.

4 Check for continuity between the terminals of the switch wiring with the switch in the various positions (e.g. switch off – no continuity, switch on – continuity) referring to the *Wiring Diagrams* at the end of this Chapter.

5 If the checks indicate a problem exists, refer to Section 23, separate the switch housing and spray the switch contacts with electrical contact cleaner. If they are accessible, the contacts can be scraped clean carefully with a knife or polished with crocus cloth. If switch components are damaged or broken, it will be obvious when the switch is disassembled.

6 Clean the inside of the switch body thoroughly and smear the contacts with silicon grease before reassembly

23 Handlebar switches –
removal and installation

Removal

1 Remove the handlebar covers and front or headlight panel as necessary to trace the wiring from the switch in question back to its connector (see Chapter 7). Disconnect the relevant wiring connector **(see illustration 22.3b)**.

2 The right-hand switch housing is integral with the throttle twistgrip housing **(see illustration)**. Undo the two screws securing the two halves of the housing together, then remove the screws and lift the switch housing off the handlebar **(see illustration)**. **Note:** *It is not necessary to displace the throttle twistgrip.*

3 On machines fitted with a rear disc brake, undo the two screws securing the two halves of the left-hand housing together, then remove the screws and lift the switch housing off the handlebar **(see illustration 23.2c)**.

4 On machines fitted with a rear drum brake, the left-hand switch housing incorporates the brake lever. Undo the two screws securing the

fitted. *On machines built before that date this may not be possible and a new ignition immobiliser may have to be fitted when the switch is renewed – check with a Peugeot dealer.*

Removal

4 Disconnect the battery negative (-ve) lead and the switch wiring connector (see Step 1). Unclip the immobiliser transponder aerial (where fitted) from the front of the switch **(see illustration)**.

5 The switch is secured to the frame by a shear bolt **(see illustration)**. To remove the bolt, drill off the bolt head, then remove the switch. The threaded section of the bolt can then be unscrewed with pliers.

Installation

Note: *A new shear-head bolt will be required.*
6 Installation is the reverse of removal. Operate the key to ensure the steering lock mechanism is correctly aligned with the frame

and steering stem before tightening the new shear-head bolt – tighten the bolt until its head snaps off.

7 Reconnect the battery negative (-ve) lead once all electrical connections have been made to the switch.

22 Handlebar switches –
check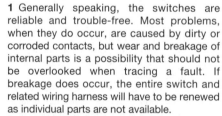

1 Generally speaking, the switches are reliable and trouble-free. Most problems, when they do occur, are caused by dirty or corroded contacts, but wear and breakage of internal parts is a possibility that should not be overlooked when tracing a fault. If breakage does occur, the entire switch and related wiring harness will have to be renewed as individual parts are not available.

2 The switches can be checked for continuity

23.2a Switch mechanism is in the rear half of the right . . .

23.2b . . . and left-hand switch housing

23.2c Undo the two screws from the front of the housing

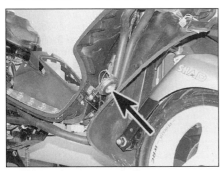

24.1a Horn location on Speedfight . . .

24.1b . . . Trekker . . .

24.1c . . . and Vivacity models

two halves of the housing together, then remove the screws and lift the switch housing off the handlebar **(see illustration 23.2c)**. **Note:** *It is not necessary to displace the brake lever.*

5 Inspect the switch contacts (see Section 22). If a component part is worn or broken, the switch housing will have to be renewed as a complete assembly.

Installation

6 Installation is the reverse of removal. Make sure the wiring connector is secure and check the operation of the switches and related components before riding the scooter.

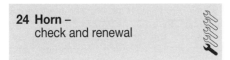

24 Horn –
check and renewal

Check

1 On Speedfight models the horn is mounted behind the right-hand front side panel; on Trekker models the horn is mounted behind the headlight panel; on Vivacity models the horn is mounted behind the front panel **(see illustrations)**. Remove any body panels as required for access (see Chapter 7).

2 Disconnect the wiring connectors from the horn and ensure that the contacts are clean and free from corrosion **(see illustration)**.

3 To test the horn, use jumper wires to connect one of the horn terminals to the battery positive (+ve) terminal and the other horn terminal to the battery negative (-ve) terminal. If the horn sounds, check the switch (see Section 22) and the wiring between the

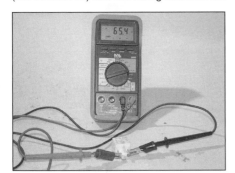

24.3 Measuring the starter relay primary resistance

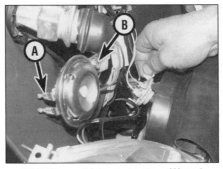

24.2 Horn wiring connectors (A) and mounting bolt (B)

switch and the horn (see the *Wiring Diagrams* at the end of this Chapter).

4 If the horn doesn't sound, renew it.

Renewal

5 Remove any body panels as required for access (see Step 1).

6 Disconnect the wiring connectors from the horn, then unscrew the bolt securing the horn and remove it **(see illustration 24.2)**.

7 Install the horn and tighten the mounting bolt securely. Connect the wiring connectors and test the horn.

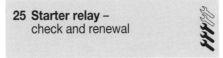

25 Starter relay –
check and renewal

Check

1 If the starter circuit is faulty, first check the fuse (see Section 5). Also check that the

25.4 Measuring the starter relay secondary resistance

25.2 Pull the starter relay out of its socket next to the battery

battery is fully-charged (see Section 3).

2 The relay is located next to the battery holder. Disconnect the battery negative (-ve) terminal, then pull the relay out of its socket and test it as follows **(see illustration)**.

3 Set a multimeter to the ohms x 1 scale and connect it across the relay's blue wire terminal and green wire terminal to measure the primary resistance **(see illustration)**.

4 Now connect the multimeter across the relay's starter motor and battery lead terminals to measure the secondary resistance. To check the operation of the relay, leave the multimeter connected, and use insulated jumper wires to connect a fully-charged 12 volt battery to the blue wire terminal (positive (+ve) terminal of the battery) and the green wire terminal (negative (-ve) terminal of the battery). At this point the relay should be heard to click and the multimeter read 0.1 to 0.5 ohms (continuity) **(see illustration)**.

5 If the relay fails either test and does not click when voltage is applied across its terminals, it is faulty and must be renewed.

6 If the relay is good, check the other components in the starter circuit as described in the relevant sections of this Chapter. If all components are good, check the wiring between the various components (see the *Wiring Diagrams* at the end of this Chapter).

Renewal

7 Disconnect the battery negative terminal.

8 Ensure the terminals in the relay socket are clean and free from corrosion and spray them with electrical contact cleaner.

9 Align the relay terminals with the socket and push it firmly into place.

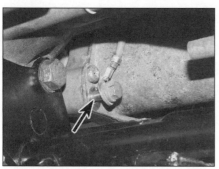

26.3 Earth wire is secured by mounting bolt (arrowed)

26 Starter motor –
removal and installation

Removal

1 The starter motor is located underneath the engine. If required, remove the belly panel (see Chapter 7).
2 Disconnect the battery negative (-ve) lead, then trace the wiring from the starter motor and disconnect it at the wiring connector. Release the wiring from any clips or ties.
3 Unscrew the two bolts securing the starter motor to the crankcase, noting the earth (ground) wire secured by the lower bolt **(see illustration)**.
4 Withdraw the starter motor from the crankcase. Remove the O-ring from the end of the motor body and discard it as a new one

26.4 O-ring is fitted to starter motor body

must be fitted on reassembly **(see illustration)**.

Installation

5 Installation is the reverse of removal. Fit a new O-ring on the end of the starter motor, making sure it is seated in its groove, and apply a smear of engine oil to it **(see illustration 26.4)**.

27 Starter motor –
disassembly, inspection and reassembly

Disassembly

Note: *No individual components are available, so if the motor is faulty, a new one must be fitted. It may be worthwhile consulting an auto electrician before buying a new motor, as*

sometimes, depending on the nature of the fault, the starter motor can be repaired.
1 Remove the starter motor (see Section 26).
2 Undo the screws securing the housing to the end cover and draw the housing off, leaving the armature in place in the cover **(see illustration)**.
3 Carefully lift the housing seal off over the armature **(see illustration)**.
4 Withdraw the armature from the cover, noting any shims or washers on either or both ends of the armature shaft, and noting how the brushes locate onto the commutator **(see illustration)**.
5 Slide the brushes out from their holders and remove the brush springs **(see illustrations)**.

Inspection

6 The parts of the starter motor that are most likely to wear and require attention are the brushes. Peugeot provide no specifications as to the minimum service length of the brushes. If any of the brushes are excessively worn, cracked, chipped, or otherwise damaged, they should be renewed. Check with an auto electrician as to the availability of new brushes – if none are available, a new starter motor must be fitted.
7 Check that the brushes are firmly attached to their terminals. If the brushes are in good condition, they may be re-used.
8 Inspect the commutator bars on the armature for scoring, scratches and discoloration **(see illustration)**. The commutator can be cleaned and polished with crocus cloth, but do not use sandpaper

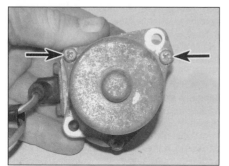

27.2 Two screws secure the starter motor housing

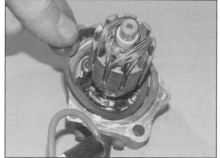

27.3 Remove the housing seal carefully . . .

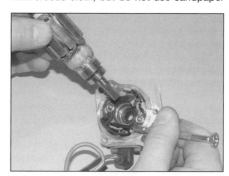

27.4 . . . then withdraw the armature from the cover

27.5a Displace the brushes . . .

27.5b . . . and remove the brush springs

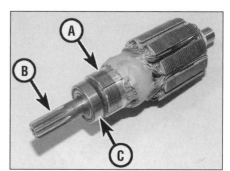

27.8 Armature commutator (A), gear teeth (B) and bearing (C)

27.9 Continuity should exist between the commutator bars

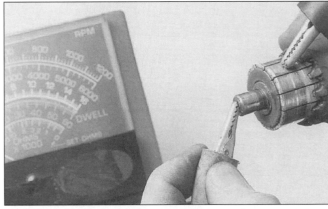

27.10 There should be no continuity between the commutator bars and the armature shaft

or emery paper. After cleaning, wipe away any residue with a cloth soaked in electrical system cleaner or denatured alcohol.
9 Using an multimeter or test light and battery, check for continuity between the commutator bars **(see illustration)**. Continuity (zero resistance) should exist between each bar and all of the others.
10 Also, check for continuity between the commutator bars and the armature shaft **(see illustration)**. There should be no continuity (infinite resistance) between the commutator and the shaft. If the checks indicate otherwise, the armature is defective.
11 Check the front end of the armature shaft for worn or chipped teeth and check the condition of the armature bearing **(see illustration 27.8)**.

Reassembly

12 Reassemble the starter motor in the reverse order of disassembly.
13 Hold the brushes back against the pressure of their springs and fit the armature into the end cover carefully to avoid damaging the seal. Check that each brush is securely pressed against the commutator by its spring and is free to move easily in its holder.
14 Lubricate the bush in the end of the housing with a smear of grease, then fit the seal and housing over the armature. Tighten the housing screws securely.

28 Charging system testing – general information and precautions

1 If the performance of the charging system is suspect, the system as a whole should be checked first, followed by testing of the individual components. **Note:** *Before beginning the checks, make sure the battery is fully charged and that all system connections are clean and tight.*
2 Checking the output of the charging system and the performance of the various components within the charging system requires the use of a multimeter (with voltage,

current and resistance checking facilities).
3 When making the checks, follow the procedures carefully to prevent incorrect connections or short circuits, as irreparable damage to electrical system components may result if short circuits occur.
4 If a multimeter is not available, the job of checking the charging system should be left to a Peugeot dealer.

29 Charging system – leakage and output test

1 If the charging system of the machine is thought to be faulty, perform the following checks.

Leakage test

2 Disconnect the battery negative (-ve) terminal.
3 Set the multimeter to the Amps function and connect its negative (-ve) probe to the battery negative (-ve) terminal, and positive (+ve) probe to the disconnected negative (-ve) lead **(see illustration)**. Always set the meter to a high Amps range initially and then bring it down to the mA (milli Amps) range; if there is a high current flow in the circuit it may blow the meter's fuse.
Caution: Always connect an ammeter in series, never in parallel with the battery, otherwise it will be damaged. Do not turn the ignition ON or operate the starter motor when the ammeter is connected – a sudden surge in current will blow the meter's fuse.
4 While Peugeot do not specify an amount, if the current leakage indicated exceeds 1 mA, there is probably a short circuit in the wiring. Disconnect the meter and connect the negative (-ve) lead to the battery, tightening it securely,
5 If leakage is indicated, use the wiring diagrams at the end of this book to systematically disconnect individual electrical components and repeat the test until the source is identified.

Output test

6 Remove the belly panel (see Chapter 7). Start the engine and warm it up to normal operating temperature, then stop the engine and turn the ignition OFF.
7 To check the unregulated voltage output, connect a multimeter set to the 0 – 50 volts AC scale (voltmeter) between the yellow wire terminal in the alternator wiring connector (see Section 31) and the battery negative terminal.
8 Start the engine and allow it to idle, then slowly increase the engine speed and note the reading obtained. The unregulated voltage should be as specified at the beginning of this Chapter. If the voltage is not within these limits, have the alternator checked by a Peugeot dealer.

30 Alternator coils – check

1 Disconnect the battery negative (-ve) terminal.
2 Remove the belly panel (see Chapter 7) and disconnect the alternator wiring connector (see Section 31).

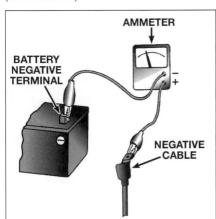

29.3 Checking the charging system leakage rate - connect the meter as shown

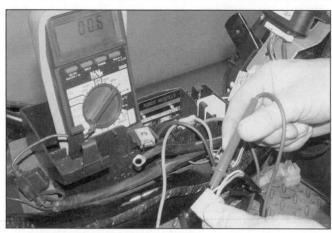

30.3 Checking the resistance in the alternator lighting coil

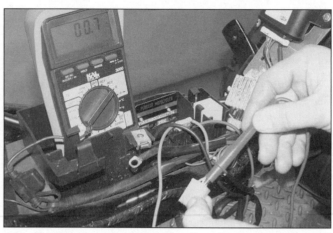

30.4 Checking the resistance in the alternator battery charge coil

3 Set a multimeter to the ohms x 1 scale and connect the meter probes to the yellow wire terminal in the alternator side of the connector and to earth (ground). This will give a resistance reading for the lighting coil which should be consistent with the Specifications at the beginning of this Chapter **(see illustration)**.

4 Connect the meter probes to the white wire terminal in the alternator side of the connector and to earth (ground). This will give a resistance reading for the battery charge coil which should be consistent with the Specifications at the beginning of this Chapter **(see illustration)**.

5 If the readings obtained differ greatly from those given, particularly if the meter indicates

a short circuit (no measurable resistance) or an open circuit (infinite, or very high resistance), the entire alternator stator assembly must be renewed as no individual components are available. However, first check that the fault is not due to a damaged or broken wire from the alternator to the connector; pinched or broken wires can usually be repaired.

31 Alternator –
removal and installation

Note: *This procedure can be carried out with the engine in the frame.*

Removal

1 Disconnect the battery negative (-ve) terminal.

2 Remove the belly panel (see Chapter 7) and disconnect the alternator wiring connector **(see illustration)**. Free the wiring from any clips or guides and feed it through to the alternator.

3 Remove the cooling fan on air-cooled engines (see Chapter 2A) or the water pump on liquid-cooled engines (see Chapter 2B).

4 To remove the rotor centre nut it is necessary to stop the rotor from turning; use either the Peugeot service tool (Pt. No. 752237) or make up a tool which engages the two large holes in

the rotor face (see Tool Tip Chapter 2C, Section 6). With the rotor securely held, unscrew the nut and discard it as a new one must be fitted on reassembly **(see illustration)**.

> **TOOL TiP** *A rotor holding tool can easily be made using two strips of steel bolted together in the middle, with a bolt through each end which locates into the slots in the rotor. Do not allow the bolts to extend too far through the rotor slots otherwise the coils could be damaged.*

5 To remove the rotor from the crankshaft it is necessary to first protect the end of the shaft; use either the Peugeot service tool (Pt. No. 68007) or a similar protective cap.

6 The rotor is mounted on a taper; to pull it off use either the Peugeot service tool (Pt. No. 750806) or a two-legged puller. To use the service tool, first screw the body of the tool all the way into the threads in the rotor. Hold the tool steady with a spanner on its flats and tighten the centre bolt, exerting steady pressure to draw the rotor off the crankshaft.

7 To use a two-legged puller, thread the puller legs into the two large holes in the rotor and tighten the centre bolt, exerting steady pressure to draw the rotor off the crankshaft **(see illustration)**. Remove the Woodruff key from the shaft for safekeeping, noting how it fits **(see illustration)**.

31.2 Disconnect the alternator wiring connector

31.4 Hold the rotor and undo the centre nut

31.7a Remove the rotor from the crankshaft with a puller . . .

31.7b . . . then remove the Woodruff key

8 The alternator stator and ignition pulse generator are wired together as an assembly. Undo the bolts securing the pulse generator and lift the wiring out of the slot in the engine case noting how the wiring grommet fits into the slot **(see illustration)**. Undo the bolts securing the stator and remove the stator and pulse generator assembly **(see illustration)**. Note: *The bolts for the pulse generator and the alternator stator differ in length. Do not mix them up.*

Installation

9 Position the alternator stator and the pulse generator in the engine case and press the wiring grommet into its slot **(see illustration 30.8b)**. Align the mounting holes for the stator and pulse generator, then install the fixing bolts and tighten them securely.

10 Clean the tapered end of the crankshaft and the corresponding mating surface on the inside of the rotor with a suitable solvent. Make sure that no metal objects have attached themselves to the magnets on the inside of the rotor. Fit the Woodruff key into its slot in the shaft, then install the rotor onto the shaft, aligning the slot in the rotor with the key **(see illustration)**.

11 Install the new rotor nut and tighten it to the torque setting specified at the beginning of this Chapter, using the method employed on removal to prevent the rotor from turning **(see illustration 31.4)**.

12 Reconnect the wiring at the connector and secure it with any clips or ties.

13 Install the remaining components in the reverse order of removal.

---

32 Regulator/rectifier –
check and replacement

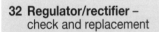

⚠️ *Warning: The check of the charging and lighting coil requires the engine to be run at between ½ and ¾ throttle. Ensure that the rear wheel is clear of the ground when the engine is running at do not retain this engine speed for longer than is necessary to take the meter reading.*

1 Remove the floor panel (see Chapter 7). The regulator/rectifier is mounted on a bracket

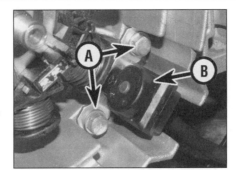

31.8a Two bolts (A) secure the pulse generator (B)

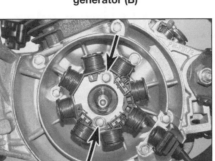

31.8c Alternator stator is secured by two bolts (arrowed)

forward of the battery holder **(see illustration)**.

2 Disconnect the battery negative (-ve) terminal. Set a multimeter to the ohms x 1 scale and connect the meter probes to the green wire terminal in the regulator/rectifier wiring connector and to the connector on the battery negative (-ve) lead **(see illustration)**. The multimeter should read 0.1 to 0.5 ohms (continuity). Disconnect the meter and reconnect the battery negative (-ve) lead to the terminal.

3 To check the battery charging voltage, set the multimeter to the 0 – 50 volts DC scale and connect its probes to the red wire and green wire terminals in the regulator/rectifier wiring connector **(see illustration)**. Start the engine and note the voltage reading at the specified throttle opening (see Specifications).

4 To check the lighting voltage, set the multimeter to the 0 – 50 volts AC scale and connect the meter probes to the yellow wire

31.8b Wiring locates in slot in engine case

31.10 Slot (arrowed) in rotor should align with Woodruff key

and green wire terminals in the regulator/rectifier wiring connector. Start the engine and note the voltage reading at the specified throttle opening (see Specifications).

5 If the voltage is not within these limits, have the regulator/rectifier checked by a Peugeot dealer.

6 Disconnect the battery negative (-ve) terminal. Disconnect the regulator/rectifier wiring connector. Undo the bolt securing the regulator/rectifier to its bracket and remove it.

7 Install the new unit and tighten the mounting bolt securely. Connect the wiring connector.

HAYNES HiNT *Clues to a faulty regulator are constantly blowing bulbs, with brightness varying considerably with engine speed, and battery overheating.*

32.1 Location of the regulator/rectifier

32.2 Checking for continuity in the regulator/rectifier earth (ground) circuit

32.3 Wiring connector should be connected to the regulator/rectifier during voltage output checks

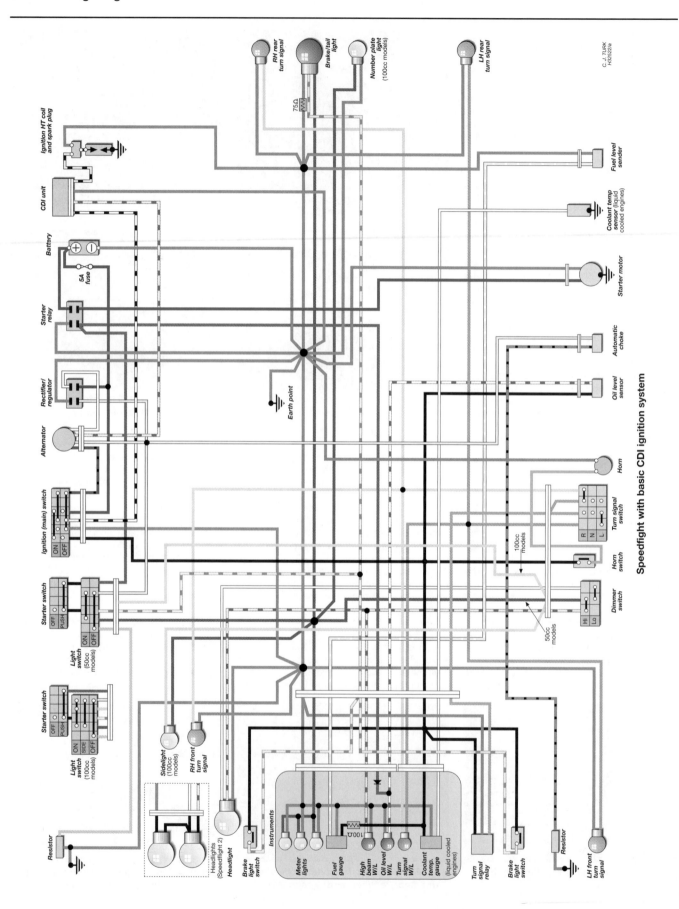

Speedfight with basic CDI ignition system

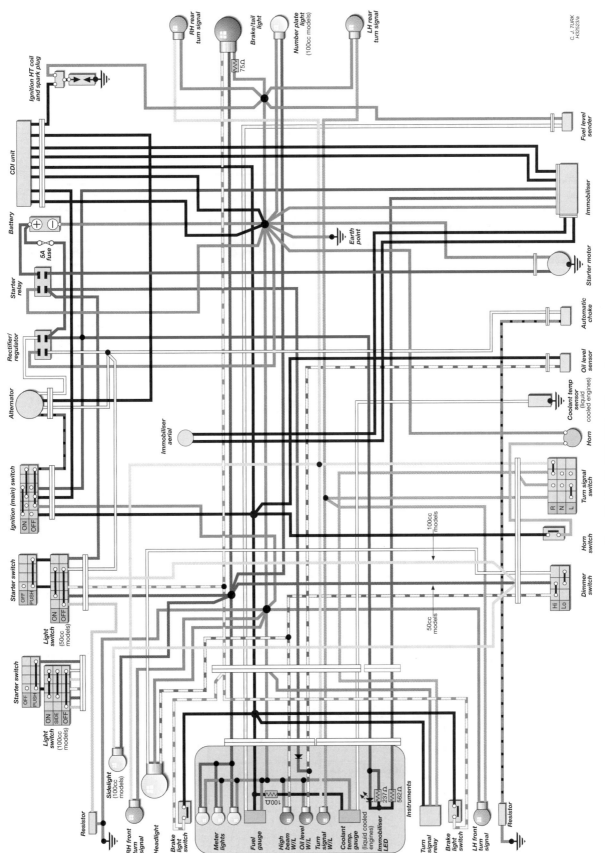

Speedfight with AEC 400 ignition system

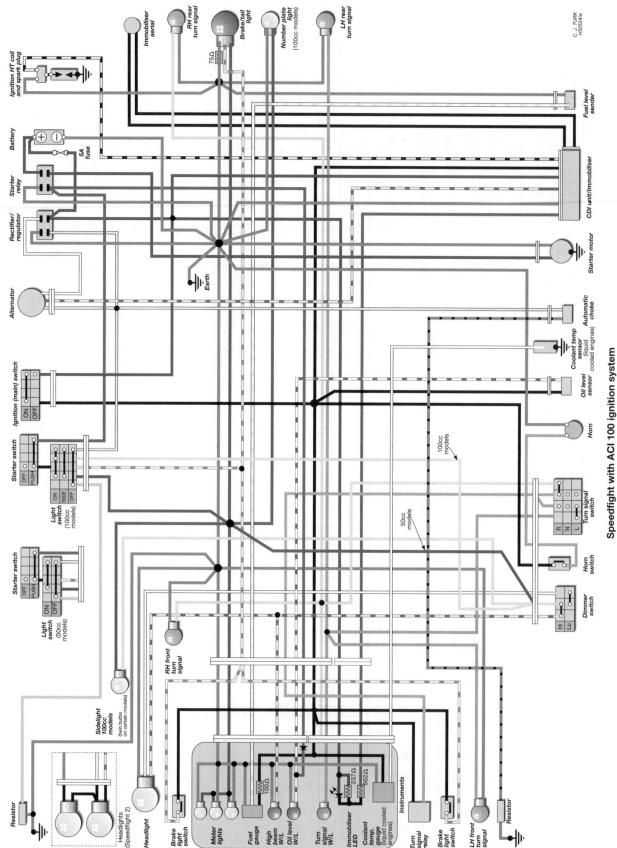

C. J. TURK
H32524/a

Speedfight with ACI 100 ignition system

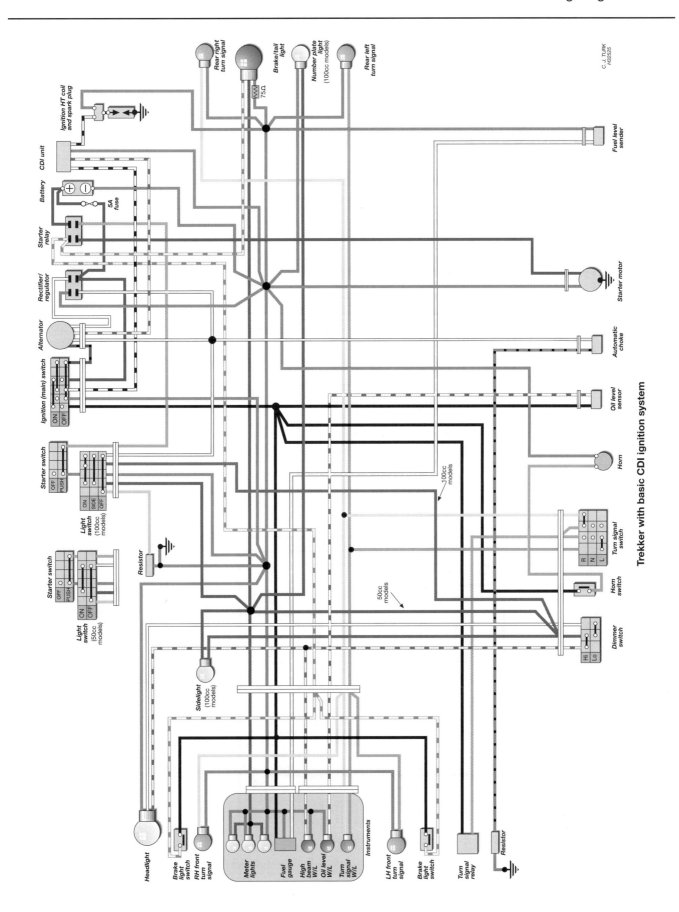

C. J. TURK
H32525

Trekker with basic CDI ignition system

Ignition HT coil and spark plug

CDI unit

Battery

5A fuse

Starter relay

Rectifier/ regulator

Alternator

Ignition (main switch)
ON / OFF

Starter switch
OFF / PUSH
ON / SIDE / OFF

Light switch (100cc models)

Starter switch
OFF / PUSH
ON / OFF

Light switch (50cc models)

Resistor

Sidelight (100cc models)

Headlight

Brake light switch

RH front turn signal

Meter lights

Fuel gauge

High beam W/L

Oil level W/L

Turn signal W/L

Instruments

LH front turn signal

Brake light switch

Turn signal relay

Resistor

Rear right turn signal

Brake/tail light

75Ω

Number plate light (100cc models)

Rear left turn signal

Fuel level sender

Starter motor

Automatic choke

Oil level sensor

Horn

100cc models

50cc models

Turn signal switch
R / N / L

Horn switch

Dimmer switch
Hi / Lo

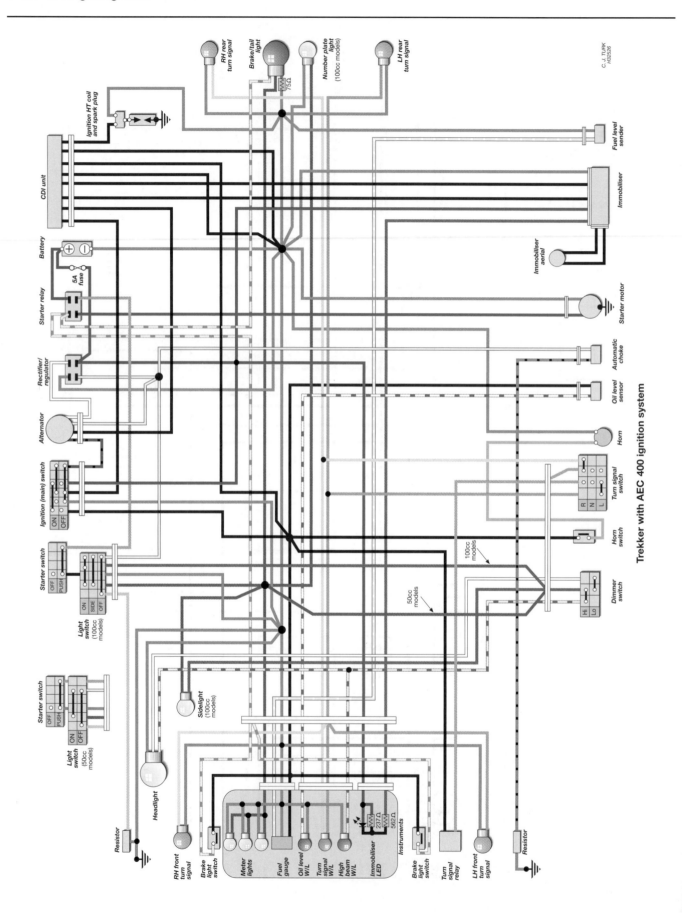

Trekker with AEC 400 ignition system

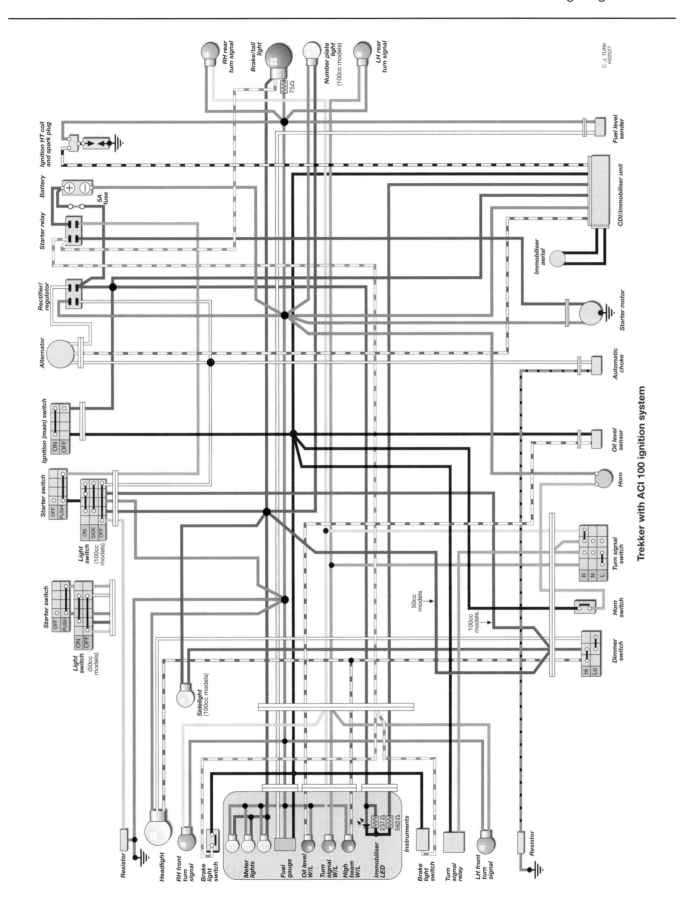

RH rear turn signal

Brake/tail light

75Ω

Number plate light (100cc models)

LH rear turn signal

C.J. TURK H32527

Fuel level sender

Ignition HT coil and spark plug

Battery

Starter relay

5A fuse

CDI/Immobiliser unit

Immobiliser aerial

Rectifier/regulator

Starter motor

Alternator

Automatic choke

Ignition (main) switch

Oil level sensor

Starter switch

Horn

Light switch (100cc models)

Turn signal switch

R N L

50cc models

Starter switch

100cc models

Horn switch

Light switch (50cc models)

Dimmer switch

Hi Lo

Sidelight (100cc models)

Resistor

Headlight

RH front turn signal

Brake light switch

Meter lights

Fuel gauge

Oil level W/L

Turn signal W/L

High beam W/L

Immobiliser LED

237Ω

562Ω

Instruments

Brake light switch

Turn signal relay

LH front turn signal

Resistor

Trekker with ACI 100 ignition system

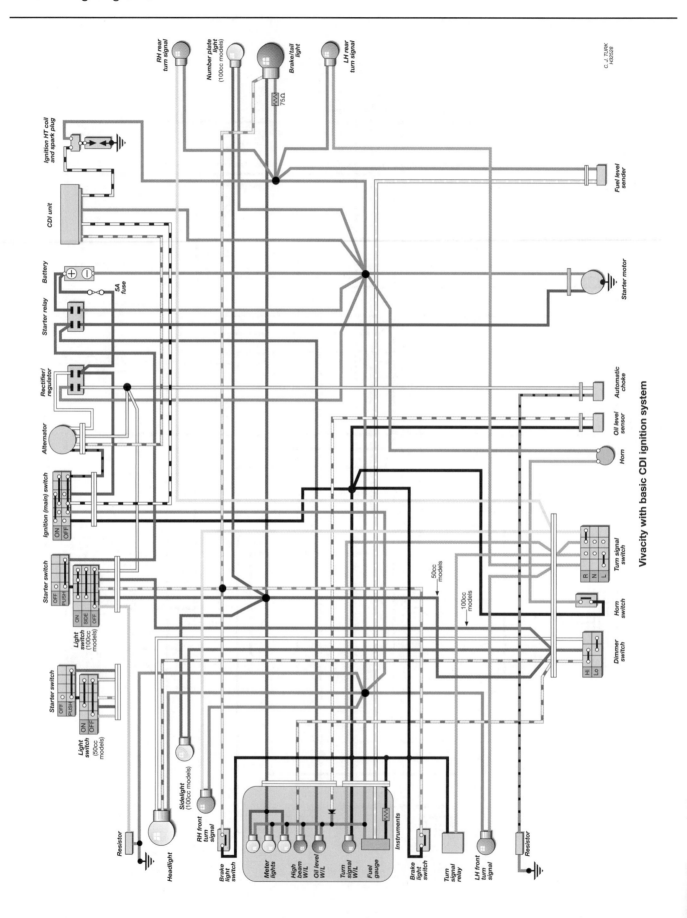

Vivacity with basic CDI ignition system

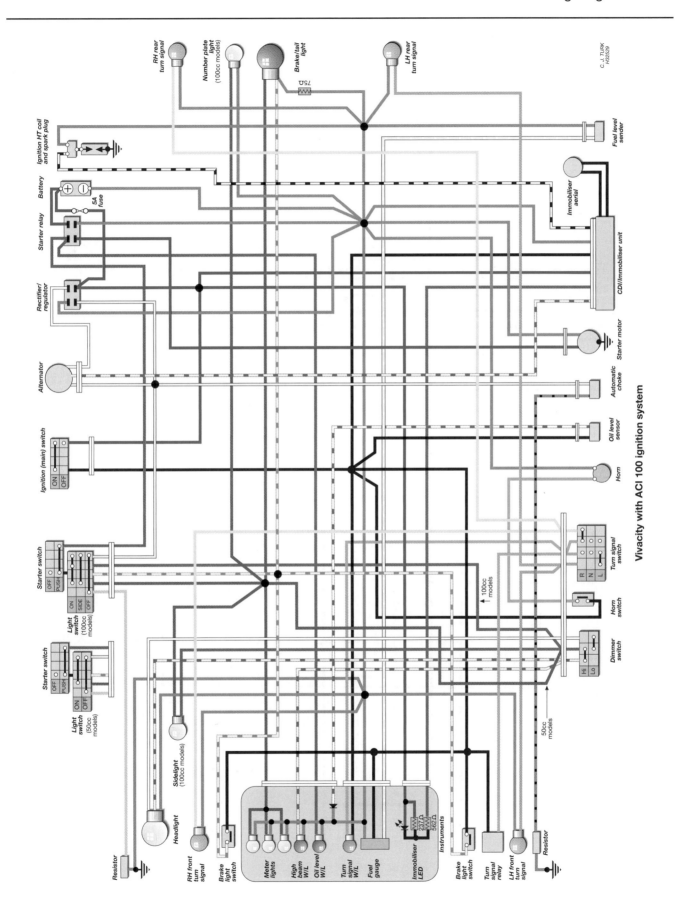

C. J. TURK
H32529

RH rear turn signal

Number plate light (100cc models)

Brake/tail light

75Ω

LH rear turn signal

Fuel level sender

Ignition HT coil and spark plug

Battery

Immobiliser aerial

Starter relay

5A fuse

Rectifier/regulator

CDI/Immobiliser unit

Alternator

Starter motor

Automatic choke

Ignition (main) switch
ON
OFF

Oil level sensor

Horn

Starter switch
OFF
PUSH

Light switch (100cc models)
ON
SIDE
OFF

Turn signal switch
R
N
L

100cc models

Horn switch

Starter switch
OFF
PUSH

Dimmer switch
HI
LO

Light switch (50cc models)
ON
OFF

50cc models

Sidelight (100cc models)

Resistor

Headlight

RH front turn signal

Brake light switch

Meter lights

High beam W/L

Oil level W/L

Turn signal W/L

Fuel gauge

Immobiliser LED

237Ω
562Ω

Instruments

Brake light switch

Turn signal relay

LH front turn signal

Resistor

Vivacity with ACI 100 ignition system

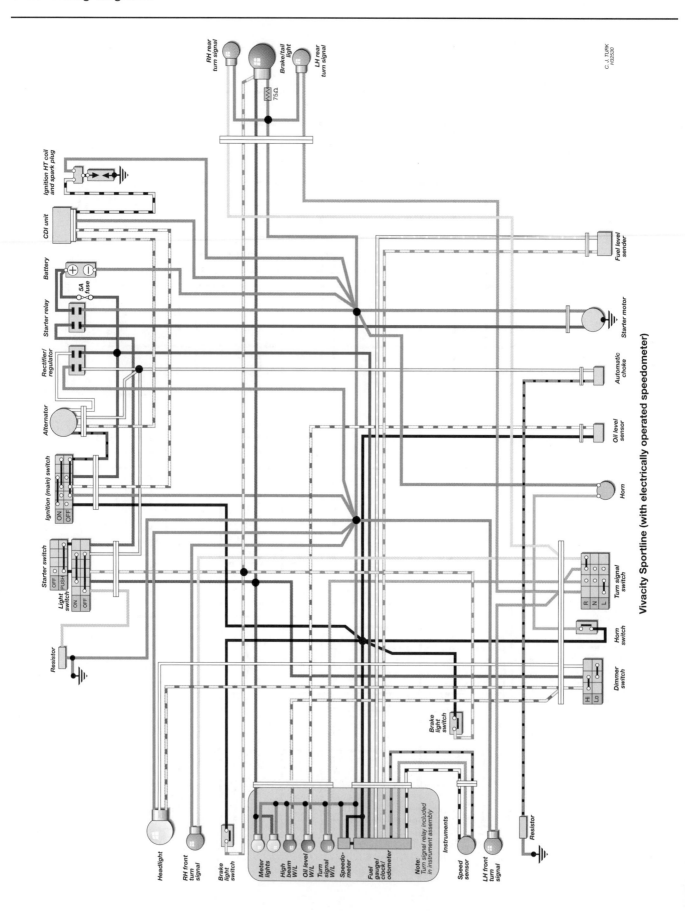

C. J. TURK
H32530

Vivacity Sportline (with electrically operated speedometer)

Length (distance)

Inches (in)	x 25.4	= Millimetres (mm)	x 0.0394	= Inches (in)
Feet (ft)	x 0.305	= Metres (m)	x 3.281	= Feet (ft)
Miles	x 1.609	= Kilometres (km)	x 0.621	= Miles

Volume (capacity)

Cubic inches (cu in; in^3)	x 16.387	= Cubic centimetres (cc; cm^3)	x 0.061	= Cubic inches (cu in; in^3)
Imperial pints (Imp pt)	x 0.568	= Litres (l)	x 1.76	= Imperial pints (Imp pt)
Imperial quarts (Imp qt)	x 1.137	= Litres (l)	x 0.88	= Imperial quarts (Imp qt)
Imperial quarts (Imp qt)	x 1.201	= US quarts (US qt)	x 0.833	= Imperial quarts (Imp qt)
US quarts (US qt)	x 0.946	= Litres (l)	x 1.057	= US quarts (US qt)
Imperial gallons (Imp gal)	x 4.546	= Litres (l)	x 0.22	= Imperial gallons (Imp gal)
Imperial gallons (Imp gal)	x 1.201	= US gallons (US gal)	x 0.833	= Imperial gallons (Imp gal)
US gallons (US gal)	x 3.785	= Litres (l)	x 0.264	= US gallons (US gal)

Mass (weight)

Ounces (oz)	x 28.35	= Grams (g)	x 0.035	= Ounces (oz)
Pounds (lb)	x 0.454	= Kilograms (kg)	x 2.205	= Pounds (lb)

Force

Ounces-force (ozf; oz)	x 0.278	= Newtons (N)	x 3.6	= Ounces-force (ozf; oz)
Pounds-force (lbf; lb)	x 4.448	= Newtons (N)	x 0.225	= Pounds-force (lbf; lb)
Newtons (N)	x 0.1	= Kilograms-force (kgf; kg)	x 9.81	= Newtons (N)

Pressure

Pounds-force per square inch (psi; lbf/in^2; lb/in^2)	x 0.070	= Kilograms-force per square centimetre (kgf/cm^2; kg/cm^2)	x 14.223	= Pounds-force per square inch (psi; lbf/in^2; lb/in^2)
Pounds-force per square inch (psi; lbf/in^2; lb/in^2)	x 0.068	= Atmospheres (atm)	x 14.696	= Pounds-force per square inch (psi; lbf/in^2; lb/in^2)
Pounds-force per square inch (psi; lbf/in^2; lb/in^2)	x 0.069	= Bars	x 14.5	= Pounds-force per square inch (psi; lbf/in^2; lb/in^2)
Pounds-force per square inch (psi; lbf/in^2; lb/in^2)	x 6.895	= Kilopascals (kPa)	x 0.145	= Pounds-force per square inch (psi; lbf/in^2; lb/in^2)
Kilopascals (kPa)	x 0.01	= Kilograms-force per square centimetre (kgf/cm^2; kg/cm^2)	x 98.1	= Kilopascals (kPa)
Millibar (mbar)	x 100	= Pascals (Pa)	x 0.01	= Millibar (mbar)
Millibar (mbar)	x 0.0145	= Pounds-force per square inch (psi; lbf/in^2; lb/in^2)	x 68.947	= Millibar (mbar)
Millibar (mbar)	x 0.75	= Millimetres of mercury (mmHg)	x 1.333	= Millibar (mbar)
Millibar (mbar)	x 0.401	= Inches of water (inH$_2$O)	x 2.491	= Millibar (mbar)
Millimetres of mercury (mmHg)	x 0.535	= Inches of water (inH$_2$O)	x 1.868	= Millimetres of mercury (mmHg)
Inches of water (inH$_2$O)	x 0.036	= Pounds-force per square inch (psi; lbf/in^2; lb/in^2)	x 27.68	= Inches of water (inH$_2$O)

Torque (moment of force)

Pounds-force inches (lbf in; lb in)	x 1.152	= Kilograms-force centimetre (kgf cm; kg cm)	x 0.868	= Pounds-force inches (lbf in; lb in)
Pounds-force inches (lbf in; lb in)	x 0.113	= Newton metres (Nm)	x 8.85	= Pounds-force inches (lbf in; lb in)
Pounds-force inches (lbf in; lb in)	x 0.083	= Pounds-force feet (lbf ft; lb ft)	x 12	= Pounds-force inches (lbf in; lb in)
Pounds-force feet (lbf ft; lb ft)	x 0.138	= Kilograms-force metres (kgf m; kg m)	x 7.233	= Pounds-force feet (lbf ft; lb ft)
Pounds-force feet (lbf ft; lb ft)	x 1.356	= Newton metres (Nm)	x 0.738	= Pounds-force feet (lbf ft; lb ft)
Newton metres (Nm)	x 0.102	= Kilograms-force metres (kgf m; kg m)	x 9.804	= Newton metres (Nm)

Power

Horsepower (hp)	x 745.7	= Watts (W)	x 0.0013	= Horsepower (hp)

Velocity (speed)

Miles per hour (miles/hr; mph)	x 1.609	= Kilometres per hour (km/hr; kph)	x 0.621	= Miles per hour (miles/hr; mph)

Fuel consumption*

Miles per gallon (mpg)	x 0.354	= Kilometres per litre (km/l)	x 2.825	= Miles per gallon (mpg)

Temperature

Degrees Fahrenheit = (°C x 1.8) + 32

Degrees Celsius (Degrees Centigrade; °C) = (°F - 32) x 0.56

It is common practice to convert from miles per gallon (mpg) to litres/100 kilometres (l/100km), where mpg x l/100 km = 282

Contents

1 Engine doesn't start or is difficult to start

Starter motor doesn't rotate

☐ Fuse blown. Check fuse and starter circuit (Chapter 9).
☐ Battery voltage low. Check and recharge battery (Chapter 9).
☐ Starter motor defective. Make sure the wiring to the starter is secure. Make sure the starter relay clicks when the start button is pushed. If the relay clicks, then the fault is in the wiring or motor.
☐ Starter relay faulty. Check it (Chapter 9).
☐ Starter switch on handlebar not contacting. The contacts could be wet, corroded or dirty. Disassemble and clean the switch (Chapter 9).
☐ Wiring open or shorted. Check all wiring connections and harnesses to make sure that they are dry, tight and not corroded. Also check for broken or frayed wires that can cause a short to earth (see wiring diagram, Chapter 9).
☐ Ignition switch defective. Check the switch according to the procedure in Chapter 9. Replace the switch with a new one if it is defective.

Starter motor rotates but engine does not turn over

☐ Starter pinion assembly defective. Inspect and repair or renew (Chapter 2).
☐ Damaged pinion assembly or starter gears. Inspect and renew the damaged parts (Chapter 2).

Starter works but engine won't turn over (seized)

☐ Seized engine caused by one or more internally damaged components. Failure due to wear, abuse or lack of lubrication. Damage can include piston, cylinder, connecting rod, crankshaft and bearings. Refer to Chapter 2A or 2B for engine disassembly.

No fuel flow

☐ No fuel in tank.
☐ Check that the fuel hose is not trapped and that tank filler cap vent is clear.
☐ Fuel tap filter clogged. Remove the tap and clean it and the filter (Chapter 4).
☐ Fuel tap vacuum hose split or detached. Check the hose.
☐ Fuel tap diaphragm split. Renew the tap (Chapter 4).
☐ Fuel hose clogged. Remove the hose and carefully blow through it.
☐ Float needle valve or carburettor jets clogged. The carburettor should be removed and overhauled if draining the float chamber doesn't solve the problem.

1 Engine doesn't start or is difficult to start (continued)

Engine flooded

☐ Float needle valve worn or stuck open. A piece of dirt, rust or other debris can jam the valve open, causing excess fuel to run into the float chamber. In this case, the float chamber should be cleaned and the needle valve and seat inspected. If the needle and seat are worn, then the leaking will persist and the parts should be replaced with new ones (Chapter 4).

No spark or weak spark

☐ Battery voltage low. Check and recharge the battery as necessary (Chapter 9).
☐ Spark plug dirty, defective or worn out. Locate reason for fouled plug using spark plug condition chart at the end of this manual and follow the plug maintenance procedures (Chapter 1). Condition is especially applicable to two-stroke engines due to the oily nature of their lubrication system.
☐ Spark plug cap or secondary (HT) wiring faulty. Check condition. Renew either or both components if cracks or deterioration are evident (Chapter 5).
☐ Spark plug cap not making good contact. Make sure that the plug cap fits snugly over the plug end.
☐ CDI unit defective. Refer to Chapter 5 for details.
☐ Pulse generator coil or source coil defective. Check the coils, referring to Chapter 5 for details.
☐ Ignition HT coil defective. Check the coil, referring to Chapter 5.
☐ Ignition switch shorted. This is usually caused by water, corrosion, damage or excessive wear. Where possible, disassemble the switch and clean the contacts, otherwire renew the switch (Chapter 9).
☐ Wiring shorted or broken. Make sure that all wiring connections are clean, dry and tight. Look for chafed and broken wires (Chapters 5 and 9).

Compression low

☐ Spark plug loose. Remove the plug and inspect its threads (Chapter 1).
☐ Cylinder head not sufficiently tightened down. If the cylinder head is suspected of being loose, then there's a chance that the gasket or head is damaged if the problem has persisted for any length of time. The head bolts should be tightened to the proper torque in the correct sequence (Chapter 2).
☐ Low crankcase compression due to worn crankshaft oil seals. Condition will upset the fuel/air mixture. Renew the seals (Chapter 2).

☐ Cylinder and/or piston worn. Excessive wear will cause compression pressure to leak past the rings. This is usually accompanied by worn rings as well. A top-end overhaul is necessary (Chapter 2).
☐ Piston rings worn, weak, broken, or sticking. Broken or sticking piston rings usually indicate a lubrication or carburation problem that causes excess carbon deposits to form on the pistons and rings. Top-end overhaul is necessary (Chapter 2).
☐ Piston ring-to-groove clearance excessive. This is caused by excessive wear of the piston ring lands. Piston renewal is necessary (Chapter 2).
☐ Cylinder head gasket damaged. If a head is allowed to become loose, or if excessive carbon build-up on the piston crown and combustion chamber causes extremely high compression, the head gasket may leak. Renew the gasket (Chapter 2).
☐ Cylinder head warped. This is caused by overheating or improperly tightened head bolts. Machine shop resurfacing or head renewal is necessary (Chapter 2).

Stalls after starting

☐ Faulty automatic choke. Check connections and movement (Chapter 4).
☐ Ignition malfunction (Chapter 5).
☐ Carburettor malfunction (Chapter 4).
☐ Fuel contaminated. The fuel can be contaminated with either dirt or water, or can change chemically if the machine is allowed to sit for several months or more. Drain the tank and carburettor (Chapter 4).
☐ Inlet air leak. Check for loose carburettor-to-inlet manifold connection, loose carburettor top (Chapter 4).
☐ Engine idle speed incorrect. Turn idle adjusting screw until the engine idles at the specified rpm (Chapter 1).

Rough idle

☐ Ignition malfunction (Chapter 5).
☐ Idle speed incorrect (Chapter 1).
☐ Carburettor malfunction (Chapter 4).
☐ Fuel contaminated. The fuel can be contaminated with either dirt or water, or can change chemically if the machine is allowed to sit for several months or more. Drain the old fuel and refill with fresh fuel of the recommended grade (Chapter 4).
☐ Inlet air leak. Check for loose carburettor-to-inlet manifold connection, loose carburettor top (Chapter 4).
☐ Air filter clogged. Clean the air filter element (Chapter 1).

2 Poor running at low speeds

Spark weak

☐ Battery voltage low. Check and recharge battery (Chapter 9).
☐ Spark plug fouled, defective or worn out. Refer to Chapter 1 for spark plug maintenance.
☐ Spark plug cap or HT wiring defective. Refer to Chapters 1 and 5 for details on the ignition system.
☐ Spark plug cap not making contact.
☐ Incorrect spark plug. Wrong type, heat range or cap configuration. Check and install correct plug listed in Chapter 1.
☐ CDI unit defective (Chapter 5).
☐ Pulse generator coil defective (Chapter 5).
☐ Ignition HT coil defective (Chapter 5).

Fuel/air mixture incorrect

☐ Pilot screw out of adjustment (Chapter 4).
☐ Pilot jet or air passage clogged. Remove and overhaul the carburettor (Chapter 4).
☐ Air bleed hole clogged. Remove carburettor and blow out all passages (Chapter 4).
☐ Air filter clogged, poorly sealed or missing (Chapter 1).
☐ Air filter housing poorly sealed. Look for cracks, holes or loose screws and replace or repair defective parts.
☐ Carburettor inlet manifold loose. Check for cracks, breaks, damaged gaskets or loose clamps.

2 Poor running at low speeds (continued)

Compression low

- ☐ Spark plug loose. Remove the plug and inspect its threads (Chapter 1).
- ☐ Cylinder head not sufficiently tightened down. If the cylinder head is suspected of being loose, then there's a chance that the gasket or head is damaged if the problem has persisted for any length of time. The head bolts should be tightened to the proper torque in the correct sequence (Chapter 2).
- ☐ Low crankcase compression due to worn crankshaft oil seals. Condition will upset the fuel/air mixture. Renew the seals (Chapter 2).
- ☐ Cylinder and/or piston worn. Excessive wear will cause compression pressure to leak past the rings. This is usually accompanied by worn rings as well. A top-end overhaul is necessary (Chapter 2).
- ☐ Piston rings worn, weak, broken, or sticking. Broken or sticking piston rings usually indicate a lubrication or carburation problem that causes excess carbon deposits to form on the pistons and rings. Top-end overhaul is necessary (Chapter 2).
- ☐ Piston ring-to-groove clearance excessive. This is caused by excessive wear of the piston ring lands. Piston renewal is necessary (Chapter 2).

- ☐ Cylinder head gasket damaged. If a head is allowed to become loose, or if excessive carbon build-up on the piston crown and combustion chamber causes extremely high compression, the head gasket may leak. Renew the gasket (Chapter 2).
- ☐ Cylinder head warped. This is caused by overheating or improperly tightened head bolts. Machine shop resurfacing or head renewal is necessary (Chapter 2).

Poor acceleration

- ☐ Carburettor leaking or dirty. Overhaul the carburettor (Chapter 4).
- ☐ Faulty automatic choke (Chapter 4).
- ☐ Timing not advancing. The pulse generator coil or the CDI unit may be defective (Chapter 5). If so, they must be replaced with new ones, as they can't be repaired.
- ☐ Brakes dragging. On disc brakes, usually caused by debris which has entered the brake piston seals, or from a warped disc or bent axle. On drum brakes, cable out of adjustment, shoe return spring broken. Repair as necessary (Chapter 8).
- ☐ Clutch slipping, drive belt worn, or speed governor faulty (Chapter 2C).

3 Poor running or no power at high speed

Firing incorrect

- ☐ Air filter clogged. Clean filter (Chapter 1).
- ☐ Spark plug fouled, defective or worn out. See Chapter 1 for spark plug maintenance.
- ☐ Spark plug cap or HT wiring defective. See Chapters 1 and 5 for details of the ignition system.
- ☐ Spark plug cap not in good contact (Chapter 5).
- ☐ Incorrect spark plug. Wrong type, heat range or cap configuration. Check and install correct plug listed in Chapter 1.
- ☐ CDI unit or HT coil defective (Chapter 5).

Fuel/air mixture incorrect

- ☐ Main jet clogged. Dirt, water or other contaminants can clog the main jet. Clean the fuel tap filter and the carburettor (Chapter 4).
- ☐ Main jet wrong size. The standard jetting is for sea level atmospheric pressure and oxygen content.
- ☐ Air bleed holes clogged. Remove and overhaul carburettor (Chapter 4).
- ☐ Air filter clogged, poorly sealed, or missing (Chapter 1).
- ☐ Air filter housing or duct poorly sealed. Look for cracks, holes or loose clamps or screws, and replace or repair defective parts.
- ☐ Carburettor inlet manifold loose. Check for cracks, breaks, damaged gaskets or loose clamps.

Compression low

- ☐ Spark plug loose. Remove the plug and inspect its threads. Reinstall and tighten securely (Chapter 1).
- ☐ Cylinder head not sufficiently tightened down. If the cylinder head is suspected of being loose, then there's a chance that the gasket or head is damaged if the problem has persisted for any length of time. The head bolts should be tightened to the proper torque in the correct sequence (Chapter 2).
- ☐ Low crankcase compression due to worn crankshaft oil seals. Condition will upset the fuel/air mixture. Renew the seals (Chapter 2).
- ☐ Cylinder and/or piston worn. Excessive wear will cause compression pressure to leak past the rings. This is usually accompanied by worn rings as well. A top-end overhaul is necessary (Chapter 2).
- ☐ Piston rings worn, weak, broken, or sticking. Broken or sticking piston rings usually indicate a lubrication or carburation problem

that causes excess carbon deposits to form on the pistons and rings. Top-end overhaul is necessary (Chapter 2).
- ☐ Piston ring-to-groove clearance excessive. This is caused by excessive wear of the piston ring lands. Piston renewal is necessary (Chapter 2).
- ☐ Cylinder head gasket damaged. If a head is allowed to become loose, or if excessive carbon build-up on the piston crown and combustion chamber causes extremely high compression, the head gasket may leak. Renew the gasket (Chapter 2).
- ☐ Cylinder head warped. This is caused by overheating or improperly tightened head bolts. Cylinder head skimming or head renewal is necessary (Chapter 2).

Knocking or pinking

- ☐ Carbon build-up in combustion chamber. Use of a fuel additive that will dissolve the adhesive bonding the carbon particles to the crown and chamber is the easiest way to remove the build-up. Otherwise, the cylinder head will have to be removed and decarbonised (Chapter 1).
- ☐ Incorrect or poor quality fuel. Old or improper grades of fuel can cause detonation. This causes the piston to rattle, thus the knocking or pinking sound. Drain the old fuel and refill with fresh fuel of the recommended grade (Chapter 4).
- ☐ Spark plug heat range incorrect. Uncontrolled detonation indicates the plug heat range is too hot. The plug in effect becomes a glow plug, raising cylinder temperatures. Install the proper heat range plug (Chapter 1).
- ☐ Improper air/fuel mixture. This will cause the cylinder to run hot, which leads to detonation. Clogged carburettor jets or an air leak can cause this imbalance. See Chapter 4.

Miscellaneous causes

- ☐ Throttle valve doesn't open fully. Adjust the throttle twistgrip freeplay (Chapter 1).
- ☐ Clutch slipping, drive belt worn, or speed governor faulty (Chapter 2C).
- ☐ Brakes dragging. On disc brakes, usually caused by debris which has entered the brake piston seals, or from a warped disc or bent axle. On drum brakes, cable out of adjustment, shoe return spring broken. Repair as necessary (Chapter 8).

4 Overheating

Engine overheats – liquid-cooled engines

☐ Coolant level low. Check and add coolant (Chapter 1).
☐ Leak in cooling system. Check cooling system hoses and radiator for leaks and other damage. Repair or renew parts as necessary (Chapter 3).
☐ Thermostat sticking open or closed. Check and renew (Chapter 3).
☐ Coolant passages clogged. Drain and flush the entire system, then refill with fresh coolant.
☐ Water pump defective. Remove the pump and check the components (Chapter 3).
☐ Clogged radiator fins. Clean them by blowing compressed air through the fins from the rear of the radiator.

Engine overheats – air-cooled engines

☐ Air cooling ducts blocked or incorrectly fitted.
☐ Problem with cooling fan.

Firing incorrect

☐ Spark plug fouled, defective or worn out. See Chapter 1 for spark plug maintenance.
☐ Incorrect spark plug.
☐ CDI unit defective (Chapter 5).
☐ Faulty ignition HT coil (Chapter 5).

Fuel/air mixture incorrect

☐ Main jet clogged. Dirt, water or other contaminants can clog the main jet. Clean the fuel tap filter and the carburettor (Chapter 4).
☐ Main jet wrong size. The standard jetting is for sea level atmospheric pressure and oxygen content.
☐ Air bleed holes clogged. Remove and overhaul carburettor (Chapter 4).
☐ Air filter clogged, poorly sealed, or missing (Chapter 1).

☐ Air filter housing or duct poorly sealed. Look for cracks, holes or loose clamps or screws, and renew or repair defective parts.
☐ Carburettor inlet manifold loose. Check for cracks, breaks, damaged gaskets or loose clamps.

Compression too high

☐ Carbon build-up in the cylinder head. Decarbonise the cylinder head (Chapter 1).
☐ Improperly machined head surface.

Engine load excessive

☐ Clutch slipping, drive belt worn, or speed governor faulty (Chapter 2C).
☐ Brakes dragging. On disc brakes, usually caused by debris which has entered the brake piston seals, or from a warped disc or bent axle. On drum brakes, cable out of adjustment, shoe return spring broken. Repair as necessary (Chapter 8).

Lubrication inadequate

☐ Oil pump out of adjustment. Adjust pump cable on models so equipped (Chapter 1).
☐ Poor quality oil or incorrect viscosity or type. Oil is rated not only according to viscosity but also according to type. Some oils are not rated high enough for use in this engine. Check the Specifications section, then drain the oil tank and refill with the correct oil (Chapter 1).

Miscellaneous causes

☐ Modification to exhaust system. Most aftermarket exhaust systems cause the engine to run leaner, which make them run hotter. When installing an accessory exhaust system, always obtain advice on rejetting the carburettor.

5 Transmission problems

No drive to rear wheel

☐ Drive belt broken (Chapter 2C).
☐ Clutch not engaging (Chapter 2C).
☐ Clutch friction material or drum excessively worn (Chapter 2C).

Transmission noise or vibration

☐ Bearings worn. Also includes the possibility that the shafts are worn. Overhaul the transmission (Chapter 2C).
☐ Gears worn or chipped (Chapter 2C)
☐ Clutch drum worn unevenly (Chapter 2C).
☐ Clutch pulley or variator pulley out of alignment (Chapter 2C).
☐ Bent or damaged transmission shaft (Chapter 2C).
☐ Loose clutch nut or variator nut (Chapter 2C).

Poor performance

☐ Variator rollers worn or insufficiently greased (Chapter 2C).
☐ Weak or broken clutch pulley spring (Chapter 2C).
☐ Clutch or drum excessively worn (Chapter 2C).
☐ Grease on clutch friction material (Chapter 2C).
☐ Drive belt excessively worn (Chapter 2C).

Clutch not disengaging completely

☐ Weak or broken clutch springs (Chapter 2C).
☐ Engine idle speed too high (Chapter 1).

6 Abnormal engine noise

Knocking or pinking

☐ Carbon build-up in combustion chamber. Decarbonise the cylinder head (Chapter 1).

☐ Incorrect or poor quality fuel. Old or improper fuel can cause detonation. This causes the piston to rattle, thus the knocking or pinking sound. Drain the old fuel and refill with fresh fuel of the recommended grade (Chapter 4).

☐ Spark plug heat range incorrect. Uncontrolled detonation indicates that the plug heat range is too hot. The plug in effect becomes a glow plug, raising cylinder temperatures. Install the proper heat range plug (Chapter 1).

☐ Improper air/fuel mixture. This will cause the cylinder to run hot and lead to detonation. Clogged jets or an air leak can cause this imbalance. See Chapter 4.

Piston slap or rattling

☐ Cylinder-to-piston clearance excessive. Caused by improper assembly. Inspect and overhaul top-end parts (Chapter 2).

☐ Connecting rod bent. Caused by over-revving, trying to start a badly flooded engine or from ingesting a foreign object into the combustion chamber. Renew the damaged parts (Chapter 2).

☐ Piston pin or piston pin bore worn or seized from wear or lack of lubrication. Renew damaged parts (Chapter 2).

☐ Piston ring(s) worn, broken or sticking. Overhaul the top-end (Chapter 2).

☐ Piston seizure damage. Usually from lack of lubrication or overheating. Renew the piston and cylinder as necessary (Chapter 2). Check that the oil pump is correctly adjusted (models with a cable-operated pump).

☐ Connecting rod small end or big end bearing clearance excessive. Caused by excessive wear or lack of lubrication. Renew crank assembly.

Other noise

☐ Exhaust pipe leaking at cylinder head connection. Caused by improper fit of pipe, loose exhaust flange or damaged gasket. All exhaust fasteners should be tightened evenly and carefully (Chapter 4). Failure to do this will lead to a leak.

☐ Crankshaft runout excessive. Caused by a bent crankshaft (from over-revving) or damage from an upper cylinder component failure.

☐ Engine mounting bolts loose. Tighten all engine unit mounting bolts (Chapter 2A or 2B).

☐ Crankshaft bearings worn (Chapter 2A or 2B).

7 Abnormal frame and suspension noise

Front end noise

☐ Steering head bearings loose or damaged. Clicks when braking. Check and adjust or renew as necessary (Chapters 1 and 6).

☐ Bolts loose. Make sure all bolts are tightened to the specified torque (Chapter 6).

☐ Fork tube (telescopic fork models) or steering stem bent. Good possibility if machine has been in an accident. Replace damaged parts with new ones (Chapter 6).

☐ Defective shock absorber with internal damage (Speedfight models). Replace shock with a new one (Chapter 6).

☐ Front axle nut or wheel bolts loose. Tighten to the specified torque (Chapter 8).

☐ Loose or worn wheel or hub bearings. Check and renew as necessary (Chapter 8).

Shock absorber noise

☐ Fluid leak caused by defective seal. Shock will be covered with oil. Replace shock with a new unit (Chapter 6).

☐ Defective shock absorber with internal damage. Replace shock with a new one (Chapter 6).

☐ Bent damper rod or damaged shock body. Replace shock with a new one (Chapter 6).

☐ Loose or worn suspension linkage components. Check and replace as necessary (Chapter 6).

Brake noise

☐ Squeal caused by dust on brake pads or shoes. Usually found in combination with glazed pads or shoes. Clean using brake cleaning solvent only (Chapter 8).

☐ Contamination of brake pads or shoes. Oil, brake fluid or dirt causing brake to chatter or squeal. Renew pads or shoes (Chapter 8).

☐ Pads or shoes glazed. Caused by excessive heat from prolonged use or from contamination. Do not use sandpaper, emery cloth, carborundum cloth or any other abrasive to roughen the pad surfaces as abrasives will stay in the pad material and damage the disc or drum. Renew pads or shoes (Chapter 8).

☐ Disc or drum warped. Can cause a chattering, clicking or intermittent squeal. Usually accompanied by a pulsating lever and uneven braking. Check the disc runout and the drum ovality (Chapter 8).

☐ Worn wheel or hub (front) or transmission (rear) bearings. Check and renew as needed (Chapters 8 or 2C).

8 Excessive exhaust smoke

White/blue smoke (oil burning)

☐ Oil pump cable adjustment incorrect. Check throttle cable/oil pump cable adjustment on models with a cable-operated pump (Chapter 1).

☐ Accumulated oil deposits in the exhaust system. If the scooter is used for short journeys only, the oil residue from the exhaust gases will condense in the cool silencer. Take the scooter for a long run to burn off the accumulated oil residue.

Black smoke (over-rich mixture)

☐ Air filter clogged. Clean or renew the element (Chapter 1).

☐ Main jet too large or loose. Compare the jet size to the Specifications (Chapter 4).

☐ Automatic choke faulty (Chapter 4).

☐ Float needle valve held off seat. Clean any sediment from the float chamber and fuel line and renew the needle and seat if necessary (Chapter 4).

Brown smoke (lean mixture)

☐ Main jet too small or blocked. Clean float chamber and jet and compare jet size to Specifications (Chapter 4).

☐ Fuel flow insufficient. Float needle valve stuck closed due to chemical reaction with old fuel.

☐ Restricted fuel supply due to blockage or trapped hose. Clean hose and float chamber.

☐ Carburettor inlet manifold loose (Chapter 4).

☐ Air filter poorly sealed or not installed (Chapter 1).

☐ Ignition timing incorrect (Chapter 5).

9 Poor handling or stability

Handlebar hard to turn

☐ Steering head bearing adjuster nut too tight. Check adjustment as described in Chapter 6.

☐ Bearings damaged. Roughness can be felt as the bars are turned from side-to-side. Renew bearings and races (Chapter 6).

☐ Races dented or worn. Denting results from wear in only one position (e.g. straight-ahead), or from an accident. Renew races and bearings (Chapter 6).

☐ Steering stem lubrication inadequate. Causes are grease getting hard from age or being washed out by high pressure car washes. Disassemble steering head and repack bearings (Chapter 6).

☐ Steering stem bent. Caused by an accident. Renew the steering stem – don't try to straighten it (Chapter 6).

☐ Front tyre air pressure too low (Daily (pre-ride) checks).

Handlebar shakes or vibrates excessively

☐ Tyres worn (Daily (pre-ride) checks).

☐ Suspension components worn. Renew worn parts (Chapter 6).

☐ Wheel rim(s) warped or damaged. Inspect wheels for runout (Chapter 8).

☐ Wheel bearings worn. Worn wheel or hub (front) or transmission bearings (rear) can cause poor stability in a straight line. Worn front bearings will cause steering wobble (Chapter 8).

☐ Handlebar mounting loose (Chapter 6).

☐ Front suspension bolts loose. Tighten them to the specified torque (Chapter 6).

☐ Engine mounting bolts loose. Will cause excessive vibration with increased engine rpm (Chapter 2A or 2B).

Handlebar pulls to one side

☐ Frame bent. Definitely suspect this if the machine has been in an accident. May or may not be accompanied by cracking near the bend. Renew the frame (Chapter 6).

☐ Wheels out of alignment. Caused by damaged wheel bearings, bent steering stem, fork tube (telescopic fork models) or frame (Chapter 6 or 8).

☐ Steering stem bent. Caused by an accident. Renew the steering stem – don't try to straighten it (Chapter 6).

☐ Fork tube bent (telescopic fork models). Disassemble the forks and renew the damaged parts (Chapter 6).

Poor shock absorbing qualities

☐ Too hard:

a) *Telescopic fork oil quantity excessive. See the Specifications in Chapter 6.*

b) *Telescopic fork oil viscosity too high. See the Specifications in Chapter 6.*

c) *Telescopic fork internal damage. See Chapter 6.*

d) *Fork tube or shock absorber bent. Causes harsh movement or suspension to stick (Chapter 6).*

e) *Shock internal damage (Chapter 6).*

f) *Tyre pressure too high (Chapter 1).*

☐ Too soft:

a) *Fork oil viscosity too light. Use the correct grade (see the Specifications in Chapter 6).*

b) *Fork or shock spring(s) weak or broken (Chapter 6).*

c) *Shock internal damage or leakage (Chapter 6).*

10 Braking problems – disc brakes

Brakes are ineffective

☐ Air in brake system. Caused by inattention to master cylinder fluid level or by leakage. Locate problem and bleed brake system (Chapter 8).
☐ Pads or disc worn (Chapters 1 and 8).
☐ Brake fluid leak. Locate problem and rectify (Chapter 8).
☐ Contaminated pads. Caused by contact with oil, grease, brake fluid, etc. Fit new pads. Clean disc thoroughly with brake cleaner (Chapter 8).
☐ Brake fluid deteriorated. Fluid is old or contaminated. Drain system, replenish with new fluid and bleed the system (Chapter 8).
☐ Master cylinder internal parts worn or damaged causing fluid to bypass. Fit new master cylinder (Chapter 8).
☐ Disc warped. Renew disc (Chapter 8).

Brake lever pulsates

☐ Disc warped. Renew disc (Chapter 8).

☐ Axle bent. Renew axle (Chapter 8).
☐ Brake caliper bolts loose (Chapter 8).
☐ Wheel warped or otherwise damaged (Chapter 8).
☐ Wheel or hub bearings damaged or worn (Chapter 8).

Brakes drag

☐ Master cylinder piston seized. Caused by wear or damage to piston or cylinder bore (Chapter 8).
☐ Lever action rough or lever stuck. Check pivot and lubricate (Chapter 8).
☐ Brake caliper piston seized in bore. Caused by wear or ingestion of dirt past deteriorated seal (Chapter 8).
☐ Brake pads damaged. Pad material separated from backing plate. Usually caused by faulty manufacturing process or from contact with chemicals. Renew pads (Chapter 8).
☐ Pads improperly installed (Chapter 8).

11 Braking problems – drum brakes

Brakes are ineffective

☐ Cable incorrectly adjusted. Check cable (Chapter 1).
☐ Shoes or drum worn (Chapters 1 and 8).
☐ Contaminated shoes. Caused by contact with oil or grease, etc. Fit new shoes. Clean drum thoroughly with brake cleaner (Chapter 8).
☐ Brake lever arm incorrectly positioned, or cam excessively worn (Chapter 8).

Brake lever pulsates

☐ Drum warped. Renew drum (Chapter 8).
☐ Axle bent. Renew axle (Chapter 8).
☐ Wheel warped or otherwise damaged (Chapter 8).
☐ Wheel or hub (front) or transmission bearings (rear) damaged or worn (Chapter 8).

Brakes drag

☐ Cable incorrectly adjusted or requires lubrication. Check cable (Chapter 1).
☐ Shoe return springs broken (Chapter 8).
☐ Lever action rough or lever stuck. Check pivot and lubricate (Chapter 8).
☐ Lever arm or cam binds. Caused by inadequate lubrication or damage (Chapter 8).
☐ Brake shoe damaged. Friction material separated from shoe. Usually caused by faulty manufacturing process or from contact with chemicals. Fit new shoes (Chapter 8).
☐ Shoes improperly installed (Chapter 8).

12 Electrical problems

Battery dead or weak

☐ Battery faulty. Caused by sulphated plates which are shorted through sedimentation. Also, broken battery terminal making only occasional contact (Chapter 9).
☐ Battery leads making poor contact (Chapter 9).
☐ Load excessive. Caused by addition of high wattage lights or other electrical accessories.
☐ Ignition (main) switch defective. Switch either earths internally or fails to shut off system. Renew the switch (Chapter 9).
☐ Regulator/rectifier defective (Chapter 9).

☐ Alternator coil open or shorted (Chapter 9).
☐ Wiring faulty. Wiring either shorted to earth or connections loose in ignition, charging or lighting circuits (Chapter 9).

Battery overcharged

☐ Regulator/rectifier defective. Overcharging is noticed when battery gets excessively warm (Chapter 9).
☐ Battery defective. Replace battery with a new one (Chapter 9).
☐ Battery amperage too low, wrong type or size. Install manufacturer's specified amp-hour battery to handle charging load (Chapter 9).

Note: *References throughout this index are in the form - "Chapter number" • "Page number"*

E

Electrical system
alternator – 9•17, 9•18
battery 1•26, 9•3, 9•4
brake light switches – 9•7
fault finding – 9•2, REF•8
fuel gauge – 9•12
fuse – 9•4
handlebar switches – 9•14
headlight – 1•33, 9•5, 9•7
horn – 1•33, 9•14
ignition (main) switch – 9•13
instruments – 9•10
licence plate light – 9•8
lighting system check – 9•4
oil level sensor – 9•13
regulator/rectifier – 9•19
resistor – 9•5
sidelight – 9•6
specifications – 9•2
starter relay and motor – 9•15, 9•16
tail/brake light – 9•7
turn signals – 9•8
wiring diagrams – 9•20
Engine
cooling fan – 2A•8
crankcases, crankshaft and connecting rod – 2A•11, 2B•6
cylinder – 2A•5, 2B•5
cylinder head – 1•33, 2A•4, 2B•4
fault finding – REF•2
idle speed – 1•31
oil level check – 0•12
oil pump – 1•29, 1•30, 2A•9, 2B•6
piston – 2A•6, 2B•5
rings – 2A•8, 2B•6
removal and installation – 2A•3, 2B•2
running-in – 2A•15, 2B•6
specificafions – 2A•1, 2B•1
Engine number – 0•8
Exhaust system – 4•13

F

Fan – 2A•8
Fault finding – REF•2 *et seq*
Filter
air – 1•26, 4•5
engine oil – 1•30
fuel – 4•3
Floor panel
Speedfight – 7•7
Trekker- 7•11
Vivacity – 7•14
Footrests – 7•1
Frame – 6•1
Frame number – 0•8
Front brake
bleeding – 8•5
caliper – 8•3
checks – 1•26

disc – 8•3
fault finding – REF•8
fluid change – 8•6
fluid level check – 0•13, 1•27
levers – 1•26, 8•7
master cylinder – 8•4
hose – 1•27, 8•5
pads – 1•27, 8•2
Front mudguard
Speedfight – 7•6
Trekker- 7•10
Vivacity – 7•13
Front panel
Speedfight – 7•5
Vivacity – 7•13
Front side panels (Speedfight) – 7•6
Front suspension
check – 6•2
forks – 6•9, 6•10, 6•11
monolever – 6•7
specifications – 6•1
Front wheel – 8•9, 8•13
Fuel system
carburettor – 1•31, 4•5 to 4•12
choke mechanism – 4•5
fuel filter – 4•3
fuel level check – 0•13
gauge and level sender – 9•12
idle fuel/air mixture adjustment – 4•4
reed valve – 4•11
system check – 1•30
tap and tank – 4•3
Fuse – 9•4

G

Gearbox
oil level check – 1•34
removal, inspection and installation – 2C•9

H

Handlebar covers
Speedfight – 7•4
Trekker- 7•9
Vivacity – 7•12
Handlebar switches – 9•14
Handlebars – 6•3
Headlight
beam alignment – 1•33
bulb – 9•5
check – 9•4
unit – 9•7
Headlight panel
Speedfight – 7•5
Trekker- 7•9
Vivacity – 7•13
Heater (carburettor) – 4•12
Horn – 1•33, 9•14
HT coil – 5•2

Preserving Our Motoring Heritage

< The Model J Duesenberg Derham Tourster. Only eight of these magnificent cars were ever built – this is the only example to be found outside the United States of America

Almost every car you've ever loved, loathed or desired is gathered under one roof at the Haynes Motor Museum. Over 300 immaculately presented cars and motorbikes represent every aspect of our motoring heritage, from elegant reminders of bygone days, such as the superb Model J Duesenberg to curiosities like the bug-eyed BMW Isetta. There are also many old friends and flames. Perhaps you remember the 1959 Ford Popular that you did your courting in? The magnificent 'Red Collection' is a spectacle of classic sports cars including AC, Alfa Romeo, Austin Healey, Ferrari, Lamborghini, Maserati, MG, Riley, Porsche and Triumph.

A Perfect Day Out

Each and every vehicle at the Haynes Motor Museum has played its part in the history and culture of Motoring. Today, they make a wonderful spectacle and a great day out for all the family. Bring the kids, bring Mum and Dad, but above all bring your camera to capture those golden memories for ever. You will also find an impressive array of motoring memorabilia, a comfortable 70 seat video cinema and one of the most extensive transport book shops in Britain. The Pit Stop Cafe serves everything from a cup of tea to wholesome, home-made meals or, if you prefer, you can enjoy the large picnic area nestled in the beautiful rural surroundings of Somerset.

John Haynes O.B.E., Founder and Chairman of the museum at the wheel of a Haynes Light 12.

< The 1936 490cc sohc-engined International Norton – well known for its racing success

The Museum is situated on the A359 Yeovil to Frome road at Sparkford, just off the A303 in Somerset. It is about 40 miles south of Bristol, and 25 minutes drive from the M5 intersection at Taunton.
Open 9.30am - 5.30pm (10.00am - 4.00pm Winter) 7 days a week, *except Christmas Day, Boxing Day and New Years Day*
Special rates available for schools, coach parties and outings Charitable Trust No. 292048